The Association of American University Presses

Directory 2008

The Association of American University Presses
71 W. 23rd Street, Suite 901
New York, NY 10010

Phone: (212) 989-1010
Faxes: (212) 989-0275 / 0176
Web site: www.aaupnet.org
E-mail: info@aaupnet.org

Published by the Association of American University Presses
71 W. 23rd St., Suite 901, New York, NY 10010
© 2007 by the Association of American University Presses, Inc.
All rights reserved.
Printed in the United States of America

International Standard Book Number 13: 978 0945103 21 9
Library of Congress Catalog Number 54-43046

Distributed to the Trade by:
The University of Chicago Press
11030 South Langley Avenue
Chicago, Illinois 60628
USA

Publication of this *Directory* was assisted by a generous grant from Edwards Brothers.

EB Life of Title®

CONTENTS

PREFACE

This *Directory* serves as a guide to the publishing programs and personnel of the 126 distinguished scholarly presses that have met the membership standards of the Association of American University Presses. Updated annually, the *Directory* provides the most comprehensive information on these publishers available from any source. It belongs on the reference shelf of anyone connected to scholarly publishing: scholars preparing materials for publication, booksellers, librarians, scholarly presses interested in joining the AAUP, and, of course, the AAUP's own members.

The *Directory* is organized particularly for the convenience of authors, librarians, and booksellers who require detailed information about AAUP members and their wide-ranging publishing programs. The "Subject Area Grid," for example, provides a quick overview of the many disciplines published by the presses, indicating those most likely to publish a work in a given area. "On Submitting Manuscripts" gives advice to potential authors on preparing and submitting a scholarly manuscript for publication.

For further detail, individual press listings provide information on their editorial programs, journals published, and key staff members. Addresses, ordering information, and information on sales representation for Canada, the UK, and Europe are also included.

The last section of the *Directory* focuses on the association and its purposes, and includes its by-laws, guidelines for admission to membership, and the names of the AAUP's Board of Directors, committees, and staff.

GENERAL INFORMATION FOR AUTHORS

What University Presses Do

University Presses perform services that are of inestimable value to the scholarly establishment, and also to the broader world of readers, and ultimately to society. If you are considering publishing with a university or other non-profit scholarly press, the following list should give you a good understanding of the scholarly publishing community.

• University Presses make available to the broader public the full range and value of research generated by university faculty.

• University Press books and journals present the basic research and analysis that is drawn upon by policymakers, opinion leaders, and authors of works for the general public.

• University Presses contribute to the variety and diversity of cultural expression at a time of global mergers and consolidation in the media industry.

• University Presses make common cause with libraries and other cultural institutions to promote engagement with ideas and sustain a literate culture.

• University Presses help to preserve the distinctiveness of local cultures through publication of works on the states and regions where they are based.

• University Presses give voice to minority cultures and perspectives through pioneering publication programs in ethnic, racial, and sexual studies.

• University Presses bring the work of overseas scholars and writers to English-language audiences by commissioning and publishing works in translation.

• University Presses rediscover and maintain the availability of works important to scholarship and culture through reprint programs.

• University Presses encourage cultural expression by publishing works of fiction, poetry, and creative nonfiction and books on contemporary art and photography.

• University Presses sponsor work in specialized and emerging areas of scholarship that do not have the broad levels of readership needed to attract commercial publishers.

• University Presses, through the peer review process, test the validity and soundness of scholarship and thus maintain high standards for academic publication.

• University Presses add value to scholarly work through rigorous editorial development; professional copyediting and design; and worldwide dissemination.

• University Presses are based at a wide array of educational institutions and thus promote a diversity of scholarly perspectives.

• University Presses encourage and refine the work of younger scholars through publication of the first books that establish credentials and develop authorial experience.

• University Presses make the works of English-language scholars available worldwide by licensing translations to publishers in other languages.

• University Presses commit resources to long-term scholarly editions and multivolume research projects, assuring publication for works with completion dates far in the future.

• University Presses add to the richness of undergraduate and graduate education by publishing most of the non-textbook and supplementary material used by instructors.

• University Presses collaborate with learned societies, scholarly associations, and librarians to explore how new technologies can benefit and advance scholarship.

• University Presses extend the reach and influence of their parent institutions, making evident their commitment to knowledge and ideas.

• University Presses demonstrate their parent institutions' support of research in areas such as the humanities and social sciences that rarely receive substantial Federal or corporate funding.

• University Presses help connect the university to the surrounding community by publishing books of local interest and hosting events for local authors.

• University Presses generate favorable publicity for their parent institutions through news coverage and book reviews, awards won, and exhibits at scholarly conferences.

• University Press staff act as local experts for faculty and administrators, providing guidance on intellectual property, scholarly communication, and the publishing process.

• University Presses provide advice and opportunities for students interested in pursuing careers in publishing.

On Submitting Manuscripts

JOURNAL ARTICLES

University presses have always been associated with publishing books of merit and distinction. This remains as true today as in the past, but less well appreciated is the extent to which university presses are active in publishing scholarly journals.

Journals form a major part of the publishing program of many presses, and more than half of the Association's members produce at least one periodical. (See page 18 for a list of presses publishing journals.) In all, university presses publish over 800 scholarly periodicals, including many of the most distinguished in their respective fields.

Authors submitting papers to a journal should check a current issue for information on where to submit manuscripts and for guidelines on length and format. Editors of journals often have very precise requirements for manuscript preparation and may return articles that do not meet their specifications.

BOOK MANUSCRIPTS

Selecting a Publisher

If you are looking for a publisher for a book-length manuscript, do some research on which press may be best for your book. You should consider the reputation in your field of various presses and their editors, the design and production quality of their books, and the range and strength of their marketing efforts. To take advantage of group promotions and past experience, presses tend to specialize in certain subjects. Occasionally a press may take on a title in an unfamiliar area, but you are more likely to be successful in your submission if you choose one that knows the field. Use the "Subject Area Grid," which begins on page 9, to find out which presses publish titles in your field. You can then find more specific information about their interests under the listings of individual presses or by consulting their catalogs. If your book has a strong regional interest, consider the lists of the university presses active in your state to determine what types of regional books they publish.

You can also learn more about the list of each publisher by studying brochures received in the mail, reading book advertisements in journals, and by visiting press exhibits at academic meetings. At these exhibits you can meet acquisitions editors from the presses most active in the discipline and talk with them about your manuscript. Such talks can be very helpful to you and the editor in deciding if your manuscript would be suitable for a particular press. If you have already decided which press you would prefer for your book, call the appropriate editor before the meeting to make an appointment.

Preparing a Manuscript Prospectus

If you have selected a publisher but do not know an editor, you can use this directory to find the appropriate editor at that press. If you are not sure which editor to approach, write to the director of the press or to its editor-in-chief. Many AAUP member presses describe their submission guidelines on their Web sites. It is best not to send the complete manuscript until you have been invited to do so. Presses vary in the amount of material they want to receive on a first submission, but some or all of the following materials are usually provided:

- a short, informative cover letter including a clear and concise description of your book and its notable features, your opinion of the audience for the book, information on the current status of the manuscript and expected completion date, and some details on the physical characteristics of the manuscript, such as length, number of illustrations, tables, appendices, etc.

- a table of contents

- a preface, introduction, or other brief sample of your manuscript

- a curriculum vitae or biographical notes

If the press is interested, the editor will invite you to submit the complete manuscript or inform you that he or she can proceed to review the materials you sent.

Preparing Your Manuscript for Review

Presses vary in their requirements for manuscript preparation. In general, the manuscript you submit for review should be as accurate and complete as possible. If a manuscript is carelessly prepared, reviewers may take offense at typographical errors or careless citations and spend precious review space discussing these problems instead of attending to the substance of your manuscript. If, for good reasons, your manuscript is incomplete, you should indicate what material is missing and provide your schedule for completion.

Although some presses will accept a single-spaced manuscript for review, it is best to double-space your text. A double-spaced manuscript is easier to read and may be required when your manuscript reaches the copyediting stage. For book publication, every element of the text should be double-spaced (including quotations, notes, bibliographies, appendices, figure legends, and glossaries). Once your manuscript is accepted for publication, your editor will advise you on any special requirements imposed by that press's house style.

The Review Process

Some university presses may give advance (i.e., conditional) contracts to experienced authors on the basis of incomplete or unreviewed manuscripts. Most, however, must obtain one or more reviews of a completed manuscript before presenting a project for the approval of the press's editorial board. As review procedures differ from press to press, check with the editor when you first submit the manuscript to find out what will be involved. He or she should be able to give you a tentative schedule for the review process. It is difficult to predict exactly how long it will take to reach a decision, since often readers' reports encourage authors to make further revisions to the manuscript and the manuscript is usually reviewed again after the author makes the revisions. If your manuscript is also under review at another publisher, be sure to let the editor know. Some editors will not review manuscripts that are under simultaneous consideration elsewhere; others will not object.

Preparing Your Manuscript for Publication

Most publishers will want an electronic version of your manuscript. Your manuscript should be keyboarded as simply as possible. There is no need to change fonts, type styles, and formats to differentiate between sections; in fact, this is counterproductive. The press's copy-editing or production department will insert the proper typesetting codes for formatting extracts, different levels of headings, and so on. And keep in mind that your book will be designed by a professional on the press's staff. Many presses will send you their own guidelines for submitting manuscripts.

FURTHER READING

Abel, Richard, Lyman W. Newlin, Katina Strauch, and Bruce Strauch, eds. *Scholarly Publishing, and Libraries in the Twentieth Century*. Indianapolis: Wiley, 2001.

American Psychological Association. *Publication Manual of the American Psychological Association*. 5th ed. Washington, DC: APA Books, 2001.

Appelbaum, Judith. *How to Get Happily Published: A Complete and Candid Guide*. 5th ed. New York: HarperResource, 1998.

Becker, Howard S. *Writing for Social Scientists: How to Start and Finish Your Thesis, Book, or Article*. Chicago: University of Chicago Press, 1986.

Day, Robert A. and Barbara Gastel *How to Write and Publish a Scientific Paper*. 6th ed. Westport, CT: Greenwood Publishing Group, Inc., 2006

Derricourt, Robin. *An Author's Guide to Scholarly Publishing*. Princeton: Princeton University Press, 1996.

Germano, William. *From Dissertation to Book*. Chicago: University of Chicago Press, 2005.

Germano, William. *Getting it Published: A Guide for Scholars and Anyone Else Serious About Serious Books*. Chicago: University of Chicago Press, 2001.

Gibaldi, Joseph and Herbert Lindenberger. *MLA Style Manual and Guide to Scholarly Publishing* 2nd ed. New York: Modern Language Association of America, 1998.

Hacker, Diana. *A Writer's Reference: 2003 MLA Update with CDROM*. 5th ed. Boston, MA: Bedford Books, 2004.

Harman, Eleanor and Ian Montagnes, eds. *The Thesis and the Book: A Guide for First-Time Academic Authors*. 2nd ed. Toronto: University of Toronto Press, 2003.

Huff, Anne Sigismund *Writing for Scholarly Publication*. Thousand Oaks, CA: SAGE Publications, 1998.

Katz, Michael J. *Elements of the Scientific Paper: A Step-by-Step Guide for Students and Professionals*. New Haven: Yale University Press, 1986.

Kasdorf, William E. *The Columbia Guide to Digital Publishing*. New York: Columbia University Press, 2003.

Luey, Beth. *Handbook for Academic Authors*. 4th ed. New York: Cambridge University Press, 2002.

Luey, Beth, ed. *Revising Your Dissertation: Advice from Leading Editors*. Berkeley: University of California Press, 2004.

Moxley, Joseph M. and Todd Taylor. *Writing and Publishing for Academic Authors*. 2nd ed. Lanham, MD: Rowman and Littlefield, 1996.

Mulvany, Nancy C. *Indexing Books*. 2nd Edition Chicago: University of Chicago Press, 2005.

Parsons, Paul. *Getting Published: The Acquisition Process at University Presses*. Knoxville: University of Tennessee Press, 1989.

Powell, Walter W. *Getting into Print: The Decision-Making Process in Scholarly Publishing*. Chicago: University of Chicago Press, 1985.

Schwartz, Marilyn and the Task Force on Bias-Free Language of the AAUP. *Guidelines for Bias-Free Writing*. Bloomington: Indiana University Press, 1995.

Strong, William S. *The Copyright Book: A Practical Guide*. 5th ed. Cambridge, MA: MIT Press, 1999.

Strunk, William J. and E. B. White. *The Elements of Style*. 4th ed. New York: Pearson Higher Education, 1999.

Swain, Dwight V. *Techniques of the Selling Writer*. Norman: University of Oklahoma Press, 1982.

Thompson, John. *Books in the Digital Age: The Transformation of Academic and Higher Education Publishing in Britain and the United States* Cambridge: Polity Press, 2005.

University of Chicago Press. *The Chicago Manual of Style*. 15th ed. Chicago: University of Chicago Press, 2003.

University of Chicago Press. *The Chicago Manual of Style Online*. 15th ed. Chicago: University of Chicago Press, 2003, http://www.chicagomanualofstyle.org/home.html

Zerubavel, Eviator. *The Clockwork Muse: A Practical Guide to Writing Theses, Dissertations, and Books*. Cambridge, MA: Harvard University Press, 1999.

For additional citations to materials on scholarly publishing, visit the association's Web site at www.aaupnet.org.

SUBJECT AREA GRID

This eight-page grid indicates the subject areas in which each press has a particularly strong interest.

Some presses are prepared to consider manuscripts of outstanding quality in areas other than those listed. For more detailed descriptions of press editorial programs, consult the individual listings in the "Directory of Members" section and contact the presses that interest you. (See also "On Submitting Manuscripts" in this directory.)

Table of subjects by publisher/institution.

	Akron	Alabama	Alaska	Alberta	A. Historical	A. Psychiatric	Amsterdam	Arizona	Arkansas	Baylor	Beacon	British Columbia	Brookings	Cairo (American)	Calgary	California	Cambridge	Carnegie Mellon	Catholic	Chicago	Chinese	Colorado	Columbia	Cork	Cornell	Duke	Duquesne	East. Washington	Florida	Fordham	Gallaudet	Georgetown
African Studies												●			●	●	●			●						●						
African American Studies		●							●		●		●			●		●		●		●	●		●	●			●	●	●	
Agriculture								●	●						●	●		●		●		●				●		●				
American Indian Studies	●	●						●	●		●	●			●	●	●			●		●			●	●		●				
American Studies	●							●	●		●				●	●	●	●		●		●	●		●	●			●	●		
Anthropology	●	●					●	●			●	●		●	●	●	●	●		●	●	●	●		●	●			●	●	●	
Cultural	●	●					●	●			●	●			●	●	●	●		●	●	●	●		●	●			●	●		
Physical	●														●	●	●	●		●			●						●			
Archaeology	●	●					●	●				●			●	●	●	●		●		●		●		●			●			
Architecture		●					●	●				●			●	●	●	●	●	●			●						●			
Art & Art History		●					●	●			●				●	●	●	●	●	●					●	●			●	●		
Asian Studies		●							●	●	●					●	●			●	●		●		●	●						
Asian American Studies		●									●					●	●			●			●		●	●						
Bibliography & Reference				●							●				●	●	●	●		●			●	●	●	●	●			●	●	
Biography	●	●	●	●			●	●			●	●			●	●	●	●	●	●	●	●	●	●	●	●			●	●	●	
Business							●					●	●		●			●	●	●		●	●		●				●			
Canadian Studies		●	●	●								●			●	●				●						●						
Caribbean Studies	●						●				●				●	●				●					●	●		●				
Child Development		●			●						●	●				●				●	●				●						●	
Classics							●			●					●	●	●		●	●			●						●			
Communications / Media	●						●		●	●	●	●		●	●	●	●	●		●	●		●			●			●			
Computer Sciences															●	●																
Creative Nonfiction	●						●			●		●				●	●											●			●	
Criminology							●					●				●	●			●			●						●			
Demography		●					●					●	●			●				●	●		●		●				●			
Economics		●					●				●	●	●	●			●			●	●		●	●					●			
Education				●							●	●	●	●			●	●		●	●		●						●	●		
Counseling																●				●									●	●		
History				●						●	●	●					●			●			●		●				●			
Learning Disabilities					●											●				●			●						●			
Theory & Method				●							●					●				●	●								●	●		
Engineering															●	●																
Environment / Conservation	●	●	●				●	●	●		●	●	●	●	●	●				●		●	●		●	●		●	●	●		●
ESL																●				●											●	●
Ethnic Studies		●	●			●	●	●	●		●	●			●	●	●			●		●			●	●			●	●		
European Studies							●				●		●	●	●	●	●						●		●	●	●		●			
Fiction											●				●	●		●											●			
Film Studies		●		●			●			●	●				●	●	●			●		●	●	●		●		●		●		
Gay and Lesbian Studies		●									●					●				●		●			●							
Gender Studies						●	●	●	●		●	●			●	●				●		●	●	●	●	●						
Geography			●							●		●				●				●	●	●	●		●	●	●					
Gerontology							●					●				●				●									●			
History	●	●	●		●		●	●			●	●			●	●	●		●	●	●	●	●		●	●			●	●		●
African					●											●	●			●						●						
American	●	●			●			●	●	●	●					●	●		●	●		●	●		●	●		●	●	●	●	●
Asian					●						●	●				●	●		●	●			●		●	●					●	
British					●							●				●	●								●					●		
Canadian		●	●	●	●						●	●			●	●	●															
Environmental	●	●	●		●			●	●		●	●				●	●			●		●			●	●		●	●			
European					●		●					●				●	●		●	●			●		●	●	●			●	●	
Latin American	●				●			●			●					●	●			●		●							●	●		
Middle Eastern					●					●	●			●		●	●			●			●						●			
Ancient					●		●									●	●	●	●	●					●							
Classical					●		●									●	●	●	●	●			●			●				●		
Modern		●	●		●		●		●		●					●	●	●	●	●	●	●	●	●	●	●			●	●		
Law		●						●				●	●		●	●	●		●	●	●	●				●				●	●	●
Language	●							●	●			●			●	●	●			●	●									●	●	●
Linguistics	●							●	●			●			●	●	●			●						●				●	●	●
Speech															●	●	●															
Latin American Studies	●						●				●		●		●	●	●			●		●		●					●			
Library Science							●									●				●												

-10-

	Akron	Alabama	Alaska	Alberta	A. Historical	A. Psychiatric	Amsterdam	Arizona	Arkansas	Baylor	Beacon	British Columbia	Brookings	Cairo (American)	Calgary	California	Cambridge	Carnegie Mellon	Catholic	Chicago	Chinese	Colorado	Columbia	Cork	Cornell	Duke	Duquesne	East. Washington	Florida	Fordham	Gallaudet	Georgetown
Literature		●	●				●	●				●				●	●	●	●	●		●	●		●	●	●	●	●	●	●	
Literary Criticism		●					●			●						●		●	●	●			●	●	●	●	●	●	●	●		
Literary History		●					●									●	●	●	●			●	●	●	●	●	●	●	●			
African																●			●				●			●			●			
African American		●						●								●			●			●			●	●			●	●		
American		●						●	●						●	●	●	●	●	●		●			●	●			●	●		
Asian																●			●	●	●		●		●			●		●		
British																●		●	●	●			●		●	●	●	●		●		
Canadian				●								●			●								●									
Classical																●	●		●	●			●		●	●				●		
Eastern																●			●				●			●						
European							●									●		●	●			●	●	●	●	●			●	●		
Medieval							●									●		●	●				●	●	●	●			●			
Renaissance							●									●		●	●			●		●	●					●		
Modern		●					●									●		●	●	●		●		●	●	●		●				
Contemporary		●					●	●								●		●	●	●		●		●		●					●	
Folklore			●					●	●										●					●	●	●		●				●
Mythology		●	●					●											●			●			●							
Translations		●	●					●				●				●	●	●	●		●		●	●		●		●			●	
Maritime Studies		●	●				●					●				●													●	●		
Mathematics																●			●													
Medicine			●		●		●									●	●			●			●									
Ethics					●											●	●								●	●		●				●
History		●	●				●							●			●		●			●	●	●	●							●
Medieval Studies							●								●	●		●	●			●			●	●	●		●			
Middle East Studies							●		●		●		●	●	●	●	●		●			●			●				●			●
Military Studies		●	●						●		●	●	●		●		●						●					●				
Near Eastern Studies											●		●	●	●		●			●					●	●						
Performing Arts							●					●				●	●	●			●				●				●	●	●	●
Dance												●				●	●			●					●				●			
Music							●					●				●	●	●			●				●				●			
Theatre							●				●	●			●	●	●			●				●		●				●	●	
Pacific Studies			●				●				●	●					●			●					●	●						
Philosophy							●					●			●		●	●	●	●		●			●	●	●			●	●	●
Ethics							●			●	●				●		●	●	●	●		●			●	●	●				●	●
History of Philosophy										●	●				●		●	●	●	●		●			●	●			●			
Photography		●														●	●	●		●		●		●				●			●	●
Poetry	●									●		●				●	●		●		●							●		●		
Political Science / Public Affairs	●		●				●		●	●	●	●	●	●	●			●	●	●		●	●	●	●	●			●		●	●
Popular Culture		●					●			●									●			●			●			●	●	●	●	
Psychiatry					●													●		●			●		●	●				●		
Psychology							●	●					●	●					●			●			●	●	●			●		
Public Health			●				●					●	●	●			●	●				●			●							
Publishing							●											●		●												
Regional Studies	●	●	●	●			●	●	●		●	●		●	●		●	●		●		●	●		●	●		●	●	●		●
Religion		●					●	●		●	●		●	●		●	●	●	●	●		●	●		●	●	●		●	●		●
Science	●		●		●		●			●	●				●	●		●	●	●		●	●	●		●		●		●		
Biological Science		●					●			●	●				●	●			●	●	●		●		●	●		●				
Botany		●							●		●	●				●							●		●	●		●				
Genetics					●						●				●		●						●							●		
Earth Science		●						●			●	●			●	●			●			●			●		●					
Geology		●						●			●	●			●	●			●			●			●		●					
Physical Science		●					●				●					●			●			●	●									
Astronomy								●								●			●			●	●									
History of Science	●	●					●	●								●			●	●	●				●	●		●				
Slavic Studies			●								●		●			●			●				●	●					●			
Sports		●																	●			●		●								
Social Work						●	●				●	●				●				●		●								●		
Sociology	●		●							●	●		●	●	●	●			●	●	●		●	●					●	●		
Urban Studies							●				●	●		●	●	●	●	●		●			●	●								●
Veterinary Sciences																●							●			●						
Women's Studies						●	●	●	●	●	●	●			●	●	●			●			●	●	●	●				●	●	●

	Georgia	Getty	Harvard	Hawaii	Howard	Illinois	Indiana Hist.	Indiana	Iowa	Island	Jewish Pub.	Johns Hopkins	Kansas	Kent State	Kentucky	Leuven	Louisiana	McGill-Queen's	Marquette	Massachusetts	MIT	Mercer	Michigan	Michigan State	Minnesota Hist.	Minnesota	Mississippi	Missouri	MLA	National Acad.	National Gallery	Naval
African Studies	●		●		●		●																●		●					●		
African American Studies	●		●		●	●	●	●				●		●	●		●		●	●		●	●	●	●	●	●	●	●	●		●
Agriculture						●	●	●							●								●							●		
American Indian Studies	●		●			●	●						●				●		●				●	●	●	●		●		●		
American Studies	●		●		●	●		●	●			●	●	●	●		●		●	●			●	●	●	●	●	●	●			
Anthropology	●		●	●	●	●		●	●						●		●						●	●		●		●				
Cultural	●		●	●	●	●		●	●						●		●						●	●		●		●				
Physical			●														●															
Archaeology		●	●						●		●				●	●							●									
Architecture		●	●			●				●							●		●	●						●		●				
Art & Art History	●	●	●		●	●											●		●	●	●		●	●							●	●
Asian Studies			●		●					●					●								●				●					
Asian-American Studies			●		●															●			●				●					
Bibliography & Reference			●			●		●				●	●													●	●					●
Biography	●		●	●	●	●	●	●	●	●			●		●	●	●	●	●	●			●	●		●	●	●	●	●		●
Business		●	●		●																●									●		
Canadian Studies																		●						●						●		
Caribbean Studies	●		●															●	●	●			●	●						●		
Child Development			●			●											●													●		
Classics	●		●			●		●			●	●					●		●				●							●		
Communications/ Media			●	●	●			●									●		●	●					●	●	●	●				
Computer Sciences																	●			●										●		
Creative Nonfiction	●		●					●	●								●						●			●	●					●
Criminology			●														●		●													●
Demography			●														●		●											●		
Economics			●	●	●	●			●								●		●	●			●	●						●		
Education			●		●	●		●				●					●		●		●		●							●	●	
Counseling																																
History			●		●	●						●	●				●					●	●									
Learning Disabilities			●			●																										
Theory & Method																	●						●							●		
Engineering			●		●												●													●		●
Environment/Conservation	●		●	●	●	●			●	●		●	●				●	●	●	●			●	●	●	●	●			●		
ESL																					●									●		
Ethnic Studies	●		●		●	●		●	●								●		●	●			●	●	●	●	●	●	●			
European Studies			●		●	●											●	●	●	●			●			●	●		●			
Fiction	●		●		●			●									●			●			●	●					●			
Film Studies	●		●	●	●	●		●					●				●	●				●				●	●	●				
Gay and Lesbian Studies																			●							●			●			
Gender Studies	●		●		●			●	●			●					●		●				●			●			●	●		
Geography	●		●						●	●							●	●	●				●	●		●						
Gerontology												●																		●		
History			●		●	●		●	●	●		●	●	●	●		●	●	●	●	●		●	●	●	●	●	●	●			●
African			●	●		●																	●									
American	●		●	●	●	●		●	●			●	●	●	●		●	●	●	●			●	●	●	●	●	●	●			●
Asian			●	●				●							●																	●
British	●		●			●									●		●										●					●
Canadian	●																●						●									●
Environmental	●		●						●	●			●		●		●	●	●				●			●						●
European			●	●				●					●				●	●	●	●				●		●		●				●
Latin American	●		●		●												●	●	●									●				●
Middle Eastern			●					●									●	●	●													
Ancient			●	●				●							●		●	●	●				●									
Classical			●					●							●		●						●									●
Modern	●		●	●	●			●						●	●		●						●				●	●				●
Law			●	●	●	●				●			●				●						●									●
Language			●	●	●	●											●		●		●		●					●				
Linguistics			●															●	●		●		●					●				
Speech				●																	●											
Latin American Studies	●	●	●		●												●		●							●				●	●	
Library Science						●											●		●													

	Georgia	Getty	Harvard	Hawaii	Howard	Illinois	Indiana Hist.	Indiana	Iowa	Island	Jewish Pub.	Johns Hopkins	Kansas	Kent State	Kentucky	Leuven	Louisiana	McGill-Queen's	Marquette	Massachusetts	MIT	Mercer	Michigan	Michigan State	Minnesota Hist.	Minnesota	Mississippi	Missouri	MLA	National Acad.	National Gallery	Naval
Literature	•		•	•	•	•		•	•			•			•		•	•		•		•	•	•	•	•	•	•	•			•
Literary Criticism	•		•	•	•	•		•				•			•		•	•	•			•	•				•	•	•	•		
Literary History	•		•			•	•	•				•			•		•	•	•			•	•				•	•	•	•		
African				•		•		•									•						•									
African American	•		•		•		•	•					•				•		•			•	•			•	•	•	•	•		
American	•		•			•		•				•			•		•	•	•	•		•	•	•	•	•	•	•	•			•
Asian			•	•				•									•						•						•			
British			•			•						•					•	•	•				•			•	•	•	•			•
Canadian																		•								•	•					
Classical		•	•									•					•		•				•					•				
Eastern																	•		•									•				
European			•									•					•		•				•			•		•	•			•
Medieval			•			•						•					•		•				•			•		•				
Renaissance			•														•		•	•			•					•				
Modern	•		•	•		•		•							•		•	•	•				•			•	•	•	•			
Contemporary	•		•	•		•		•									•	•	•				•			•	•	•	•			
Folklore	•		•	•		•		•								•	•							•	•		•	•				
Mythology			•														•		•				•					•				
Translations			•			•		•									•									•	•	•				•
Maritime Studies			•														•					•	•	•							•	•
Mathematics												•					•													•		
Medicine			•		•	•		•				•					•					•				•				•		
Ethics			•			•		•				•					•					•								•		
History			•	•		•						•					•					•										
Medieval Studies			•														•	•	•			•				•		•				
Middle East Studies			•					•					•		•	•						•				•						
Military Studies			•	•		•	•	•					•	•	•		•	•			•			•		•	•	•		•		•
Near Eastern Studies			•					•			•						•				•	•						•				
Performing Arts			•	•		•		•	•											•			•			•	•	•				
Dance			•	•		•		•												•			•									
Music			•	•		•											•			•			•			•	•					
Theatre			•	•		•		•	•											•			•				•					
Pacific Studies			•														•											•				
Philosophy			•	•	•	•		•			•						•	•	•	•						•		•				
Ethics			•			•					•						•	•	•	•		•						•				
History of Philosophy			•	•		•											•	•	•									•				
Photography	•	•			•	•	•										•	•		•	•		•			•	•	•		•		
Poetry	•								•								•	•	•	•			•			•						
Political Science/Public Affairs	•		•	•	•	•		•				•	•		•	•	•	•		•	•		•	•	•	•	•	•	•	•		•
Popular Culture		•	•											•						•						•	•	•	•			
Psychiatry			•									•					•									•				•		
Psychology			•		•	•						•					•						•			•				•		
Public Health			•		•	•			•			•					•	•								•				•		
Publishing						•															•									•		
Regional Studies	•		•	•		•	•	•	•			•	•	•		•	•	•	•	•			•	•	•	•	•	•				
Religion			•	•	•	•		•		•		•				•	•	•	•			•				•	•					
Science	•		•	•		•		•	•		•						•				•									•		•
Biological Sciences	•		•	•		•		•	•		•						•				•									•		
Botany	•		•	•				•	•												•									•		
Genetics			•					•	•				•								•									•		
Earth Sciences			•	•				•	•								•				•									•		
Geology			•					•	•												•									•		
Physical Science			•	•					•								•				•									•		
Astronomy			•																		•									•		
History of Science			•	•		•			•			•					•						•						•	•		•
Slavic Studies			•							•							•	•										•				
Social Work				•	•																									•		
Sociology			•	•	•	•											•		•	•						•				•		
Sports							•								•		•								•	•		•				
Urban Studies	•		•	•	•	•			•				•	•			•	•	•	•			•		•	•				•		
Veterinary Sciences																														•		
Women's Studies	•		•	•	•	•		•	•		•	•	•		•		•	•	•			•		•	•	•	•	•	•	•		•

	Nebraska	Nevada	New England	New Mexico	New York	North Carolina	North Texas	Northern Illinois	Northwestern	Notre Dame	Ohio	Oklahoma	Oregon State	Ottawa	Oxford	Pennsylvania	Penn State	Pittsburgh	PISA	Princeton	Puerto Rico	Purdue	RAND	Resources/RFF	Rockefeller	Russell Sage	Rutgers	Soc. Biblical Lit.	South Carolina	Southern Illinois
African Studies	●										●																			
African American Studies	●		●	●	●	●	●			●		●				●	●	●	●							●	●		●	●
Agriculture	●											●				●				●		●	●							
American Indian Studies	●	●	●	●		●						●	●	●		●		●									●			
American Studies	●	●	●	●	●	●	●				●		●			●	●	●									●		●	●
Anthropology	●	●		●	●				●		●	●	●			●	●			●	●	●					●	●		
Cultural	●	●	●		●				●		●	●	●			●	●			●	●	●		●			●			
Physical		●		●												●		●									●			
Archaeology	●	●	●	●		●					●	●				●		●											●	
Architecture			●	●	●		●						●			●	●	●	●			●								
Art & Art History			●	●	●		●	●					●			●	●	●		●	●	●							●	
Asian Studies	●										●					●	●			●								●	●	
Asian-American Studies					●											●				●							●	●		
Bibliography & Reference			●							●		●	●	●		●				●	●	●								
Biography	●	●	●	●	●	●	●	●	●	●		●				●	●	●		●	●		●			●	●		●	●
Business		●			●	●			●							●				●	●	●	●						●	
Canadian Studies	●												●																	
Caribbean Studies	●	●			●	●				●						●		●				●						●	●	
Child Development						●							●	●		●					●						●	●		
Classics						●					●					●	●			●	●	●							●	
Communications / Media			●		●		●		●							●				●		●					●			●
Computer Sciences																●				●	●	●								
Creative Nonfiction	●	●	●		●	●			●	●			●			●		●		●		●					●	●		●
Criminology		●			●		●									●				●	●	●					●			●
Demography												●	●			●				●	●	●		●			●			
Economics						●		●				●	●			●				●	●	●	●				●			
Education			●			●							●			●				●	●	●					●			
Counseling													●																	
History						●	●						●							●	●									
Learning Disabilities																					●									
Theory & Method													●							●	●	●					●			
Engineering																●				●		●								
Environment / Conservation	●	●	●	●		●	●				●	●	●			●		●	●	●	●	●	●	●			●			
ESL																●														
Ethnic Studies	●	●	●	●	●	●	●	●		●		●				●		●			●						●	●		
European Studies			●	●		●	●		●		●					●		●		●		●								
Fiction		●		●			●		●	●	●							●		●		●								
Film Studies	●			●					●							●				●		●					●			●
Gay and Lesbian Studies						●	●																							
Gender Studies	●	●	●	●		●	●	●					●			●		●		●		●					●	●		●
Geography	●	●	●			●						●	●	●		●				●		●					●			
Gerontology																●				●	●	●				●	●			
History	●	●	●	●	●	●	●	●			●	●		●		●	●	●	●	●	●	●		●	●		●		●	●
African												●				●													●	
American	●	●	●	●	●	●			●	●		●	●			●	●	●			●						●	●	●	●
Asian												●				●					●						●			
British			●			●		●				●	●			●	●													
Canadian	●					●		●					●	●																
Environmental	●	●	●			●	●	●			●	●	●			●		●	●						●		●			
European			●	●		●	●		●	●						●	●	●	●	●		●								
Latin American	●			●		●			●							●	●	●			●						●			
Middle Eastern			●		●	●										●				●								●		
Ancient						●					●					●	●			●	●							●		
Classical						●					●	●	●			●				●	●	●						●		
Modern		●	●		●	●	●	●			●	●				●		●									●		●	●
Law					●	●	●		●		●				●	●		●		●		●					●	●	●	
Language	●	●							●			●				●	●												●	
Linguistics	●			●					●				●	●		●				●		●							●	
Speech																													●	
Latin American Studies	●			●		●					●	●	●			●		●	●		●					●	●			
Library Science																														

	Nebraska	Nevada	New England	New Mexico	New York	North Carolina	North Texas	Northern Illinois	Northwestern	Notre Dame	Ohio	Oklahoma	Oregon State	Ottawa	Oxford	Pennsylvania	Penn State	Pittsburgh	PISA	Princeton	Puerto Rico	Purdue	RAND	Resources/RFF	Rockefeller	Russell Sage	Rutgers	Soc. Biblical Lit.	South Carolina	Southern Illinois
Literature	●	●	●	●		●		●	●	●	●	●		●	●	●	●			●	●	●					●		●	●
Literary Criticism	●	●	●	●		●		●	●	●	●			●	●	●	●			●	●	●					●	●	●	●
Literary History	●	●	●			●		●		●	●			●	●	●				●	●	●							●	
African										●				●						●										
African American			●			●			●					●						●							●		●	
American	●	●	●	●		●		●	●	●	●	●		●	●					●							●		●	●
Asian										●				●						●							●			
British						●			●	●				●	●					●							●		●	
Canadian													●																	
Classical						●		●	●		●			●	●					●								●		
Eastern										●				●						●										
European		●						●	●		●			●	●			●		●									●	
Medieval									●		●			●	●	●			●											
Renaissance									●		●			●	●				●											
Modern		●			●		●				●			●	●					●							●		●	●
Contemporary	●	●	●	●		●	●	●	●				●		●			●	●	●							●		●	●
Folklore		●	●	●		●	●						●		●	●	●				●									
Mythology		●									●	●		●						●										
Translations	●		●	●				●	●			●		●		●			●	●	●						●			
Maritime Studies		●			●					●							●		●								●			
Mathematics			●											●			●	●	●											
Medicine		●	●		●				●	●		●	●			●				●			●		●		●			
Ethics		●	●		●					●		●	●			●											●			
History		●							●	●													●		●					
Medieval Studies					●		●		●		●	●	●		●	●														
Middle East Studies		●			●			●						●						●							●			
Military Studies	●			●	●	●			●	●				●						●									●	●
Near Eastern Studies					●									●													●			
Performing Arts		●		●		●		●						●			●			●										●
Dance						●								●																
Music		●			●		●							●			●													
Theatre		●					●							●			●													●
Pacific Studies						●								●																
Philosophy		●		●	●	●	●	●	●		●	●		●	●	●	●	●	●	●		●			●	●				●
Ethics		●			●	●	●	●		●	●		●	●	●	●	●		●	●		●								
History of Philosophy			●			●	●	●	●		●	●		●	●	●	●	●	●	●										
Photography	●		●	●		●							●							●							●			●
Poetry		●			●		●	●	●					●		●		●		●										●
Political Science / Public Affairs		●	●	●	●		●		●		●		●	●	●	●	●	●	●	●		●	●		●					
Popular Culture		●	●	●	●	●												●												●
Psychiatry														●					●											
Psychology				●		●								●				●		●				●						
Public Health		●			●								●	●			●	●	●	●			●	●	●					
Publishing		●						●									●													
Regional Studies	●	●	●	●	●	●	●	●	●		●	●	●		●	●	●	●				●		●			●	●	●	●
Religion		●	●	●	●	●	●	●		●	●		●	●	●	●				●			●				●	●	●	
Science	●	●	●		●				●		●	●		●			●	●	●		●		●		●		●		●	
Biological Sciences		●	●		●				●	●		●			●	●	●		●		●				●		●		●	
Botany		●			●						●			●			●	●	●						●				●	
Genetics												●			●	●									●				●	●
Earth Sciences	●	●			●				●	●		●			●	●		●		●										
Geology	●									●		●			●	●														
Physical Science	●	●			●							●			●	●	●	●		●										
Astronomy												●			●	●	●													
History of Science				●			●		●			●			●	●	●	●	●		●			●		●				
Slavic Studies						●	●				●			●	●	●	●		●											
Social Work		●								●	●		●	●			●		●			●			●			●		
Sociology	●	●		●		●				●	●		●		●	●	●		●			●		●	●					
Sports		●		●									●																	
Urban Studies		●	●		●	●					●	●		●		●	●		●	●		●	●		●					
Veterinary Sciences																	●		●											
Women's Studies	●	●	●	●	●	●	●	●		●	●		●	●	●	●	●			●		●			●	●			●	●

	S. Methodist	Stanford	SUNY	Syracuse	Teachers	Temple	Tennessee	Texas	Texas A&M	Texas Christian	Texas Tech	Texas Western	Tokyo	Toronto	United Nations	U.S. Inst. Peace	Upjohn	Urban Inst.	Utah	Utah State	Vanderbilt	Virginia	Washington	Wash. State	Wayne State	Wesleyan	West Indies	West Virginia	Wilfrid Laurier	Wisconsin	Woodrow Wilson	Yale
African Studies													●	●	●	●												●		●	●	●
African American Studies		●	●	●	●	●	●	●		●			●	●	●							●	●	●	●	●	●	●				●
Agriculture									●				●		●																	
American Indian Studies		●	●	●			●	●	●				●	●		●			●	●		●	●	●						●		●
American Studies	●	●	●			●	●	●		●	●	●	●						●	●	●	●	●		●			●		●	●	●
Anthropology	●	●		●		●	●	●	●				●	●					●			●	●		●	●	●	●	●	●		●
Cultural		●				●		●					●	●					●			●			●	●	●	●		●		●
Physical							●				●	●	●	●					●									●				●
Archaeology						●	●	●	●				●	●					●		●	●	●	●				●				●
Architecture						●	●	●	●	●			●	●							●	●	●		●						●	●
Art & Art History	●	●				●		●					●	●							●	●	●	●				●				●
Asian Studies	●	●			●								●	●	●		●	●				●								●	●	●
Asian American Studies	●			●	●								●									●										●
Astronomy													●																			●
Bibliography & Reference													●	●								●		●			●					●
Biography	●	●	●	●		●	●	●					●	●					●		●		●							●	●	●
Business	●	●											●	●	●																	●
Canadian Studies													●	●					●		●	●	●	●				●	●	●		●
Caribbean Studies		●			●								●									●					●					●
Child Development				●									●																			●
Classics		●					●						●	●									●					●	●			●
Communications / Media		●	●		●		●						●	●									●							●	●	●
Computer Sciences	●												●																			●
Creative Nonfiction	●		●	●			●				●											●	●					●				●
Criminology	●	●			●		●						●																			●
Demography													●	●										●								
Economics	●	●		●	●		●						●	●	●		●	●										●		●		●
Education	●	●		●	●		●						●				●		●	●								●				●
Counseling				●									●							●								●				●
History		●											●	●						●								●				●
Learning Disabilities				●	●								●							●								●				●
Theory & Method		●		●	●								●	●						●								●				●
Engineering													●																			●
Environment / Conservation		●	●		●	●	●	●	●				●	●	●	●			●	●			●	●	●	●				●		●
ESL				●									●																			●
Ethnic Studies	●	●	●		●		●	●		●	●	●	●	●		●			●	●		●	●	●		●	●		●	●		●
European Studies		●	●					●					●	●		●														●	●	●
Fiction	●		●						●	●																	●					
Film Studies	●		●	●		●		●					●									●		●	●			●	●	●		●
Gay and Lesbian Studies		●											●						●									●		●		
Gender Studies		●	●		●	●	●						●	●	●				●			●	●	●	●			●		●		●
Geography			●		●		●	●					●	●	●	●			●			●								●		●
Gerontology													●																			
History	●	●			●	●	●	●	●	●	●	●	●			●			●		●	●	●	●	●	●		●		●	●	●
African													●			●					●							●		●		●
American	●	●	●		●	●	●	●	●	●	●	●	●			●			●	●	●	●	●					●		●	●	●
Asian	●	●							●		●		●			●							●							●	●	●
British	●	●							●		●		●		●	●												●		●	●	●
Canadian				●									●	●									●	●	●				●		●	●
Environmental				●			●	●		●			●	●		●			●			●	●	●	●			●		●	●	●
European	●	●	●						●		●		●			●						●		●						●	●	●
Latin American	●	●				●			●	●		●	●			●				●							●		●	●		●
Middle Eastern	●	●	●					●					●			●					●									●		●
Ancient								●					●	●																		●
Classical								●					●	●															●	●		●
Modern	●			●		●					●		●	●	●														●	●	●	●
Law	●				●								●	●																		●
Language		●					●						●	●	●				●				●					●				●
Linguistics													●	●	●				●						●			●				●
Speech																							●									●
Latin American Studies	●	●			●		●				●	●			●	●				●						●			●	●	●	●
Library Science													●	●																		●

	S. Methodist	Stanford	SUNY	Syracuse	Teachers	Temple	Tennessee	Texas	Texas A&M	Texas Christian	Texas Tech	Texas Western	Tokyo	Toronto	United Nations	U.S. Inst. Peace	Upjohn	Urban Inst.	Utah	Utah State	Vanderbilt	Virginia	Washington	Wash. State	Wayne State	Wesleyan	West Indies	West Virginia	Wilfrid Laurier	Wisconsin	Woodrow Wilson	Yale
Literature		•	•	•		•	•	•	•	•	•	•		•					•		•	•	•		•		•		•			•
Literary Criticism		•	•	•			•	•		•			•	•							•	•	•		•				•		•	•
Literary History				•			•	•		•	•		•	•							•	•	•		•							•
African		•																			•				•							•
African American		•																			•	•	•		•		•					•
American		•	•	•		•	•	•	•	•	•		•								•	•	•		•							•
Asian		•											•									•										•
British		•								•			•								•	•										•
Canadian														•									•				•					•
Classical		•						•					•														•					•
Eastern		•																														
European		•	•	•				•					•								•	•										•
Medieval		•	•										•															•				•
Renaissance													•																			•
Modern		•	•			•	•	•		•			•								•	•										•
Contemporary		•	•			•	•						•								•											•
Folklore			•			•	•	•	•		•		•				•	•			•				•		•					•
Mythology			•										•				•								•					•		•
Translations		•	•	•				•					•										•	•	•		•					•
Maritime Studies								•					•		•								•	•								•
Mathematics													•																			
Medicine	•												•	•													•					•
Ethics	•			•									•								•				•							•
History													•								•				•							•
Medieval Studies			•	•									•	•														•				•
Middle East Studies		•	•				•						•		•	•					•									•	•	•
Military Studies		•	•			•		•		•	•		•	•	•						•									•	•	•
Near Eastern Studies			•	•			•						•	•	•	•					•									•	•	•
Performing Arts	•			•									•	•											•				•		•	•
Dance																									•				•		•	•
Music				•																					•			•				•
Theatre	•			•									•																			•
Pacific Studies		•											•	•	•	•						•	•							•	•	•
Philosophy	•	•	•	•									•	•															•		•	•
Ethics	•	•	•										•	•	•	•					•								•		•	•
History of Philosophy		•											•	•																		•
Photography				•			•	•					•	•								•										•
Poetry													•				•	•							•				•			•
Political Science / Public Affairs		•	•	•		•		•	•			•	•	•	•	•	•	•			•	•	•	•		•						•
Popular Culture		•	•					•					•								•				•			•				•
Psychiatry													•	•							•											•
Psychology		•											•	•							•						•					•
Public Health		•										•	•	•	•		•				•											•
Publishing	•												•	•																		•
Regional Studies	•	•	•	•		•	•	•	•	•	•	•		•			•				•	•	•	•	•	•		•	•			•
Religion	•	•	•	•		•	•	•					•	•	•	•					•				•			•		•	•	•
Science				•			•	•		•	•		•	•	•				•		•				•			•		•		•
Biological Sciences							•	•		•			•	•	•						•				•			•				•
Botany			•				•			•			•								•							•				•
Genetics													•																			
Earth Sciences						•	•		•	•			•		•				•													•
Geology						•	•	•		•			•						•													•
Physical Science													•																			•
Astronomy													•																			
History of Science		•					•						•								•				•							•
Slavic Studies													•	•							•									•	•	•
Social Work													•	•	•	•			•									•				•
Sociology		•	•	•		•		•					•	•			•				•							•		•		•
Sports	•		•	•	•																											
Urban Studies		•	•			•		•					•	•	•		•	•			•				•						•	•
Veterinary Sciences													•																			
Women's Studies			•	•		•	•	•		•	•	•	•	•			•		•		•		•	•	•	•	•	•		•		•

PRESSES PUBLISHING JOURNALS

University presses have always been associated with publishing books of merit and distinction. This remains as true today as in the past, but less well appreciated is the extent to which university presses are active in publishing scholarly journals.

Journals form a major part of the publishing program of many presses, and more than half of the association's members produce at least one periodical. In all, university presses publish more than 800 scholarly periodicals, including many of the most distinguished in their respective fields. The following is a list of those presses that publish journals.

Each individual press listing also gives the number of journals, if any, that a press publishes and usually lists the titles of journals under the press's editorial program. Many journals are available in both print and electronic versions. For information concerning a specific periodical, readers are advised to consult a copy of the publication before communicating with the press concerned.

The following AAUP member presses publish journals.

The University of Alabama Press
American Historical Association
American Psychiatric Press, Inc.
American University in Cairo Press
Amsterdam University Press
The University of Arkansas Press
Brookings Institution Press
University of Calgary Press
The University of California Press
Cambridge University Press
The Catholic University of America Press
The University of Chicago Press
The Chinese University Press
University Press of Colorado
Cork University Press
Duke University Press
Fordham University Press
Georgetown University Press
The University of Hawai'i Press
The University of Illinois Press
Indiana University Press
The Johns Hopkins University Press
The Kent State University Press
The University Press of Kentucky
Leuven University Press
Marquette University Press
The MIT Press
The Michigan State University Press

Minnesota Historical Society Press
University of Minnesota Press
Modern Language Association of America
National Gallery of Art
Naval Institute Press
The University of Nebraska Press
The University of North Carolina Press
University of North Texas Press
Northwestern University Press
University of Ottawa Press
Oxford University Press
Penn State University Press
Pisa University Press
Princeton University Press
The University of Puerto Rico Press
RAND Corporation
The Rockefeller University Press
Society of Biblical Literature
State University of New York Press
University of Texas Press
Texas Tech University Press
University of Toronto Press, Inc.
Washington State University Press
Wayne State University Press
Wesleyan University Press
University of the West Indies Press
West Virginia University Press
Wilfrid Laurier University Press
The University of Wisconsin Press

DIRECTORY OF MEMBERS

This section includes a wealth of information on the AAUP's 126 member presses, including current street and mailing addresses, phone and fax numbers, and Web site and e-mail addresses. Most presses also list their sales representatives / distributors for Canada, the UK, and Europe. (Addresses for these representatives are included at the end of the section.)

Each entry contains important information describing that press's editorial program. This includes a list of disciplines published, special series, joint imprints, copublishing programs, and the names of journals published, if any.

Press staff are listed, wherever possible, by the following departments / order: director and administrative staff, acquisitions editorial, electronic publishing, manuscript editorial, design and production, marketing, journals, business, and information systems. In most cases the first person listed within a department is its head. Readers should note, however, that this method of organization is intended to promote ease of use, and is not always indicative of the lines of authority within an individual press.

Information on each press's membership status follows the staff listing. This includes date of press founding, type of membership (full, international, or associate), year admitted to AAUP, title output for 2006 and 2007, the number of journals published, and the total number of titles currently in print.

The University of Akron Press

Akron, OH 44325-1703

Phone: (330) 972-5342
Fax: (330) 972-8364
E-mail: uapress@uakron.edu
Web site: www.uakron.edu/uapress

Customer Service / Order Fulfillment:
Phone: (330) 972-6953
Toll-free: (877) UAPRESS (827-7377)
Fax: (330) 972-8364

Staff
Interim Director: Andrew Borowiec (330/972-6202; e-mail: borowiec@uakron.edu)
Production Coordinator: Amy Freels (330/972-5342; e-mail: production@uakron.edu)
Business Manager: Carol Slatter (330/972-2795; e-mail: slatter@uakron.edu)
Marketing Representative: Julie Gammon (330/972-6254; e-mail: jgammon@uakron.edu)
Distribution Manager: Mike Palumbo (330/972-6953; e-mail: uapress@uakron.edu)

Full Member
Established: 1988
Title output 2006: 9
Titles currently in print: 94

Admitted to AAUP: 1997
Title output 2007: 6

Editorial Program
Scholarly books and poetry, with special interests in environmental studies and regional history. The Press distributes the publications of Principia Press.
Special series: Akron Series in Poetry, with Akron Poetry Prize Competition; Ohio History and Culture; Ohio Politics; Technology and the Environment

The University of Alabama Press

Street Address:
200 Hackberry Lane
Tuscaloosa, AL 35401

Phone: (205) 348-5180
Fax: (205) 348-9201
E-mail: (user I.D.)@uapress.ua.edu
Web site: www.uapress.ua.edu

Mailing Address:
Box 870380
Tuscaloosa, AL 35487-0380

Order Fulfillment:
The University of Alabama Press
Chicago Distribution Center
11030 South Langley Avenue
Chicago, IL 60628
Phone: (773) 568-1550
Fax: (773) 660-2235

UK / European Distributor:
Eurospan

Canadian Representative:
Scholarly Book Services

Staff
Director: Daniel J.J. Ross (205/348-1560; e-mail: danross)
 Assistant to the Director: Denise Rickman (205/348-5180; e-mail: drickman)
 Rights and Permissions Coordinator: Claire Evans (205/348-1561; e-mail: cevans)

Acquisitions Editorial: Daniel J.J. Ross (history, Judaic studies, regional, trade)
  Senior Acquisitions Editor: Judith Knight (archaeology, anthropology, ethnohistory, Native American studies) (205/348-1568; e-mail: jknight)
  Acquisitions Editor, Humanities: Dan Waterman (literature and criticism, rhetoric and communication, African American studies, public administration, theater, environmental studies) (205/348-5538; e-mail: waterman)
  Acquisitions Editor: Elizabeth Motherwell (natural history and the environment) (205/348-7108; e-mail: emother)
Electronic Publishing: Claire Evans, Associate Editor for Digital and Electronic Publishing (205/348-1561; e-mail: cevans)
Manuscript Editorial: Suzette Griffith, Managing Editor (205/348-9708; e-mail: sgriffit)
  Assistant Managing Editor: Joanna Jacobs (205/348-1563; e-mail: jjacobs)
  Project Editor: Jon Berry (205/348-1565; e-mail: jberry)
  Editorial Assistant: Carol Connell (205/348-5183; e-mail: cconnell)
Design and Production: Rick Cook, Production Manager (205/348-1571; e-mail: rcook)
  Designer: Michele Quinn (205/348-1570; e-mail: mquinn)
  Production Editor and Assistant Production Manager: Chris Heller (205/348-9665; e-mail: cheller)
Marketing: Elizabeth Motherwell, Sales Manager (205/348-7108; e-mail: emother)
  Assistant Marketing Manager and Publicity Director: Shana Rivers (205/348-9534; e-mail: srrivers)
  Advertising, Direct Mail, and Exhibits Manager: (205/348-1566)
Business: Rosalyn Carr, Manager (205/348-1567; e-mail: rcarr)
  Accounting Specialist: Allie Harper (205/348-1564; e-mail: aharper)

Full Member

Established: 1945	Admitted to AAUP: 1964
Title output 2006: 82	Title output 2007: 81
Titles currently in print: 1,191	Journals published: 3

Editorial Program

African American studies; American history; American literature and criticism; American religious history; American social and cultural history; anthropology; archaeology, American, Caribbean, southern and historical; creative non-fiction; ethnohistory; Judaic studies; Latin-American studies; linguistics, esp. dialectology; military history; Native American studies; natural history and environmental studies; public administration; regional studies; rhetoric and communication; southern history and culture; sports history; theatre. Submissions are not invited in poetry, fiction, or drama. The Press distributes for Samford University Press.
Journals: *Theatre History Studies*; *Theatre Symposium*; *Fairy Tale Review*
Special series: Alabama: The Forge of History; Caribbean Archaeology and Ethnohistory; Classics in Southeastern Archaeology; Contemporary American Indian Studies; Deep South Books; Judaic Studies; Library of Alabama Classics; Modern and Contemporary Poetics; The Modern South; Religion and American Culture; Rhetoric, Culture, and Social Critique; Studies in American Literary Realism and Naturalism
Imprints: Fiction Collective 2; Fire Ant Books

University of Alaska Press

Mailing Address:
PO Box 756240
Fairbanks, AK 99775-6240

Phone: (888) 252-6657; (907) 474-5831
Fax: (907) 474-5502
E-mail: fypress@uaf.edu
Web site: www.uaf.edu/uapress

Street Address:
794 University Avenue, Suite 220
Fairbanks, AK 99709

Orders Outside Alaska:
University of Alaska Press
Chicago Distribution Center
11030 South Langley Avenue
Chicago, IL 60628-3892
Phone: (800) 621-2736
Fax: (800) 621-8476

Staff
Director: Robert Mandel (907/474-2776; e-mail: fnrm@uaf.edu)
Assistant to the Director: Amy Simpson (907/474-5832; e-mail: fnals@uaf.edu)
Managing Editor: Elisabeth Dabney (907/474-6389; e-mail: e.dabney@uaf.edu)
Production Editor: Sue Mitchell (907/474-6413; e-mail: ffsm@uaf.edu)
Marketing & Sales Coordinator: Becky Hall (907/474-5831; e-mail: fypress@uaf.edu)

Full Member
Established: 1967
Title output 2006: 12
Titles currently in print: 149

Admitted to AAUP: 1992
Title output 2007: 14

Editorial Program
Nonfiction, all disciplines relating to Alaska, the Pacific Rim, and Circumpolar North. American history, politics, and literature; anthropology; Native American studies and art; energy and conservation; environmental studies; geography; American biography and autobiography; new and classic fiction of Alaska and the American West; children's books. Submissions are invited in fiction and poetry related to Alaska and the Pacific Northwest.

The Press distributes publications for Vanessapress, Alaska Sea Grant Program, Alaska Native Knowledge Network, Alaska Native Language Center, Limestone Press, White Mammoth, University of Alaska Museum of the North, Geophysical Institute, Anchorage Museum Association, Alutiiq Museum, Alaska Quarterly Review, Dryad Press, Far to the North Press, and Arctic Studies Center of the Smithsonian Institution.

Special series: Classic Reprint; Lives of Great Explorers; Oral Biography; Rasmuson Library Historical Translation; Snowy Owl (trade book imprint); International Polar Year (2007-2009) Studies

The University of Alberta Press

Ring House 2
Edmonton, AB T6G 2E1
Canada

Phone: (780) 492-3662
Fax: (780) 492-0719
E-mail: (user I.D.)@ualberta.ca
Web site: www.uap.ualberta.ca

Customer Service / Order Fulfillment:
Phone: (780) 492-3662
Fax: (780) 492-0719

UK / European Distributor:
Gazelle Drake Academic

Canadian Distributor:
GTW Limited
34 Armstrong Avenue
Georgetown ON L7G 4R9 Canada
Phone: (905) 873-9781
Fax: (905) 873-6170
E-mail: orders@gtwcanada.com
Web site: www.gtwcanada.com

US Distributor:
Michigan State University Press
1405 South Harrison Road, Suite 25
East Lansing MI 48823-5202
Phone: (517) 355-9543
Fax: (517) 432-2611
Web site: www.msupress.msu.edu

Staff
Director: Linda D. Cameron (780/492-0717; e-mail: linda.cameron)
Editor: Mary Mahoney-Robson (on extended leave)
Acquisitions Editor: Michael Luski (780/492-4945; e-mail: michael.luski)
Managing Editor: Peter Midgley (780/492-7714; e-mail: petem)
Design / Production: Alan Brownoff (780/492-8285; e-mail: abrownof)
Sales & Marketing Manager: Cathie Crooks (780/492-5820; e-mail: ccrooks)
  Sales / Marketing Assistant: Jeffrey Carpenter (780/492-7493; e-mail: jsc1)
Administrative Assistant: Yoko Sekiya (780/492-3662; e-mail: yoko.sekiya)

Full Member
Established: 1969
Title output 2006: 27
Titles currently in print: 169

Admitted to AAUP: 1983
Title output 2007: 26

Editorial Program
The University of Alberta Press (UAP) publishes in the areas of biography, history, literature, natural history, regional interest, travel narratives, and reference books.
Special series: Mountain Cairns—a series on the history and culture of the Canadian Rockies; cuRRents—a Canadian literature series

American Historical Association

400 A Street., S.E.
Washington, DC 20003-3889

Phone: (202) 544-2422
Fax: (202) 544-8307
E-mail: aha@historians.org
Web site: www.historians.org

Staff
Executive Director: Arnita A. Jones (202/544-2422 ext. 100; e-mail: ajones@historians.org)
Controller: Randy Norell (202/544-2422 ext.109; e-mail: rnorell@historians.org)
Editor, *American Historical Review*: Robert A. Schneider (812/855-7609; e-mail: raschnei@indiana.edu)
Assistant Director, Publications: Robert B. Townsend (202/544-2422 ext. 118; e-mail: rtownsend@historians.org)
Internet Projects Coordinator: Vernon Horn (202/544-2422 ext. 122; e-mail: vhorn@historians.org)
Editor, *Perspectives*: Pillarisetti Sudhir (202/544-2422 ext. 121; e-mail: psudhir@historians.org)
Production Manager: Christian A. Hale (202/544-2422 ext. 133; e-mail: chale@historians.org)
Publication Sales: Meaghan Gay (202/544-2422 ext. 108; e-mail: mgay@historians.org)

Associate Member
Established: 1884
Title output 2006: 9
Titles currently in print: 64

Admitted to AAUP: 2005
Title output 2007: 12
Journals published: 2

Editorial Program
The AHA publishes a wide variety of periodical, annual, and other publications of service and interest to the historical profession and the general public. Primary publications are the journals, the *American Historical Review* (published by the Journals Division of the University of Chicago Press) and the monthly news magazine *Perspectives*. The Association's other major publication is the annual *Directory of History Departments, Historical Organizations, and Historians*. Beyond that, the AHA publishes a wide range of topical booklets (generally 32 to 120 pages long) on the practice of history and historical topics. On the Web, the Association publishes a wide range of documentary and bibliographic materials, as well as a daily blog, for those interested in the study of the past and the practice of history.

American Psychiatric Publishing, Inc.

1000 Wilson Blvd., Suite 1825
Arlington, VA 22209

Phone: (703) 907-7322
Fax: (703) 907-1092
E-mail: appi@psych.org
Indiv: (user I.D.)@psych.org
Web site: www.appi.org

Orders:
Phone: (800) 368-5777; (703) 907-7322
Fax: (703) 907-1091

European Distributor:
Eurospan

Canadian Representative:
Login Brothers Canada

Staff
Chief Executive Officer: Ronald E. McMillen (703/907-7876; e-mail: rmcmillen)
  Executive Assistant: Bessie Jones (703/907-7892; e-mail: bjones)
Editor-in-Chief: Robert E. Hales (703/907-7892)
  Editorial Director, Books: John McDuffie (703/907-7871; e-mail: jmcduffie)
  Book Acquisitions Coordinator: Bessie Jones (703/907-7892; e-mail: bjones)
Director of e-Publishing: Pam Harley (703/907-7870; e-mail: pharley)
Managing Editor, Books: Greg Kuny (703/907-7872; e-mail: gkuny)
Director of Sales and Marketing: Robert Pursell (703/907-7893; e-mail: bpursell)
  Assistant Director of Marketing: Christie Couture (703/907-7877; e-mail: ccouture)
  Marketing and Sales Manager: Trang Duong (703/907-8538; e-mail: tduong)
Editorial Director, Journals: Michael Roy (703/907-7894; e-mail: mroy)
Director of Finance and Business Operations: Kathy Stein (703/907-7875; e-mail: kstein)
  Director of Customer Service: Linda Phillips (703/907-8571; e-mail: lphillips)

Associate Member
Established: 1981
Title output 2006: 51
Titles currently in print: 780

Admitted to AAUP: 1993
Title output 2007: 26
Journals published: 7

Editorial Program
Clinical books and monographs in psychiatry and related fields; research monographs; medical textbooks; study guides; nonfiction trade books in mental health; annual review; and journals.
Journals: *Academic Psychiatry; American Journal of Psychiatry; FOCUS; Journal of Neuropsychiatry; Psychiatric News; Psychiatric Services; Psychosomatics*
Special series: Concise Guides
Special imprints: American Psychiatric Association; Group for the Advancement of Psychiatry; American Psychopathological Association
Copublishing programs: The World Health Organization

The American University in Cairo Press

113 Kasr el Aini Street
PO Box 2511
Cairo, Egypt 11511

Phone: + 202 2797 6926
Fax: +202 2794 1440
E-mail: aucpress@aucegypt.edu
Indiv: (user I.D.)@aucegypt.edu
Web site: www.aucpress.com

US Office:
420 Fifth Avenue
New York, NY 10018-2729

Phone: (212) 730-8800
Fax: (212) 730-1600

US and Canadian Distributor:
International Publishers Marketing
PO Box 605
Herndon, VA 20172
Phone: + 703 661 1586; 800 758-3756
Fax: + 703 661 1501
E-mail: ipmmail@presswarehouse.com

UK / European Distributor:
Eurospan
c/o Turpin Distribution
Pegasus Drive, Stratton Business Park
Biggleswade, Bedfordshire SG18 8TQ
United Kingdom
Tel: +44 (0)176 760 4972
Fax: +44 (0)176 760 1640
E-mail: eurospan@turpin-distribution.com

Staff
Director: Mark Linz (+202 2797-6888; e-mail: linz)
  Assistant to the Director: Tawhida Sherif (+202 2797-6926; e-mail: tina)
  Editorial: Neil Hewison, Associate Director for Editorial Programs (+202 2797-6892;
  e-mail: rnh)
Managing Editor: Nadia Naqib (+202 2797-6887; e-mail: nnaqib)
Production: Miriam Fahmy, Production Manager (+202 2797-6937; e-mail: miriam)
Sales Manager: Tahany el-Shammaa (+202 2797-6985; e-mail: tahanys)
  Promotion Manager: Nabila Akl (+202 2797 6896; e-mail: akl)

International Member
Established: 1960
Title output 2006: 80
Titles currently in print: 850

Admitted to AAUP: 1986
Title output 2007: 85
Journals published: 2

Editorial Program
The Press is recognized as the leading English-language publisher in the Middle East, and
publishes a wide range of scholarly monographs, texts and reference works, and general inter-
est books on ancient and modern Egypt and the Middle East, as well as Arabic literature in
English translation, most notably the works of Egyptian Nobel laureate Naguib Mahfouz.
Journals: *Alif: Journal of Comparative Poetics, Cairo Papers in Social Science*
Copublishing programs: Numerous copublishing programs with US, UK and European
universities and trade publishers.

Amsterdam University Press

Herengracht 221
1016 BG Amsterdam
The Netherlands

Phone: +31-20-4200050
Fax: +31-20-4203214
E-mail: info@aup.nl
Indiv: (user I.D.)@aup.nl
Web site: www.aup.nl

US & Canadian Sales Representative:
University of Chicago Press
Phone: (800) 621-2736

UK Representative:
UPM

European Representative:
Durnell Marketing

Staff
Director: Saskia C. J. de Vries (e-mail: s.c.j.devries)
Deputy Director and Head of Sales and Marketing: Martin Voigt (e-mail m.voigt)
Administration: Frans Havelaar (e-mail: f.havelaar); Daniela Pinnone (e-mail: d.pinnone)
Senior Acquisitions Editors: Pauline Retel (humanities, art) (e-mail: p.retel);
   Erik van Aert (social studies) (e-mail: e.vanaert); Jeroen Sondervan (film studies)
   (e-mail j.sondervan)
Electronic Publishing: Eelco Ferwerda, Publisher Digital Products (e-mail: e.ferwerda)
Manuscript Editorial: Jaap Wagenaar, Editor (social sciences) (e-mail: j.wagenaar)
   Assistant Editor: Chantal Nicolaes (e-mail: c.nicolaes)
Production: Arnout van Omme, Production Manager (e-mail: a.vanomme)
International Marketing: Martin Voigt (e-mail: m.voigt); Magdalena Hernas
   (e-mail: m.hernas)
   Orders: Jelle Bloem (e-mail: j.bloem)

International Member
Established: 1992
Title output 2006: 120
Titles currently in print: 620

Admitted to AAUP: 2000
Title output 2007: 120
Journals published: 5

Editorial Program
Scholarly and some trade titles (English and Dutch language) in anthropology; archaeology; art and art history; Asian studies; classical studies; cultural studies; economics; film and television studies; gender studies; history; Judaica; language and linguistics; law; literature; medieval and Renaissance studies; music; philosophy; political science; social sciences; theater and performing arts; regional titles. Textbooks for universities and higher education. AUP distributes for the University of Leiden (Leiden University Press).

Journals: *Academische Boekengids* (Academic Book Review); *Mens & Maatschappij* (People and Society); *Tijdschrift voor Muziektheorie* (Dutch Journal of Music Theory); *GJSS: Graduate Journal of Social Science* (www.GJSS.org); *Tbilisi Mathematical Journal* (ncst.org.ge/Journals/TMJ/indexj)

English series: Amsterdam Archaeological Studies; Changing Welfare States; Film Culture in Transition; MARE Publications.Series In German: Justiz und NS-Verbrechen (A collection of postwar German trial judgments concerning Nazi crimes of a homicidal nature committed during World War II)

Imprints: Vossiuspers UvA, Salomé, Pallas Publications.

Copublications: Mercatorfonds (Belgium), Princeton University Press, University of California Press

The University of Arizona Press

355 S. Euclid Avenue, Suite 103
Tucson, AZ 85719-6654

Phone: (520) 621-1441
Fax: (520) 621-8899
E-mail: uapress@uapress.arizona.edu
Indiv: (user I.D.)@uapress.arizona.edu
Web site: www.uapress.arizona.edu

Canadian Representative:
University of British Columbia Press

Orders:
Phone: (520) 626-4218; (800) 426-3797

Warehouse:
330 S. Toole Avenue
Tucson, Arizona 85701-1813

European Representative:
William Gills

Staff

Director: Christine R. Szuter (520/621-1441; e-mail: szuter)
  Assistant to the Director / Permissions: Sarah O'Mahen (520/621-3911; e-mail: somahen)
Senior Acquiring Editor: Patti Hartmann (Chicano/Latino studies and literature, Native American studies and literature, environmental literature and creative nonfiction, environmental and western history, Latin American studies, regional) (520/621-7920; e-mail: hartmann)
  Acquiring Editor: Allyson Carter (anthropology, archaeology, environmental sciences, astronomy and space sciences, regional) (520/621-3186; e-mail: acarter)
  Editorial Assistants: Kristen Buckles (520/621-5919; e-mail: kbuckles); Natasha Varner (520/621-5919; e-mail: EditorialAssistant)
Editing and Production Manager: Harrison Shaffer (520/621-5916; e-mail: hshaffer)
  Assistant Managing Editor: Alan M. Schroder (520/621-5814; e-mail: aschroder)
  Manuscript Editor: Nancy Arora (520/621-5915; e-mail: narora)
  Production Assistant: Miriam Fisher (520/621-7916; e-mail: mfisher)
Sales and Marketing: Kathryn Conrad, Manager (520/621-9109; e-mail: kconrad)
  Publicity Manager: Holly Dolan (520/621-3920; e-mail: hdolan)
  Advertising and Direct Mail Manager: Keith LaBaw (520/621-8656; e-mail: klabaw)
  Exhibits Manager: Leigh McDonald (520/621-4913; e-mail: lmcdonald)
Business Manager: Shay Cameron (520/621-7919; e-mail: scameron)
  Accounts Payable: Melissa Sotomayor (520/626-3041; e-mail: msotomayor)
  Customer Relations: Barbara Armstrong (520/621-7923; e-mail: barmstrong)
  Accounting Specialist: Aidan Harte (520/621-9865; e-mail: aharte)
  Customer Service Representative: Arin Cumming (520/621-5813; e-mail: acumming)
  Fulfillment Manager: Adam Duckworth (520/621-3289; e-mail: aduckworth)
  Shipping and Fulfillment: Greg Morton (520/621-3289; e-mail: gmorton); Liz Vargas (520/621-3289; e-mail: lvargas); Charles Touseull (520/621-3289; e-mail: ctouseull)
Information Systems Manager: Beth Swain (520/621-5815; e-mail: swain)

Full Member

Established: 1959
Title output 2006: 56
Titles currently in print: 832

Admitted to AAUP: 1962
Title output 2007: 60

Editorial Program
Specialties strongly identified with the universities in the state and other significant nonfiction of regional and national interest. Especially strong fields include the American West; anthropology and archaeology; Chicano/Latino studies and literature; ecology and environmental sciences; environmental studies and literature; Latin American studies; Native American studies and literature; space sciences; western and environmental history.

The Press also distributes titles from Ironwood Press; the Arizona State Museum; Statistical Research, Inc.; SWCA, Inc.; Northern Arizona University Bilby Research Center; Center for Desert Archaeology; University of Arizona Critical Languages Program; Oregon State University Press; and Left Coast Press, Inc.

Special series: Amerind Studies in Archaeology; Anthropological Papers of the University of Arizona; The Archaeology of Colonialism in North America; Arizona Sonora Desert Museum Studies In Natural History; Camino del Sol; Desert Places; Environmental History of the Borderlands; Environmental Science, Law, and Policy; Experiencing the Southwest; Frank Hamilton Cushing and the Hemenway Southwestern Archaeological Expedition: A Documentary History, 1882-1893; The Mexican-American Experience; Modern American West; Native Peoples of the Americas; Society, Environment, and Place; Southwest Center Series; Space Science Series; Sun Tracks; Women's Western Voices

The University of Arkansas Press

McIlroy House
201 Ozark Avenue
Fayetteville, AR 72701-1201

Canadian Representative:
Scholarly Book Services

Phone: (800) 626-0090
Phone: (479) 575-3246
Fax: (479) 575-6044
E-mail: uapress@uark.edu
Indiv: (user I.D.)@uark.edu
Web site: www.uapress.com

UK / European Representative:
Eurospan

Staff
Director and Editor: Lawrence J. Malley (479/575-3096; e-mail: lmalley)
   Assistant to the Director: Julie Watkins (479/575-7242; e-mail: jewatki)
Acquisitions Editorial: Lawrence J. Malley
Manuscript Editorial, Design, and Production: Brian King, Assistant Director and Director of Editorial, Design, and Production (479/575-6780; e-mail: brking)
   Production Manager: David Scott Cunningham (479/575-5767; e-mail: dscunni)
Marketing: Tom Lavoie, Assistant Director and Director of Marketing and Sales (479/575-6657; e-mail: tlavoie)
   Marketing and Advertising Designer: Charlie Shields (479/575-7258; e-mail: cmoss)
   Publicity and Promotions: Melissa King (479/575-7715; e-mail: mak001)
Business: Mike W. Bieker, Assistant Director and Business Manager (479/575-3859; e-mail: mbieker)

Assistant Business Manager: Carolyn Brt (479/575-3459; e-mail: cbrt)
Customer Service: Kathleen Z. Willis (479/575-3634, e-mail: kwillis)
Warehouse Manager: Sam Ridge (479/575-3858; e-mail: sridge)
Business Office Fax: (479/575-5538)

Full Member

Established: 1980	Admitted to AAUP: 1984
Title output 2006: 18	Title output 2007: 23
Titles currently in print: 525	Journals published: 1

Editorial Program
African American history; civil rights studies; Civil War studies; cultural studies; history; Middle East studies; music; poetry and poetics; regional studies; southern history; and women's studies. Submissions are not invited in general fiction, textbooks, or children's books.

The Press also publishes the winner of the University of Arkansas Press Award for Arabic Literature in Translation and the winners of the University of Arkansas Press Poetry Series.
Journal: *Philosophical Topics*
Special series: Arkansas Classics; The Carter Collection; The Civil War in the West; The Histories of Arkansas; Portraits of Conflict; The University of Arkansas Press Poetry; The William Gilmore Simms Collection

Baylor University Press

Street Address:	Mailing Address:
1920 South 4th Street	One Bear Place # 97363
Waco, TX 76706 -2529	Waco, TX 76798-7363

Phone: (254) 710-3164	Orders:
Fax: (254) 710-3440	Baylor University Press
Web site: www.baylorpress.com	c/o Hopkins Fulfillment Service
	P.O. Box 50370
	Baltimore, MD 21211-4370
	Phone: (800) 537-5487 or (410) 516-6956
	Fax: (410) 516-6998

UK Representative:	Canadian Representative:
Alban Books Ltd.	Scholarly Book Services

Staff
Director: Carey Newman (254/710-3522; e-mail: Carey_Newman@baylor.edu)
  Associate Director / Production Manager: Diane E. Smith
  (254/710-2563; e-mail: Diane_Smith@baylor.edu)
  Operations Manager: Stacy Buford (254/710-3522; e-mail: Stacy_Buford@baylor.edu)
Acquisitions: Casey Blaine, Editor (254/710-2846; e-mail: Casey_Blaine@baylor.edu)
  Editorial Assistants: Myles Werntz (254/710-1465; e-mail: Myles_Werntz@baylor.edu);
  Jessica Hooten (254/710-1465; e-mail: Jessica_Hooten@baylor.edu)
Manuscript Editorial: Elisabeth Wolfe, Editorial Assistant (254/710-3164; e-mail: Elisabeth_Wolfe@baylor.edu)

Design and Production: Diane E. Smith, Associate Director / Production Manager (254/
710-2563; e-mail: Diane_Smith@baylor.edu)
　Copy Editor: Ellen Condict (254/710-3164; e-mail: Ellen_Condict@baylor.edu)
Marketing Manager: Jennifer Hannah (254/710-4800; e-mail:
　Jennifer_Hannah@baylor.edu)
　Advertising and Publicity Coordinator: Laura Barth (254/710-1460; e-mail:
　Laura_Barth@baylor.edu)
　Events Coordinator: Amanda Toller (254/710-4116; e-mail: Amanda_Toller@baylor.edu)

Full Member

Established: 1897　　　　　　　　　　　Admitted to AAUP: 2007
Title output 2006: 22　　　　　　　　　Title output 2007: 35
Titles currently in print: 130

Editorial Program

Established in 1897, Baylor University Press publishes thirty new titles each year in the
following academic areas: religion & public life; rhetoric & religion; religious studies &
theology; religion & literature; religion & philosophy; religion & higher education. In accordance with Baylor University's mission, the Press strives to serve the academic community
by producing works of excellent quality that integrate faith and understanding.
Special series: Baylor Handbook on the Greek New Testament; Baylor Handbook on the
Hebrew Bible; Edmondson Historical Lecture; Latino/a Religious Thought for the New
Millennium; The Making of Christian Imagination; Provost's Series; Studies in Rhetoric and
Religion; Studies in Christianity and Literature; Studies in Religion and Higher Education

Beacon Press

Mailing Address:　　　　　　　　　　Street Address:
25 Beacon Street　　　　　　　　　　41 Mt. Vernon Street
Boston, MA 02108-2892　　　　　　　Boston, MA 02108

Phone: (617) 742-2110　　　　　　　　European Representative:
Fax: (617) 723-3097　　　　　　　　　Publishers Group UK
Marketing/Publicity/Subsidiary
Rights Fax: (617) 742-2290　　　　　　Canadian Representative:
E-mail: (user I.D.)@beacon.org　　　　　Fitzhenry & Whiteside
Web site: www.beacon.org

Staff

Director: Helene Atwan (e-mail: hatwan)
　Assistant to the Director: Alex Kapitan (e-mail: akapitan)
Editorial: Gayatri Patnaik, Senior Editor (e-mail: gpatnaik)
　Senior Editor: Amy Caldwell (e-mail: acaldwell)
　Editor: Brian Halley (e-mail: bhalley)
　Assistant Editor: Allison Trzop (e-mail: atrzop)
Production: PJ Tierney, Production Director & Digital Publishing Director (e-mail: ptierney)

Managing Editor: Lisa Sacks (e-mail: lsacks)
Creative Director: Bob Kosturko (e-mail: bkosturko)
Marketing: Tom Hallock, Associate Publisher, Director of Sales, Marketing, and SubRights (e-mail: thallock)
  Associate Publicist: Leah Riviere (e-mail: lriviere)
  Publicity Director: Pamela MacColl (e-mail: pmaccoll)
  Publicist: Gina Frey (e-mail: gfrey)
  Sales & Marketing Associate: Katie Spencer (e-mail: kspencer)
  Rights & Permissions Associate: Joanna Green (e-mail: jgreen)
Business: John Wong, Chief Financial Officer (e-mail: jwong)
  Business Operations Manager: Greg Kanter (e-mail: gkanter)
  Accounts Payable/Receivable: C.C. Hardy (e-mail: chardy)

Associate Member

Established: 1854   Admitted to AAUP: 1988
Title output 2006: 51   Title output 2007: 54
Titles currently in print: 758

Editorial Program

Beacon Press, the non-profit publisher owned by the Unitarian Universalist Association, publishes works for the general reader, specializing in African American, Native American, and Asian American studies; anthropology; current affairs; education; environmental studies; gay and lesbian studies; nature writing; personal essays; philosophy; regional books; religion; and women's studies.

Special series and joint publishing programs: Bluestreak; The Concord Nature Library; the Beacon Press / Simmons College series on Race, Education, and Democracy; Queer Action / Queer Ideas

University of British Columbia Press

2029 West Mall
University of British Columbia
Vancouver, BC V6T 1Z2
Canada

Phone: (604) 822-5959
Toll-free (in Canada): (877) 377-9378
Fax: (604) 822-6083
Toll-free (in Canada): (800) 668-0821
E-mail: (user I.D.)@ubcpress.ca
Web site: www.ubcpress.ca

Canadian Orders and Returns:
University of Toronto Press
5201 Dufferin Place
Toronto, ON M3H 5T8
Canada
Phone: (416) 667-7791
Fax: (416) 667-7832
Toll-free (in Canada): (800) 565-9523
Toll-free fax (in Canada): (800) 221-9985
E-mail: utpbooks@utpress.utoronto.ca

US Orders and Returns:
University of Washington Press
PO Box 50096
Seattle, WA 98145-4115
Phone: (800) 441-4115
Fax: (800) 669-7993
E-mail: uwpord@u.washington.edu

UK Distributor:
Eurospan

Staff

Director: Peter Milroy (604/822-3807; e-mail: milroy)
  Assistant to the Publisher: Megan Brand (604/822-4161; e-mail: brand)
  Assistant Director, Eastern Canada Manager, (Toronto): Melissa Pitts (416/778-7193; e-mail: pitts)
Acquisitions Editorial: Jean Wilson, Associate Director—Editorial (604/822-6376; e-mail: wilson) (regional Canadian history, regional, native studies, health / medical studies, sexuality studies, Northern studies, education)
  Senior Editor: Emily Andrew (Nelson office) (250/352-0992; e-mail: andrew) (Asian, politics, military history, general Canadian history, film and media studies)
  Acquisitions Editors: Randy Schmidt (Kelowna) (250/764-4761; e-mail: schmidt) (forestry, law and society, environmental studies, geography, urban studies and planning, sustainable development); Melissa Pitts (Toronto office) (416/778-7193; e-mail: pitts) (Canadian history, sociology, urban studies and planning)
Production Editorial: Holly Keller, Assistant Director—Production and Editorial Services (604/822-4545; e-mail: keller)
  Project Editor: Camilla Blakeley (416/762-7361; e-mail: blakeley)
  Editors: Ann Macklem (604/822-0093; e-mail: macklem); Darcy Cullen (604/822-5744; e-mail: cullen); Anna Eberhard Friedlander (604/822-4548; e-mail: acef)
Marketing: George Maddison, Associate Director Marketing and Operations (604/822-2053; e-mail: maddison)
  Academic Sales, Course Sales, and Marketing Manager: Elizabeth Whitton (604/822-8226; e-mail: whitton)
  Awards and Exhibits Manager: Kerry Kilmartin (604/822-8244; e-mail: kilmartin)
  Advertising and Catalogues Manager: Jason Congdon (604/822-4546; e-mail: congdon)
  Marketing Assistant: Valerie Nair (604/822-9462; e-mail: frontdesk)
Finance/Distribution: Devni De Silva, Finance Manager (604/822-8938; e-mail: desilva)
  Finance Assistant: Harmony Johnson (604/822-5370; e-mail: johnson)
  Inventory Manager / Academic Sales: Shari Martin (604/822-1221; e-mail: martin)

Full Member

Established: 1971   Admitted to AAUP: 1972
Title output 2006: 56   Title output 2007: 60
Titles currently in print: 595

Editorial Program

Scholarly books and serious nonfiction, with special interest in archaeology; Asian and Pacific studies; economics; education; environment; fisheries; forestry; geography; history; law; Northwest Coast art; Native studies; Pacific maritime studies; political science; sociology; urban studies; and women's studies.

Special series: Canadian Yearbook of International Law; Contemporary Chinese Studies; First Nations Languages; Nature/History/Society; Pioneers of British Columbia; Sexuality Studies; Sustainability and the Environment; UBC Laboratory of Archaeology Monographs; Urbanization in Asia

Brookings Institution Press

1775 Massachusetts Avenue, N.W.
Washington, DC 20036-2103

Phone: (202) 797-6000; (202) 797-6311
E-mail: bibooks@brookings.edu
Indiv: (firstinitial)(lastname)@brookings.edu
Web site: www.brookings.edu

<u>Warehouse (RETURNS ONLY):</u>
Brookings Press—Book Returns
c/o Maple Press Distribution
Lebanon Distribution Center
704 Legionaire Drive
Fredericksburg, PA 17026

<u>Customer Service / Orders:</u>
Hopkins Fulfillment Service
P.O. Box 50370
Baltimore, MD 21211-4370
Phone: (800) 537-5487 or (410) 516-6956
Fax: (410) 516-6998

<u>UK Representative:</u>
University Presses Marketing

<u>Canadian Representative:</u>
UBC Press

Staff

Vice President & Director: Robert L. Faherty (202/536-3636)
   Program and Web Administrator: Renuka Deonarain (202/536-3637)
   Web / Electronic Promotion Coordinator: Jessica Howard (202/536-3609)
   Rights Coordinator & Assistant to the VP: Chelsea Stevens (202/536-3604)
Acquisitions Editor: Mary Kwak (202/536-3617)
Manuscript Editorial: Janet Walker, Managing Editor (202/536-3613)
   Editors: Eileen Hughes (202/536-3614); Anthony Nathe (202/536-3615)
Design and Production: Lawrence Converse, Production Manager (202/536-3618)
   Art Coordinator: Susan Woollen (202/536-3619)
Marketing Director/Senior Acquisitions Editor: Christopher Kelaher (202/536-3606)
   Direct Marketing Manager: Tom Parsons (202/536-3610)
   Publicity Manager: Susan Soldavin (202/536-3611)
   Publicity & Exhibits Coordinator: Jaime Fearer (202/536-3608)
   Sales and Marketing Assistant: Robin Becht (202/536-3607)
Distribution Services Manager: Terrence Melvin (202/797-6429)
   Distribution Services Assistant: Fred King (202/797-6311)

Full Member

Established: 1916
Title output 2006: 42
Titles currently in print: 1,002

Admitted to AAUP: 1958
Title output 2007: 52
Journals published: 6

Editorial Program

Economics, government, and international affairs, with emphasis on the implications for public policy of current and emerging issues confronting American society. The Press publishes books written by the Institution's resident and associated staff members employed or commissioned to carry out projects defined by the directors of Brookings research programs, as well as manuscripts acquired from outside authors.

   The Institution also publishes Brookings Papers on Economic Activity; Brookings Papers on Education Policy; Brookings Trade Forum; Brookings-Wharton Papers on Urban Affairs; Economia (copublished with the Latin American and Caribbean Economic Association);

and The Future of Children (copublished with the Woodrow Wilson School of Public and International Affairs, Princeton University).

The Press distributes publications of the Bertelsmann Foundation, the Carnegie Endowment for International Peace, the Centre for Economic Policy Research, the Century Foundation Press, Council on Foreign Relations, Economica, the Center for Global Development, the Institute for Latin American Studies, the International Labor Organization, the Japan Center for International Exchange, the OECD, the Royal Institute for International Affairs, the Trilateral Commission, the United Nations University Press, and the Washington Institute for Near East Policy.

University of Calgary Press

2500 University Drive N.W.
Calgary, AB T2N 1N4
Canada

Phone: (403) 220-7578
Fax: (403) 282-0085
E-mail: ucpress@ucalgary.ca
Indiv: (user I.D.)@ucalgary.ca
Web site: www.uofcpress.com

US Orders:
Michigan State University Press
1405 South Harrison Road, Suite 25
Manly Miles Building
East Lansing, MI 48823-5202
Phone: (517) 355-9543
Fax: (517) 432-2611; (800) 678-2120
E-mail: msupress@msu.edu

Canadian Distribution & Orders:
uniPRESSES
c/o Georgetown Terminal Warehouses
34 Armstrong Avenue
Georgetown, ON L7G 4R9
Canada
Phone (toll-free): (877) 864-8477
Fax (toll-free): (877) 864-4272
E-mail: orders@gtwcanada.com

UK / European Distributor:
Gazelle Book Services, Ltd.

Staff

Director: TBA
Director of Operations & Permissions / Copyright Officer: Wendy Stephens (403/220-3721; e-mail: wstephen)
Senior Editor & Acquisitions: John King (403/220-4208; e-mail: jking)
   Staff Editor: Peter Enman (403/220-2606; e-mail: enman)
   Editorial Secretary: Karen Buttner (403/220-3979; e-mail: kbuttner)
Grants Writer: Kellie Moynihan (403/210-8511; e-mail: moynihan)
Graphic Designer: Melina Cusano (403/220-8719; e-mail: mcusano)
Marketing Manager: Barb Murray (403/220-5284; e-mail: bmurray)
Promotions Coordinator: Greg Madsen (403/220-4343; e-mail: gmadsen)
Journals Manager: Judy Powell (403/220-3512; e-mail: powell)
Fulfillment/Subscriptions: Megan Travis (403/220-3514; e-mail: ucpmail)

Full Member

Established: 1981

Admitted to AAUP: 2002
(Affiliate member: 1992-95)

Title output 2006: 30

Title output 2007: 25

Titles currently in print: 237

Journals published: 6 print, 2 electronic

Editorial Program

University of Calgary Press publishes academic and trade books and journals that engage academic, industry/business, government, and public communities. The Press focuses on works that give voice to the heartland of the continent (the Canadian Northwest, the American West, including the mountain region and the Great Plains). The University of Calgary Press is experimental and offers alternative perspectives on established canons and subjects. The Press strives to bring diverse voices and views to the forefront and endeavors to help new scholars and writers break in to the academic and trade markets.

Print journals: *ARIEL—A Review of International English Literature*; *Canadian Journal of Counselling*; *Canadian Journal of Latin American and Caribbean Studies*; *Canadian Journal of Philosophy*; *Canadian Journal of Program Evaluation*; *Mousieon—Journal of the Classical Association of Canada*

Online only journals: *Currents: New Scholarship in the Human Services*; *The International Electronic Journal for Leadership in Learning*

Special series: African Missing Voices; African Occasional Papers; Art in Profile; Beyond Boundaries (Canadian Defence and Strategic Studies); Canadian Archival Series; Cinemas Off Centre; Industry Canada Research; Latin American and Caribbean Studies; Legacies Shared; Northern Lights; Open Spaces; Parks and Heritage; Supplementary volumes of the Canadian Journal of Philosophy; Turning Points Occasional Papers in Latin American Studies

Copublishing programs: The Arctic Institute of North America; Industry Canada; Latin American Research Centre

University of California Press

2120 Berkeley Way
Berkeley, CA 94704-1012

Phone: (510) 642-4247
Fax: (510) 643-7127
E-mail: askucp@ucpress.edu
Indiv: (firstname.lastname)@ucpress.edu
Web site: www.ucpress.edu

Journals:
2000 Center Street, Suite 303
Berkeley, CA 94704
Phone: (510) 643-7154
Fax: (510) 642-9917
Journals Web site: www.ucpress.edu/journals

California Warehouse:
1095 Essex Street
Richmond, CA 94801
Phone: (510) 642-4240
Fax: (510) 215-0237

Order Fulfillment:
California Princeton Fulfillment Services
1445 Lower Ferry Road
Ewing, NJ 08618-1424
Orders: (800) 777-4726
Fax: (800) 999-1958
Customer Service: (609) 883-1759

UK / European Office:
University Presses of California,
Columbia, and Princeton, Ltd.
1 Oldlands Way, Bognor Regis
West Sussex P022 9SA
United Kingdom
Phone: +44 1243 842165
Fax: +44 1243 842167

Staff

Director: Lynne Withey (510/642-5393)
   Assistant to the Director: Hannah Love (510/642-0189)
   Associate Director and Publisher: Sheila Levine (510/642-4246)
   Director, Journals and Digital Publishing Division: Rebecca Simon (510/642-5536)
   Assistant Director / Chief Financial Officer: Anna Weidman (510/642-4388)
   Assistant Director and Director of Development: Deborah Kirshman (510/643-7704)
   Associate Director of Development and Public Relations: Erin Marietta (510/643-8465)
Acquisitions Editorial: Sheila Levine, Associate Director and Publisher (food, regional studies) (510/642-4246)
   Executive Editors: Naomi Schneider (sociology, anthropology, gender studies) (510/642-6715); Stanley Holwitz (anthropology, public health, Jewish studies) (510/642-4244)
   Publisher, Science Group: Charles R. Crumly (natural sciences)
   Sponsoring Editors: Laura Cerruti (poetry, literature) (510/642-9793); Reed Malcolm (religion, Asian studies) (510/643-1812); Stephanie Fay (art history) (510/642-6733); Deborah Kirshman (art history, museum copublications) (510/643-7704); Niels Hooper (history) (510/643-8331); Blake Edgar (biology, archaeology, viticulture) (510/643-4643); Mary Francis (music, film) (510/642-4147); Jenny Wapner (natural history) (510/642-4229)
Managing Editor: Marilyn Schwartz (510/642-6548)
   Assistant Managing Editor: Kate Warne (510/643-6858)
   Project Editors: Rachel Berchten (510/642-0133); Suzanne Knott (510/642-8981); Dore Brown (510/642-4591); Jacqueline Volin (510/642-0061); Stephanie Fay (510/642-6733);

Sue Heinemann (510/643-8979); Rose Vekony (510/642-6521); Cindy Fulton (510/642-6734); Laura Harger (510/643-9081); Mary Severance (510/643-8555)

Design and Production: Anthony C. Crouch, Director (510/642-5394)

Production Coordinators: Robin Demers (510/642-9758); Peggy Golden (510/643-6859); Spencer Perry (510/643-1673); Sam Rosenthal (510/642-8102); Janet Villanueva (510/642-9805); Ren Thompson (510/642/4245); Pam Augspurger (510/642-5395)

Design: Lia Tjandra (510/643-7982); Nola Burger (510/643-9167); Jessica Grunwald (510/643-2213); Sandy Drooker

Marketing: Julie Christianson, Director of Sales and Marketing (510/642-4051)

Advertising Manager: Marta Gasoi (510/642-2649)

Direct Mail Manager: Christine Longmuir (510/642-5054)

Publicity Manager: Alexandra Dahne (510/643-5036)

Electronic Rights and Text Promotion Manager: Erich van Rijn (510/643-8915)

Intellectual Property and Subsidiary Rights Manager: R. Jill Phillips (510/642-4261)

Sales: Amy-Lynn Fischer, Associate Director of Sales (510/642-9373)

Associate Sales Manager: Mark Anderson

Sales Associate: Chris Schraeder (510/643/2023)

Special Sales Manager: Don McIlraith (510/642-6685)

Journals & Digital Publishing: Rebecca Simon, Director, Journals & Digital Publishing (510/642-5536)

Sales and Marketing Director: Rebekah Darksmith (510/643-0952)

Production Manager: Susanna Tadlock (510/642-6221)

Business Manager: Carmen Williams (510/642-7993)

Information Technology Manager: Gabriel Alvaro (510/642-4961)

Marketing Manager: Nick Lindsay (510/642-8883)

Library Relations Specialist: Rachel Lee (510/643-4366)

Customer Service Manager: Khalil el-Kareh (510/642-6188)

Advertising Coordinator: Corey Gerhard (530/750-0515)

Business: Karla Golden, Manager (510/642-7944)

California Warehouse: Theresa (Ta) Trevette (510/642-8744)

Human Resources: Doris Floyd (510/642-5338)

Administrative Services Manager: Pam Wimberly (510/642-6934)

Human Resources Specialist: Shannon Kotter (510/643-9796)

Information Systems: Patrick King, Director (510/642-6522)

Full Member

Established: 1893

Title output 2006: 229

Titles currently in print: 4,000

Admitted to AAUP: 1937

Title output 2007: 230

Journals published: 34

Editorial Program

Anthropology, art history, Asian studies, biology, classical studies, film, food, history, music, natural history, poetry, public health, regional studies, religion, sociology, viticulture, Mark Twain series. Submissions are not invited in original poetry or fiction.

Journals: *Asian Survey; The Auk; Classical Antiquity; The Condor Contexts: Understanding People in Their Social Worlds; Federal Sentencing Reporter; Film Quarterly; Gastronomica: Historical Studies in the Natural Sciences; Huntington Library Quarterly; Index to Foreign Legal Periodicals; Journal of the American Musicological Society; Journal of Empirical Research on*

Human Research Ethics; The Journal of Food and Culture; The Journal of Musicology; Journal of Palestine Studies; Journal of Vietnamese Studies; Jung Journal: Culture & Psyche; Law and Literature; Mexican Studies / Estudios Mexicanos; Music Perception; Music Theory Spectrum; NAPA Bulletin; New Criminal Law Review; Nineteenth-Century Music; Nineteenth-Century Literature; Nova Religio; Pacific Historical Review; PoLAR, The Public Historian; Religion and American Culture; Representations; Rhetorica; Sexuality Research and Social Policy; Social Problems; Sociological Perspectives; Symbolic Interaction

Cambridge University Press

Cambridge University Press, Americas
32 Avenue of the Americas
New York, NY 10013-4211

Phone: (212) 337-5000
Fax: (212) 691-3239
E-mail: (firstinitial)(lastname)@cambridge.org
Web site: www.cambridge.org

Distribution Center:
100 Brook Hill Drive
West Nyack, NY 10994-2133
Phone: (845) 353-7500
Fax: (845) 353-4141

Head (UK) Office:
The Edinburgh Building
Shaftesbury Road
Cambridge CB2 2RU
UK

Staff
Chief Executive: Stephen Bourne (UK)

NY Office: (212) 924-3900
President, Americas: Richard L. Ziemacki (212/337-5052)
Special Projects Director: Pauline Ireland (212/337-5090)
Academic Publishing: Frank Smith, Editorial Director (212/337-5960)
Publishing Director, STM: Marc Strauss (212/337-5992)
Publishing Director, Humanities: Beatrice Rehl (212/337-5096)
    Academic Editors: Beth Barry (medicine) (212/337-5075); Lewis Bateman (political science) (212/337-5965); Andrew Beck (linguistics, religion) (212/337-5941); John Berger (law) (212/337-5958); Heather Bergman (computer science) (212/337-5099); Lauren Cowles (math, computer science) (212/337-5962); Eric Crahan (history, political science) (212/337-5952); Christopher Curcio (life sciences) (212/337-6567); Peter Gordon (engineering) (212/337-5944); Scott Parris (economics, business) (212/337-5964); Edward Parsons (social sciences) (212/337-5961); Allan Ross (life sciences) (212/337-5993); Eric Schwartz (psychology, cognitive science) (212/337-5947)
Marketing: Liza Murphy, Sales and Marketing Director (212/337-5066)
    Associate Director, HSS Marketing: Catherine Friedl (212/337-5049)
    Associate Director, STM Marketing: Aleta Kalkstein (212/337-5967)
    Associate Director, Trade Sales & Marketing: Melissanne Scheld (212/337-5988)

Associate Director, College Sales & Marketing: Kerry Cahill (212/337-5065)
Library Sales & Marketing Manager: Mary Beth Jarrad (212/337-5991)
Marketing & Promotions Manager: Gary Suarez (212/337-5085)
Publicity Manager: Gregory Houle (212/337-5058)
Exhibits Manager: James Murphy (212/337-5074)
Rights and Permissions Manager: Marc Anderson (212/337-5048)
Journals: Edward Barnas, Senior Editor, STM Journals (212/337-5004)
Senior Editor, HSS Journals: Mark Zadrozny (212/337-5012)
Journals Editor: Robert Dreesen (212/337-5981)
Production Manager: Edward Carey (212/337-5985)
Marketing Manager: Susan Soule (212/337-5019)
Business Development Manager, Journals: Andrea Cernichiari (212/337-5022)
ELT Publishing
Publishing Director: Louisa Hellegers (212/337-5042)
Senior Publishing Manager: Janet Aitchison (grammar, reference, exams, pronunciation, vocabulary, EAP, e-publishing) (212/337-6574)
Senior Publishing Manager: Debbie Goldblatt (adult courses, skills and conversation courses) (212/337-5003)
Publishing Managers: Lesley Koustaff (secondary & primary courses) (212/337-5043); Louise Jennewine (Latin America, market research) (212/337-5025)
Production Manager: Sandra Pike (212/337-5029)
Production / Manufacturing Manager: Tami Savir (212/337-5968)
International Marketing / Business Development Director: Howard Siegelman (212/337-5002)
US/Canada Sales and Marketing Director: Kenneth Clinton (212/337-5010)
Marketing Manager: Carine Mitchell (212/337-5006)
Senior Sales and Marketing Manager: Andy Martin (212/337-5007)
Senior National Sales Manager: James Anderson
Production: Catherine Felgar, Production Director (212/337-5094)
Information Systems: David Kwederis, Information Services Manager (212/337-5060)
HR: Carol New, HR Director (212/337-5045)
West Nyack: (845) 353-7500
Press Distribution Director: Ian Bradie (ext. 4339)
Chief Financial Officer: George Rubich (ext. 4342)
Computer Department: Joan Bernstein, Software Development Manager (ext. 4325)
MIS Manager: George Ianello (ext. 4324)
Credit Manager: Randy Zeitlin (ext. 4322)
Customer Service Manager: Marianne Headrick (ext. 4409)
Inventory Control Manager: Holly Verrill (ext. 4306)
Warehouse Operations Manager: Don Federico (ext. 4321)

Full Member
Established: 1534

American Branch: 1949	Admitted to AAUP: 1950
Title output 2006: over 2,000	Title output 2007: over 2,000
Titles currently in print: about 14,000	Journals published: 211

Editorial Program

A broad range of academic titles in the humanities; social sciences; biological and physical sciences; mathematics; medicine; psychology; law; religious studies; reference works; and English language teaching.

Journals: *Acta Numerica; Ageing and Society; AI EDAM: Artificial Intelligence for Engineering Design, Analysis and Manufacturing; AJS Review; American Political Science Review; Ancient Mesoamerica; Anglo-Saxon England; animal; Animal Health Research Reviews; Annual Review of Applied Linguistics; Antarctic Science; Applied Psycholinguistics; Arabic Sciences and Philosophy; Archaeological Dialogues; arq: Architectural Research Quarterly; Behavioral and Brain Sciences; Behavioural and Cognitive Psychotherapy; Bilingualism: Language and Cognition; Biofilms; Bio-Societies; Bird Conservation International; Breast Cancer Online; British Journal of Anaesthetic and Recovery Nursing; The British Journal for the History of Science; British Journal of Music Education; British Journal of Nutrition; British Journal of Political Science; Bulletin of Entomological Research; Bulletin of the School of Oriental and African Studies; Cambridge Archaeological Journal; The Cambridge Law Journal; Cambridge Opera Journal; Cambridge Quarterly of Healthcare Ethics; Canadian Journal of Political Science/Revue canadienne de science politique; Cardiology in the Young; Central European History; Chinese Journal of Agricultural Biotechnology; The China Quarterly; The Classical Quarterly; The Classical Review; Combinatorics, Probability and Computing; Comparative Studies in Society and History; Compositio Mathematica; Contemporary European History; Continuity and Change; Development and Psychopathology; Du Bois Review; Early Music History; Earth and Environmental Sciences Transactions of the Royal Society of Edinburgh; Ecclesiastical Law Journal; Econometric Theory; Economics and Philosophy; Edinburgh Journal of Botany; Eighteenth-Century Music; English Language and Linguistics; English Today; Environment and Development Economics; Environmental Conservation; Environmental Practice; Epidemiology and Infection; Equine and Comparative Exercise Physiology; Ergodic Theory and Dynamical Systems; European Business Organization Law Review; European Constitutional Law Review; European Journal of Anaesthesiology; European Journal of Applied Mathematics; European Journal of Sociology; European Review; European Review of Economic History; Experimental Agriculture; Expert Reviews in Molecular Medicine; Fetal and Maternal Medicine Review; Financial History Review; Foreign Policy Bulletin; Genetical Research; Geological Magazine; Glasgow Mathematical Journal; Greece and Rome; Harvard Theological Review; Health Economics, Policy and Law; The Historical Journal; International Journal of Asian Studies; International Journal of Astrobiology; International Journal of Cultural Property; International Journal of Law in Context; International Journal of Middle East Studies; The International Journal of Neuropsychopharmacology; International Journal of Technology Assessment in Health Care; International Journal of Tropical Insect Science; International Labor and Working-Class History; IO: International Organization; International Psychogeriatrics; International Review of Social History; International Review of the Red Cross; Japanese Journal of Political Science; The Journal of African History; Journal of African Law; The Journal of Agricultural Science; Journal of American Studies; The Journal of Asian Studies; Journal of Biosocial Science; Journal of Child Language; Journal of Dairy Research; The Journal of Ecclesiastical History; The Journal of Economic History; Journal of Fluid Mechanics; Journal of French Language Studies; Journal of Functional Programming; Journal of Germanic Linguistics; Journal of Global History; Journal of Helminthology; Journal of the Institute of Mathematics of Jussieu; Journal of Institutional Economics; Journal of the International Neuropsychological Society; Journal of the International*

Phonetic Association; The Journal of Laryngology and Otology; Journal of Latin American Studies; Journal of Linguistics; Journal of the Marine Biological Association of the United Kingdom; The Journal of Modern African Studies; Journal of Navigation; Journal of Pension Economics and Finance; Journal of Plasma Physics; Journal of Psychiatric Intensive Care; Journal of Public Policy; Journal of Radiotherapy in Practice; Journal of the Royal Asiatic Society; Journal of Social Policy; Journal of the Society for American Music; Journal of Southeast Asian Studies; Journal of Systematic Palaeontology; Journal of Tropical Ecology; Knowledge Engineering Review; Language in Society; Language Teaching; Language Variation and Change; Laser and Particle Beams; Legal Information Management; Legal Theory; Leiden Journal of International Law; The Lichenologist; Macroeconomic Dynamics; Mathematical Proceedings of the Cambridge Philosophical Society; Mathematical Structures in Computer Science; Microscopy and Microanalysis; Modern Asian Studies; Modern Intellectual History; Natural Language Engineering; Netherlands International Law Review; Netherlands Yearbook of International Law; Neuron Glia Biology; New Testament Studies; New Theatre Quarterly; Nordic Journal of Linguistics; Nurse Prescriber; Nutrition Research Reviews; Organised Sound; Oryx; Palliative & Supportive Care; Parasitology; Perspectives on Politics; Philosophy; Phonology; Plainsong and Medieval Music; Plant Genetic Resources; Polar Record; Politics & Gender; Popular Music; Primary Health Care Research & Development; Probability in the Engineering and Informational Sciences; Proceedings of the Edinburgh Mathematical Society; Proceedings of the International Astronomical Union; Proceedings of the Nutrition Society; Proceedings of the Royal Society of Edinburgh: Section A Mathematics; Progress in Neurotherapeutics and Neuropsychopharmacology; PS: Political Science & Politics; Psychological Medicine; Public Health Nutrition; Quarterly Reviews of Biophysics; ReCALL; Religious Studies; Renewable Agriculture and Food Systems; Review of International Studies; The Review of Politics; Reviews in Clinical Gerontology; Robotica; Royal Historical Society Camden Fifth Series; Royal Historical Society Transactions; Rural History; Science in Context; Scottish Journal of Theology; Seed Science Research; Social Philosophy and Policy; Social Policy and Society; Studies in American Political Development; Studies in Second Language Acquisition; Systematics and Biodiversity; Tempo; Thalamus and Related Systems; Theatre Research International; Theatre Survey; Theory and Practice of Logic Programming; Twentieth-Century Music; Urban History; Utilitas; Victorian Literature and Culture; Visual Neuroscience; World Trade Review; World's Poultry Science Journal; Yearbook of International Humanitarian Law; Zygote

Special series, joint imprints, and/or copublishing programs (partial list): Cambridge Companions to Philosophy; Cambridge Earth Science Series; Cambridge Edition of the Works of F. Scott Fitzgerald; Cambridge Edition of the Works of D. H. Lawrence; Cambridge Film Classics; Cambridge History of China; Cambridge History of Japan; Cambridge History of Science; Cambridge Medical Reviews; Cambridge Studies in Medieval Life and Thought; Cambridge Monographs on Mathematical Physics; Cambridge Opera Handbooks; Cambridge Studies in American Literature and Culture; Cambridge Studies in Ecology; Cambridge Studies in Mathematical Biology; Cambridge Studies in Publishing and Printing History; Cambridge Studies in Environment and History, Cambridge Tracts in Mathematics; Cambridge Texts in the History of Political Thought; Developmental and Cell Biology Series; Econometric Society Monographs; Hematological Oncology; Neurobiology and Psychiatry; New Directions in Language Teaching; Publications of the German Historical Institute; Studies in Natural Language Processing

Carnegie Mellon University Press

5032 Forbes Avenue
Pittsburgh, PA 15289-1021

Phone: (412) 268-2861
Fax: (412) 268-8706
Web site: www.cmu.edu/universitypress

Order Fulfillment:
CUP Services
750 Cascadilla Street
Ithaca, NY 14850

Customer Service:
Phone: (800) 666-2211
Fax: (800) 688-2877
E-mail: orderbook@cupserv.org

Staff

Director: Gerald Costanzo (poetry editor) (e-mail: gc3d@andrew.cmu.edu)
Senior Editor: Cynthia Lamb (nonfiction acquisitions) (e-mail: cynthial@andrew.cmu.edu)
Interim Fiction Editor: Gerald Costanzo
Drama / Entertainment Technology Editor: Donald Marinelli (e-mail: thedon@cmu.edu)
Production Manager: Connie Amoroso (e-mail: connieamoroso@yahoo.com)
Accounts Administrator: Anna Houck (e-mail: am2x@andrew.cmu.edu)

Full Member

Established: 1972
Title output 2006: 20
Titles currently in print: 450

Admitted to AAUP: 1991
Title output 2007: 16

Editorial Program

Carnegie Mellon's particular strength lies in literary publishing: Carnegie Mellon Series in Short Fiction, Carnegie Mellon Poetry Series, the Carnegie Mellon Classic Contemporaries Series (the reissuing of significant early books by important contemporary poets; beginning in 2008, the Classic Contemporaries Series will include fiction), and the Poets in Prose Series (memoir in the form of poets writing about their writing lives, poetry criticism, and the epistolary novel). Additionally, the Press has an emerging program in the publishing of texts related to entertainment technology. Carnegie Mellon is unique among US universities in offering interactive studies in the fine arts and computer technology. A future of ubiquitous broadband, nanotechnology, robotics, artificial intelligence, the blurring of reality between the 'material' world and the 'virtual' world augur well for the growth of entertainment computing as a legitimate academic discipline. Entertainment computing focuses on how enhanced computing power may be utilized to create ever more incredible entertainment possibilities.

The Press also publishes in art, music, the performing arts, critical analysis, education, university history, and social history.

The Catholic University of America Press

240 Leahy Hall
620 Michigan Avenue, N.E.
Washington, DC 20064

Phone: (202) 319-5052
Fax: (202) 319-4985
E-mail: (user I.D.)@cua.edu
Online catalog: cuapress.cua.edu

<u>Warehouse (Returns only):</u>
Hopkins Fulfillment Service
RETURNS
c/o Maple Press Co.
Lebanon Dist. Center
704 Legionaire Drive
Fredericksburg, PA 17026

<u>Customer Service:</u>
Hopkins Fulfillment Service
PO Box 50370
Baltimore, MD 21211
Phone: (800) 537-5487
Fax: (410) 516-6998

<u>UK Representative:</u>
Eurospan

<u>Canadian Representative:</u>
Scholarly Book Services

Staff

Director: David J. McGonagle (e-mail: mcgonagle)
  Administrative Assistant: Jessica Spotswood (e-mail: emanuel)
Acquisitions Editor: James C. Kruggel (philosophy, theology) (e-mail: kruggel); David J.
  McGonagle (all other fields)
Managing Editor: Theresa Walker (e-mail: walkert)
  Editorial Assistant: Tanjam Jacobson (e-mail: jacobsot)
Design and Production: Anne Kachergis (Kachergis Book Design, 14 Small Street North,
  Pittsboro, NC 27312)
Marketing Manager: Elizabeth Benevides (e-mail: benevides)
  Marketing Assistant: Abigail Padou (e-mail: padou)
Journals: Hubert Ngueha, Administrative Assistant (e-mail: ngueha)

Full Member

Established: 1939
Title output 2006: 36
Titles currently in print: 431

Admitted to AAUP: 1985
Title output 2007: 36
Journals published: 4

Editorial Program

American and European history (both ecclesiastical and secular); American and European
literature; philosophy; political theory; theology. Periods covered range from late antiquity
to modern times, with special interest in late antiquity, early Christianity, and the medieval
period. Submissions are not invited in fiction, poetry, mathematics, the natural sciences, and
related professional fields.

Journals: *The Americas; The Catholic Historical Review; Pierre d'Angle;*
U. S. Catholic Historian

Special series: Catholic Moral Thought; The Fathers of the Church: A New Translation;
Medieval Texts in Translation; Patristic Monograph Series of the North American Patristics
Society; Publications of the American Maritain Association (distributed); Studies in Philoso-
phy and the History of Philosophy; Thomas Aquinas in Translation

The University of Chicago Press

1427 E. 60th Street
Chicago, IL 60637-2954

Phone (Books): (773) 702-7700
Phone (Journals): (773) 702-7600
Fax: (773) 702-2705 (Books Acquisitions)
    (773) 702-9756 (Books Marketing)
    (773) 702-0172 (Journals Marketing)
    (773) 702-0694 (Journals Production)
E-mail: (firstinitial)(lastname)@press.uchicago.edu
Web site and online catalog: www.press.uchicago.edu;
www.press.uchicago.edu/presswide/

Chicago Distribution Center:
11030 South Langley Avenue
Chicago, IL 60628
Phone: (773) 702-7000
Fax: (773) 702-7212

UK Representative:
University Press Marketing

Canadian Representative:
The University Press Group

Staff

Director: Garrett P. Kiely (773/702-8878)
    Deputy Director: Christopher Heiser (773/702-2998)
    Assistant to the Director and Deputy Director: Ellen M. Zalewski (773/702-8879)
Books Division:
Manager: Robert Lynch (773/702-3160)
    Department Administrator: Teresa Fagan (773/834-1829)
Acquisitions Editorial:
    Editorial Directors: Alan Thomas (humanities & sciences) (773/702-7644); John Tryneski (social sciences & paperbacks) (773/702-7648)
    Editors: Susan Bielstein (art, architecture, ancient archeology, classics, film studies) (773/702-7633); T. David Brent (anthropology, philosophy, psychology, psychiatry) (773/702-7642); Robert P. Devens (American history, regional publishing) (773/702-0158); Elizabeth Branch Dyson (ethnomusicology, education, philosophy) (773/702-7637); Kathleen Hansell (music) (773/702-0427); Christie Henry (life sciences, geography, cartography) (773/702-0468); Jennifer Howard (physical sciences, mathematics) (773/702-3145); Douglas Mitchell (history, sociology, sexuality studies, rhetoric) (773/702-7639); Randolph Petilos (medieval studies, poetry in translation) (773/702-7647); Karen Darling (history, philosophy, and social studies of science); David Pervin (economics, business, law) (773/702-7638); Alan Thomas (literature, religion) (773/702-7644); John Tryneski (political science, law and society) (773/702-7648)
    Managing Editor, Phoenix Poets: Randolph Petilos (773/702-7647)
    Paperback Editor: Margaret Hivnor (773/702-7649)
    Assistant Paperback Editor: Janet Deckenbach (773/702-7034)
Reference: Paul Schellinger, Editorial Director (773/702-2376)
    Senior Editor: David Morrow (773/702-7465)
    Senior Project Editor: Mary Laur (773/702-7326)
Contracts and Subsidiary Rights Manager: Perry Cartwright (773/702-6096)
    Foreign Rights Manager: Gretchen Linder (773/702-7741)
Manuscript Editorial: Anita Samen, Managing Editor (773/702-5081)

Design and Production: Sylvia Hecimovich, Design and Production Director (773/702-7924)
  Associate Design and Production Director / Design Manager: Jill Shimabukuro (773/702-7653)
Digital Media Group: Andrew Brenneman, Digital Media and Systems Manager (773/702-8521)
  E-commerce / E-marketing Manager: Dean Blobaum (773/702-7706)
Marketing: Carol Kasper, Director (773/702-7733)
  Distributed Books Coordinator: Saleem Dhamee (773/702-4916)
  Marketing Manager for Reference & Regional Projects: Ellen Gibson (773/702-3233)
  Reference Special Sales Coordinator / Promotions Manager: Laura Anderson (773/702-3233)
  Marketing Design Manager: Mary Shanahan (773/702-7697)
  Senior Marketing Designer: Alice Reimann (773/702-7849)
  Direct Marketing Manager: Joe Weintraub (773/702-0377)
  Associate Direct Marketing Manager: Stuart Kisilinsky (773/702-8924)
  Direct Mail Associate: Casimir Psjuchek (773/702-7887)
Sales: John Kessler, Associate Marketing Director/Sales Director (773/702-7248)
  Sales and Distribution Associate: Robert Hoffman (773/702-0340)
  Sales and Inventory Associate: Joseph Peterson (773/702-7723)
  International Sales Manager: TBA (773/702-7898)
  Sales Representatives: Bailey Walsh (Midwest); Blake De Lodder (East Coast); Gary Hart (West Coast)
  Sales Assistant: Vertelle Kanyama (773/702-7899)
Publicity and Promotions: Mark Heineke, Promotions Director (773/702-3714)
  Advertising Manager: Anne Osterman (773/702-0289)
  Advertising, Marketing, and Marketing Coordinator: Lara Maksymonko (773/702-2945)
  Exhibits Manager and Seasonal Catalog Coordinator: Carrie Adams (773/702-4216)
  Exhibits Associate: Stephanie Maieritech (773/702-0285)
  Publicity Manager: Levi Stahl (773/702-7897)
  Senior Promotions Manager: Stephanie Hlywak (773/702-0376)
  Promotions Managers: Robert Hunt (773/702-0279); Megan Marz (773/702-7490); Lindsey Dawson (773/702-1964); Kristi McGuire (773/702-2548
  Trade Promotion Coordinator: Harriett Green (773/702-4217)

<u>Journals Division</u>

Journals Division Manager: Nawin Gupta (773/702-8785)
  Publications Management Director: Debra McBride (773-702-7359)
  Publications Managers: Andrew Baumann (773/702-7087); Tess Mullen (773/702-7442); Michael Cunningham (773/702-7678)
  Publicity Coordinator: Suzanne Wu (773/834-0386)
  Circulation Development Manager: Jeralynn Lee (773/702-5549)
  Director of Business Development: Mary Summerfield (773/702-2383)
  Publications Acquisition Manager: Kari Roane (773/702-7362)
  Medical Publisher & Publishing Operations Director: Everett Conner (773/753-2669)
  Production Manager, Medical Journals: Ashley Towne (773/753-4241)
  Operations Manager, Astronomy Journals: Mary Guillemette (773/753-3373)
  Project Manager & IT Operations Director: Barry Bernier (773/834-3085)
  Publishing Technology Manager: John Muenning (773/753-3376)

IT Operations Manager: Kerry Kroffe (773/702-2621)
Subscription Fulfillment Manager: Don Pavoni (773/753-4243)
Licensing & Permissions Manager: Katharine Duff (773/702-7688)
Advertising Sales & Services Manager: Carmella Barhany (773-702-3120)
Advertising Sales Manager: Tim Hill (773/702-8187)
Advertising and List Rental Coordinator: Cheryl Jones (773/702-7361)
Chief Manuscript Editor, General Journals: Mary E. Leas (773/702-7961)
Chief Manuscript Editor, Science Journals: Barbara Condon (773/702-3993)
Chief Manuscript Editor, Astronomy Journals: Elizabeth Huyck (773/753-8021)
Chicago Distribution Center Services:
President of Chicago Distribution Services: Donald A. Collins (773/702-7020)
Chief Operations Officer: Karen Barch (773/702-7024)
   UHRM/Administrator: Sharon Klausner (773/702-7010)
   Distribution Services Coordinator: Sue Tranchita (773/702-7014
   Customer Service Manager: Karen Hyzy (773/702-7109)
   Assistant Manager, Customer Service/Instructor Trainer Title Management: Latrice Allen (773/702-7112)
   Credit and Collections, A/R Manager: Nick Cole (773/702-7164)
   Director of Accounting: Bob Peterson (773/702-7036)
   Chicago Digital Distribution Center Manager: Jeanne Weinkle (773/702-7238)
   M.I.S. Manager: Christopher Jones: (773/702-7229)
   Royalty/Rights, Return Manager: Cassandra Wisniewski (773/702-7062)
   Warehouse Distribution Manager: Gail Candreva-Szwet (773/702-7080)
   Journals Warehouse Manager: Don P. Collins (773/702-7245)
BiblioVault:
BiblioVault Operations and Web Coordinator: Kate Davey (773/834-4417)

Full Member

Established: 1891	Admitted to AAUP: 1957
Title output 2006: 195	Title output 2007: 235
Titles currently in print: 5,013	Journals published: 47

Editorial Program

Sociology; anthropology; political science; business and economics; history; English; American and foreign literature; literary criticism; biological and physical sciences and mathematics; conceptual studies of science; law; philosophy; linguistics; geography and cartography; art history; classics; architecture; history of photography; education; psychiatry and psychology; musicology. Submissions are not invited in fiction or poetry or in conventional textbooks.

Journals (* available online): *American Art*; American Journal of Education*; The American Historical Review, American Journal of Sociology*; The American Naturalist*; The Astronomical Journal*; The Astrophysical Journal*; The Astrophysical Journal Supplement Series*; Classical Philology*; Clinical Infectious Diseases*; Comparative Education Review*; Critical Inquiry*; Current Anthropology*; Economic Development and Cultural Change*; The Elementary School Journal*; Ethics*; History of Religions*; Infection Control and Hospital Epidemiology*; International Journal of American Linguistics*; International Journal of Plant Sciences*; Isis*; Journal of British Studies*; Journal of Consumer Research*; The Journal of Geology*; Journal of Human*

Capital; *The Journal of Infectious Diseases**; *Journal of Labor Economics**; *The Journal of Law and Economics**; *The Journal of Legal Studies**; *The Journal of Modern History**; *Journal of Near Eastern Studies**; *Journal of Political Economy**; *The Journal of Religion**; *The Library Quarterly**; *Modern Philology**; *Philosophy of Science**; *Physiological and Biochemical Zoology**; *Publications of the Astronomical Society of the Pacific**; *The Quarterly Review of Biology**; *Signs**; *Social Service Review**; *Winterthur Portfolio**

Annuals: *Crime and Justice*; *Osiris**; *Supreme Court Economic Review*; *The Supreme Court Review*

Special imprints: Phoenix Books (trade paperbacks); Midway Reprints (short-run paperback reprints)

The Chinese University Press

The Chinese University Press
Shatin, New Territories, Hong Kong

Phone: +852 2946-5300
Fax: +852 2603-6692
E-mail: cup@cuhk.edu.hk
Indiv: (user I.D.)@cuhk.edu.hk
Web site: www.chineseupress.com

North American Distributor:
Columbia University Press
Phone: (800) 944-8648 / (914) 591-9111
Fax: (800) 944-1844 / (914) 591-9201

UK and European Distributor:
Eurospan

Staff

Director: Qi Gan (+852 2946-5399; e-mail: ganqi)
Secretary to the Director: Tina Chan (+852 2946-5398; e-mail: tinachan)
Editorial: Wai Keung Tse, Senior Editor (+852 2946-5397; e-mail: waikeungtse)
Production: Kingsley Ma, Manager (+852 2946-5391; e-mail: kwaihungma)
Business/Marketing: Angelina Wong, Manager (+852 2946-5386; e-mail: laifunwong)

International Member

Established: 1977
Title output 2006: 54
Titles currently in print: 654

Admitted to AAUP: 1981
Title output 2007: 60
Journals published: 6

Editorial Program

Bilingual publication of academic and general trade titles. Areas of interest include Chinese studies in literature, history, philosophy, languages, and the arts. The Press also publishes books on business, government, medicine, natural sciences, as well as dictionaries and general books in both the English and Chinese languages.

The Press also has joint imprints with Columbia University Press and École Française d'Extrême-Orient.

Journals: *Asian Anthropology*; *Asian Journal of English Language Teaching*; *The China Review*; *Hong Kong Drama Review*; *Journal of Psychology in Chinese Societies*; *Journal of Translation Studies*

Special series: Bibliography and Index Series; Bilingual Series on Modern Chinese Literature; Ch'ien Mu Lectures in History and Culture; Educational Studies Series; Hong Kong Taxation; Institute of Chinese Studies Monograph Series; Young Scholars Dissertation Awards

University Press of Colorado

5589 Arapahoe Avenue
Suite 206C
Boulder, CO 80303

Phone: (720) 406-8849
Fax: (720) 406-3443
E-mail: (user I.D)@upcolorado.com
Web site: www.upcolorado.com

Distributor:
University of Oklahoma Press
2800 Venture Drive
Norman, OK 73069-8216
Orders: (800) 627-7377
Fax: (800) 735-0476; (405) 364-5798

European Representative:
Gazelle Book Services

Staff

Director and Acquisitions Editor: Darrin Pratt (e-mail: darrin)
Managing Editor: Laura Furney (e-mail: laura)
Production Manager: Dan Pratt (e-mail: dan)
Marketing & Sales Manager: Ann Wendland (e-mail: ann)

Full Member

Established: 1965
Title output 2006: 26
Titles currently in print: 319

Admitted to AAUP: 1982
Title output 2007: 24

Editorial Program

Physical sciences; natural history; ecology; American history; Western history; anthropology; archaeology; and regional titles.

The Press also copublishes with and distributes titles for the Denver Museum of Natural History, the Colorado Historical Society Colorado State University's Cooperative Extension, and the Center for Literary Publishing.

Special series: Atomic History & Culture; Mesoamerican Worlds; Mining the American West; Timberline Books

Columbia University Press

61 West 62nd Street
New York, NY 10023-7015

Phone: (212) 459-0600
Fax: (212) 459-3677
E-mail: (user I.D.)@columbia.edu
Web site: www.columbia.edu/cu/cup

Customer Service:
Phone: (800) 944-8648
Fax: (914) 591-9201

Business Office & Warehouse:
136 South Broadway
Irvington-on-Hudson, NY 10533-2508

Phone: (914) 591-9111
Fax: (914) 591-9201

UK Office:
University Presses of California,
Columbia, and Princeton, Ltd.
Southern Cross Trading Estate
1 Oldlands Way, Bognor Regis
West Sussex PO22 9SA
United Kingdom
Phone: +44 1243 842165
Fax: +44 1243 842167

Staff

New York City (212/459-0600):
President and Director: James D. Jordan (ext. 7118; e-mail: jj2143)
   Chief Financial Officer: David Hetherington (exts. 7122/6211; e-mail: dh2321)
   Assistant to the Director: Afua Adusei (ext. 7117; e-mail: aa2337)
   Publishing Director and Director of Rights and Contracts: Clare Wellnitz (ext. 7147;
   e-mail: cw270)
   Subsidiary Rights Associate: Justine Evans (ext. 7128; e-mail: je2217)
Acquisitions Editorial: Jennifer Crewe, Associate Director and Editorial Director (Asian
   humanities, film studies, literary and cultural studies) (ext. 7145; e-mail: jc373)
   Senior Executive Editors: Peter Dimock (political philosophy, American history, Middle
   East history) (ext. 7119; e-mail: pd304); Wendy Lochner (religion, philosophy, animal
   studies) (ext. 7121; e-mail: wl2003)
   Executive Editor: Lauren Dockett (social work, psychology) (ext. 7107; e-mail: ld2237)
   Publisher for the Life Sciences: Patrick Fitzgerald (ext. 7136; e-mail: pf2134)
   Publisher for Finance and Economics: Myles Thompson (ext. 7161; e-mail: mt2312)
   Executive Editor: Anne Routon (Asian history, international relations, anthropology) (ext.
   7116; e-mail: akr36)
   Associate Editor: Juree Sondker (journalism, food history, film) (ext. 7204; e-mail: js2403)
Reference / Electronic Publishing: Karen Casey, Director of Reference and Electronic
   Publishing (ext. 7137; e-mail: kc2282)
Manuscript Editorial: Anne McCoy, Managing Editor (ext. 7111; e-mail: aam10)
   Electronic Manuscripts Administrator: Leslie Bialler (ext. 7109; e-mail: lb136)
Design and Production: Linda Secondari, Creative Director, Manufacturing and Technology
   (ext. 7102; e-mail: ls241)
   Senior Book Designer: Milenda Lee (ext. 7103; e-mail: ml2657)
   Production Manager: Jennifer Jerome (ext. 7177; e-mail: jj352)
Marketing: Brad Hebel, Director of Marketing and Sales (ext. 7130; e-mail: bh2106)

Publicity Director: Meredith Howard (ext. 7126; e-mail: mh2306)
Electronic Marketing Manager: Philip Leventhal (ext. 7159; e-mail: pl2164)
Sales Representative for Electronic Products: John Babcock (ext. 7158; e-mail: jb2579)
Direct Mail Manager: Todd Lazarus (ext. 7152; e-mail: tdl10)
Advertising Manager: Elena Iaffa (ext. 7124; e-mail: ei2131)
East Coast Sales Representative: Catherine Hobbs (ext. 7809; e-mail: chobss@rlc.net)
Mid-West Sales Representative: Kevin Kurtz (ext. 7806; e-mail: kkurtz5@earthlink.net)
West Coast Sales Representative: William Gawronski (ext. 7807; e-mail: wgawronski@earthlink.net)
IT: Courtney Lew, Network Manager (ext. 7153; e-mail: cl800)
Systems Support Specialist: Sean Chen (ext. 7106; e-mail: sc2566)
Irvington (914/591-9111):
Controller and Business Manager: Sarah Vanderbilt (ext. 6227; e-mail: scv12)
Assistant to the CFO and Business Manager: Sylvia Martinez (ext. 6231; e-mail: sm2862)
Human Resources Manager: James Pakiela (ext. 6217; e-mail: jp2483)
Warehouse Manager: Thomas Lofgren (ext. 6218; e-mail: tl2147)
Royalty Coordinator: Louise Erickson (ext. 6229; e-mail: le66)
Customer Service Manager: Diane Pillinger (ext. 6240; e-mail: pd182)

Full Member

Established: 1893   Admitted to AAUP: 1937
Title output 2006: 162   Title output 2007: 167
Titles currently in print: 2,558

Editorial Program

General reference works in print and electronic formats. Scholarly, general interest, and professional books, upper-level textbooks in the humanities, social sciences, and earth and life sciences. Subjects include animal studies; anthropology; Asian Studies; botany; conservation and environmental science; ecology; evolutionary studies; film; finance and economics; gender studies; history; international affairs; literary and cultural studies; media studies; Middle East studies; philosophy; political science; religion and social work. The Press publishes poetry, fiction, and drama in translation only.

Columbia University Press is the distributor in the United States, Canada, and Latin America for Kegan Paul, University of Tokyo Press, Wallflower Press, East European Monographs, and Chinese University Press of Hong Kong, and distributes for Edinburgh University Press in the United States, Canada and Latin America.

Special series, joint imprints, and/or co-publishing programs: American Lectures on the History of Religions; American Museum of Natural History Biodiversity Series; Arts and Traditions of the Table; Asia Perspectives; Bampton Lectures in America; Between Men—Between Women; Biology and Resource Management; CERI Series in Comparative Politics and International Studies; Columbia Classics in Anthropology; Columbia Classics in Philosophy; Columbia Guides to American History; Columbia Guides to American Indian History; Columbia Guides to Asian History; Columbia History of Urban Life; Columbia Readings of Buddhist Literature; Columbia Series in Science and Religion; Columbia Studies in Contemporary American History; Columbia Studies in International History; Columbia Studies in Political Thought; Columbia Themes In Philosophy; Complexity in Ecological Systems;

Critical Moments in Earth History; Cultures of History; Empowering the Powerless; End of Life Care; European Perspectives; Film and Culture; Foundations of Social Work Knowledge; Gender and Culture; Gender, Theory and Religion; Global Chinese Culture; Harriman Lectures; History and Society of the Modern Middle East; History of Urban Life; Initiative for Policy Dialogue; Introduction to Asian Civilizations; Insurrections: Critical Studies in Religion, Politics, and Culture; Issues, Cases, and Methods in Biodiversity Conservation; Italian Academy in America Lectures; John Dewey Essays in Philosophy; Leonard Hastings Schoff Lectures; Maps of the Mind; Modern Asian Literature; Modern Chinese Literature from Taiwan; The Neurosciences, Social Sciences, and the Arts; New Directions in Critical Theory; Popular Cultures, Everyday Lives; Records of Western Civilization; Religion and American Culture; Translations from the Asian Classics; Treasury of the Indic Sciences; Weatherhead Books on Asia; Wellek Library Lectures; Woodbridge Lectures

Cork University Press

Youngline Industrial Estate, Pouladuff Road
Cork, Ireland

Phone: +353 (21) 490 2980
Fax: + 353 (21) 431 5329
E-mail: corkuniversitypress@ucc.ie
Web site: www.corkuniversitypress.com

US Representative:
Stylus Publishing
22883 Quicksilver Drive
Sterling, VA 20166-2012
Phone: (703) 661-1504
Fax: (703) 661-1501
E-mail: stylusmail@presswarehouse.com

UK Representative:
Marston Book Services

Irish Representative:
Gill & MacMillan

Staff
Director: Mike Collins (e-mail: mike.collins@ucc.ie)
Editorial: Sophie Watson (e-mail: corkuniversitypress@ucc.ie)
Production: Maria O'Donovan (e-mail: m.odonovan@ucc.ie)

International Member
Established: 1925
Title output 2006: 12
Titles currently in print: 176

Admitted to AAUP: 2002
Title output 2007: 23
Journals published: 1

Editorial Program
While the Press specializes in the broad field of Irish Cultural, its subject range extends across the fields of music, art history, literary criticism and poetry. However, the focus of our list is in the areas of Irish cultural history, archaeology and landscape studies.
Journal: *Irish Review*
Special series: Field Day Monographs; Ireland into Film

Cornell University Press

Street Address:
Sage House
512 East State Street
Ithaca, NY 14850

Mailing Address:
PO Box 250
Ithaca, NY 14851

Phone: (607) 277-2338
Fax: (607) 277-2374
E-mail: (user I.D.)@cornell.edu
Web site: www.cornellpress.cornell.edu

UK Representative:
University Presses Marketing

Order Fulfillment:
CUP Services
750 Cascadilla Street
Ithaca, NY 14850
Phone: (800) 666-2211
Fax: (800) 688-2877

UK / European Distributor:
NBN International

Canadian Representative:
Lexa Publishers' Representatives

Staff

Director: John G. Ackerman (ext. 209; e-mail: jga4)
  Assistant Director & CFO: Roger A. Hubbs (607-277-2696; e-mail: rah9)
  Assistant Director & Managing Editor: Priscilla Hurdle (ext. 244; e-mail: plh9)
  Personnel Manager: Sally McClure-Parshall (ext. 228; e-mail: sjm19)
  Assistant to the Director: Michael Morris (ext. 210; e-mail: mam278)
Acquisitions Editorial: Peter J. Potter, Editor-in-Chief (classics, Medieval studies, literature)
  (ext. 241; e-mail: pjp33)
  Editorial Director, ILR Press: Frances Benson (labor studies and workplace issues, health
  care, business) (ext. 222; e-mail: fgb2)
  Executive Editor: Roger Haydon (politics, international relations, philosophy, history of
  science, Asian studies) (ext. 225; e-mail: rmh11)
  Editors: John G. Ackerman (European history, music, philosophy of religion, Russian
  history) (ext. 209; e-mail: jga4); TBA (American history, US politics, law, New York state
  and regional books) (ext. 233); Heidi Lovette (science: entomology, herpetology, natural
  history, ornithology, plant sciences) (ext. 234; e-mail: hsl22); Peter Wissoker (anthropology,
  geography, sociology, urban studies) (ext. 224; e-mail: pw87)
Manuscript Editorial: Priscilla Hurdle, Managing Editor (ext. 244; e-mail: plh9)
  Manuscript Editors: Candace Akins (ext. 260; e-mail: cja3); Teresa Jesionowski (ext. 249;
  e-mail: tj15); Ange Romeo-Hall (ext. 243; e-mail: asr8); Karen Hwa (ext. 245; e-mail:
  kth9); Karen Laun (ext. 236; e-mail: kml35)
Design and Production: Karen Kerr, Manager (ext. 235; e-mail: kg99)
  Associate Production Manager: George Whipple (ext. 237; e-mail: gtw2)
  Senior Designers: Lou Robinson (ext. 262; e-mail: lr11); Scott Levine (ext. 263;
  e-mail: sel37)
  Senior Production Coordinators: Christopher Basso (ext. 240; e-mail: cmb224);
  Diana Silva (ext. 257; e-mail: drs68)
  Production Coordinator: Karen Beebe (ext. 239; e-mail: kjb5)

Marketing: Mahinder Kingra, Marketing Manager (ext. 255; e-mail: msk55)
  Sales Manager: Nathan Gemignani (ext. 251; e-mail: ndg5)
  Publicity Manager: Jonathan Hall (ext. 252; e-mail: jlh98)
  Subsidiary Rights Manager: Tonya Cook (e-mail: cup-subrights)
  Advertising Coordinator: Amelia Wise (ext. 256; e-mail: arw45)
  Publicity Coordinator: Jennifer Longley (ext. 254; e-mail: jal225)
  Exhibits Coordinator: David Mitchell (ext. 248; e-mail: dwm23)
  Copy Supervisor/Awards Coordinator: Susan Barnett (ext. 259; e-mail: scb33)
  Permissions Coordinator: Stephanie Munson (ext. 231; e-mail: sm120)
Business: (607/277-2696)
  Chief Financial Officer: Roger A. Hubbs (ext. 132; e-mail: rah9)
  Accounting & Operations Coordinator: Cindy Snyder (ext. 133; e-mail: chs6)
  Procurement, Disbursements & Title Accounting: Trudy Cism (ext. 139; e-mail: tec7)
CUP Services Distribution Center:
  CUP Services Manager: Christopher Quinlan (607/277-2211, ext. 125; e-mail: cq@cupserv.org)
  Client Services, Accounts Receivable: Christine Jolluck (607/277-2037, ext. 126; e-mail: cj@cupserv.org)
  MIS: Patrick Garrison (607/277-2969, ext. 149; e-mail: plg6@cupserv.org)
  Customer Service: Sheila Maleski (607/277-2211, ext. 137; e-mail: orderbook@cupserv.org)
  Warehouse and Shipping: Jon Austin (607/277-2827, ext. 151; e-mail: ja@cupserv.org)

Full Member

Established: 1869   Admitted to AAUP: 1937
Re-established in present form: 1930
Title output 2006: 142   Title output 2007: 124
Titles currently in print: 2,200

Editorial Program

Serious nonfiction, with particular strengths in anthropology; Asian studies; classics; history; industrial and labor relations; life science; literary criticism and theory; music; natural history; philosophy; politics and international relations; race studies; religion; Slavic studies; sociology; and women's studies. Submissions are not invited in poetry or fiction.

Cornell University Press is the distributor in the United States and Canada for Leuven University Press.

Special imprints: Comstock Publishing Associates; ILR Press

Special series, joint imprints, and/or copublishing programs: Agora Editions; Ancient Commentators on Aristotle; Collection on Technology and Work; Conjunctions of Religion and Power in the Medieval Past; Cornell Studies in Classical Philology/Townsend Lectures; Cornell Studies in Money; Cornell Studies in Political Economy; Cornell Studies in Security Affairs; The Cornell Wordsworth; The Cornell Yeats; The Culture and Politics of Health Care Work; Culture and Society after Socialism; Cushwa Center Studies of Catholicism in Twentieth-Century America; Islandica; Knowledge and Practice; Literature of American Labor; Masters of Latin Literature; Metropolitan Ethnographies; Psychoanalysis and Social Theory; The United States in the World

Duke University Press

Street Address:
905 West Main Street
Suite 18-B
Durham, NC 27701

Mailing Address:
Box 90660
Durham, NC 27708- 0660

Phone: (919) 687-3600
Faxes: (919) 688- 4574 (Books)
(919) 688-3524 (Journals)
(919) 688-4391 (Marketing)
E-mail: info@dukepress.edu
Indiv:
(firstinitial)(lastname)@dukeupress.edu
(unless otherwise indicated)
Web site: www.dukeupress.edu

Orders and Customer Service:
Phone: (888) 651-0122; (919) 688-5134
Fax: (888) 651-0124; (919) 688-2615

Warehouse:
Duke University Press
Distribution Center
120 Golden Drive
Durham, NC 27705
Phone: (919) 384-0733

UK / European Representative:
Combined Academic Publishers

Canadian Representative:
Lexa Publishers' Representatives

Staff

Director: Stephen A. Cohn (919/687-3606)
  Assistant to the Director/Development Coordinator: Kristin Anderson (919/687-3685)
  Manager, Central Administration: Robyn L. Miller (919/687-3633)
  Subsidiary Rights and Permissions: Diane Grosse (919/687-8007)
Acquisitions Editorial: Ken Wissoker, Editorial Director (anthropology, cultural studies, post-colonial theory, lesbian and gay studies, construction of race, gender and national identity, literary criticism, film and television, popular music, visual studies) (919/687-3648; e-mail: kwiss@duke.edu)
Executive Editor: J. Reynolds Smith (literary theory and history, cultural theory and practice, religion, American studies, Latin American studies, Asian studies, race and ethnicity, science and technology, sociology, contemporary music) (919/687-3637; e-mail: j.smith@duke.edu)
Senior Editor: Valerie Millholland (Latin American studies, South Asian studies, European history and politics, US history, women's history, environmental studies, race and ethnicity studies, law) (919/687-3628; e-mail: vmill@duke.edu)
Assistant Editors: Miriam Angress (religion, women's studies, history, humanities, cultural studies) (919/687-3601); Courtney Berger (political theory, feminist theory, film and television, food and wine) (919/687-3652)
Manuscript Editorial: Fred Kameny, Managing Editor (919/687-3603)
  Assistant Managing Editors: Pamela Morrison (919/687-3630); Justin Faerber (919/687-3669); Mark Mastromarino (919/687-3660)
Marketing: Emily Young, Associate Director and Marketing Manager (919/687-3654)
  Associate Marketing Manager: H. Lee Willoughby-Harris (919/687-3646; e-mail: hlwh)
  Sales Manager: Michael McCullough (919/687-3604)
  Catalog Copywriting Coordinator: Katie Courtland (919/687-3663)

Advertising Coordinator: Dafina Diabate (919/687-3649)
Exhibits Coordinator: Helena Knox (919/687-3647)
Publicity Assistant: TBA (919/687-3650)
Design and Production: Deborah Wong, Design & Production Manager (919/687-3629)
  Assistant Design & Production Manager: Cherie Westmoreland (919/687-3643)
  Book Designer: Amy Buchanan (919/687-3651; e-mail: arbuchanan); Heather Hensley (919/687-3658)
  Graphic Designer: Jennifer Hill (919/687-3676)
  Senior Production Assistant: Christina Pelech (919/687-3668)
  Administrative Assistant: Patty Van Norman (919/687-3622)
Journals: Rob Dilworth, Editorial & Administrative Manager (919/687-3624)
  Senior Managing Editor: Laurel Ferejohn (919/687-3688)
  Marketing Manager: Donna Blagdan (919/687-3631)
  Assistant Marketing Manager: Cason Lynley (919/687-3653)
  Library Relations Manager: Kim Steinle (919/687-3655)
  Advertising & Publicity Coordinator: Mandy Dailey-Berman (919/687-3636)
  Direct Marketing and Exhibits Coordinator: Jocelyn Dawson (919/687-3687)
  Senior Marketing Assistant: Leslie Grignolo (919/687-3627)
  Production & Finance Manager: Michael Brondoli (919/687-3605)
  Art Director / Journals Designer: Sue Hall (919/687-3620; e-mail: suehall)
  Assistant Designer: Jeff Mahorney (919/687-3697)
  Production Supervisor: Allison Belan (919/687-3619)
Business Office and Distribution: Norris Langley, Chief Financial Officer (919/687-3607)
  Warehouse Manager: Lloyd Moore (919/384-1244)
  Warehouse Supervisor: Margie Clayton (919/384-0733)
  Customer Service—Journals: Lesley Jones (919/687-3617)
  Customer Service—Books: (919/687-3610)
  Customer Service Manager: TBA (919/687-3684)
  Accounts Payable and Royalty Supervisor: Michelle Wright (919/687-3614)
Information Systems: Pamela Spaulding, Manager (919/687-3641)
  Assistant Manager: Martin Leppitsch (919/687-3662)
  Database Administrator / Unison Programmer: Ling Mao (919/687-3665)
  Unison / STM Programmer: Gavril Chiver (919/687-3611)
  Help Desk Manager: Marcus Butts (919/687-3635)

Full Member

Established: 1921 (as Trinity College Press)	Admitted to AAUP: 1937
Title output 2006: 118	Title output 2007: 116
Titles currently in print: 2,157	Journals published: 33

Editorial Program

Scholarly books in the humanities and social sciences, with lists in art criticism and history; cultural studies; literary theory and history; legal studies; gay and lesbian studies; gender studies; American history; African American studies; Asian American studies; Latin American anthropology, history, literature, and politics; Slavic studies; European history and politics; cultural anthropology; minority politics and post colonial issues; music; film and TV; environmental studies; political science and political philosophy; religion; sociology; and science studies.

Journals (*journals available online): *American Literature*; American Literary Scholarship*; American Speech*; boundary 2*; Camera Obscura*; The Collected Letters of Thomas and Jane Welsh Carlyle; Common Knowledge*; Comparative Studies of South Asia, Africa and the Middle East*; differences; Duke Gifted Letter, Duke Mathematical Journal*; Eighteenth-Century Life*; Ethnohistory*; French Historical Studies*; GLQ: A Journal of Lesbian and Gay Studies*; Hispanic American Review*; History of Political Economy*; Journal of Health Politics, Policy and Law*; Journal of Medieval and Early Modern Studies*; Labor: Studies in Working Class History of the Americas*; Mediterranean Quarterly*; Modern Language Quarterly*; Neurology-Oncology*; New German Critique*; Pedagogy: Critical Approaches to Teaching Literature, Language, Culture & Composition*; Philosophical Review*; Poetics Today*; positions: east Asia cultures critique*; Public Culture*; Radical History Review*; SAQ: South Atlantic Quarterly*; Social Science History*; Social Text*; Theater**

Special series, joint imprints and/or copublishing programs: American Encounters: Global Interactions; Asia-Pacific: Culture, Politics and Society; Collected Letters of Thomas and Jane Welsh Carlyle; Console-ing Passions; Constitutional Conflicts; Body/Commodity/ Text; the C. Eric Lincoln Series on the Black Experience; Ecologies for the Twenty-First Century; International and Comparative Working-Class History; Latin America in Translation; Latin America Otherwise: Languages, Empires, Nations; Latin America Readers; Living with the Shore; New Americanists; Next Wave: New Directions in Women's Studies; Objects/ Histories: Perverse Modernities; Politics, Culture & History; Post-Contemporary Interventions; Public Planet; Radical Perspectives: A Radical History Review Book Series; Refiguring American Music; Science and Cultural Theory; Series Q: SIC

Duquesne University Press

600 Forbes Avenue
Pittsburgh, PA 15282

Phone: (412) 396-6610
Fax: (412) 396-5984
Web site: www.dupress.duq.edu

UK Representative:
Gazelle Book Sevices

Distribution / Orders:
CUP Services
Box 6525
750 Cascadilla Street
Ithaca, NY 14851-6525
Orders only: (800) 666-2211
Fax: (607) 272-6292
Customer Service: (607) 277-2211

Staff

Director: Susan Wadsworth-Booth (412/396-5684; e-mail: wadsworth@duq.edu)
Marketing & Business Manager: Lori R. Crosby (412/396-5732; e-mail: crosbyl@duq.edu)
Production Editor: Kathy McLaughlin Meyer (412/396-1166; e-mail: meyerk@duq.edu)
Editorial Assistant: Akiko Motomura (412/396-4866)
Promotions/Marketing Assistant: Joanna Taylor (412/396-4863)

Full Member

Established: 1927

Title output 2006: 11
Titles currently in print: 108

Admitted to AAUP: 1995
(Former membership: 1962-72)
Title output 2007: 10

Editorial Program

Literary studies, specifically of late medieval, Renaissance and seventeenth-century literature; ethics; philosophy; psychology; religious studies. The Press does not publish fiction, poetry, or unrevised dissertations.

Special series: Medieval & Renaissance Literary Studies; Levinas Studies: An Annual Review

Eastern Washington University Press

534 E. Spokane Falls Blvd.
Spokane, WA 99202

Phone: (509)368-6596; (800) 508-9095
Fax: (509) 623-4283
E-mail: ewupress@mail.ewu.edu
Indiv: (user I.D.)@mail.ewu.edu, unless otherwise indicated
Web site: ewupress.ewu.edu

Orders:
Eastern Washington University Press
Phone: (800) 508-9095
E-mail: ewupress@mail.ewu.edu

Staff

Director: Ivar Nelson (509/623-4286; e-mail: inelson)
Senior Editor: Christopher Howell (509/623-4291; e-mail: cnhowell)
Managing Editor: Pamela Holway (509/623-4351; e-mail: pholway)
Sales and Publicity Manager: Steve Meyer (509/623-4215; e-mail: smeyer)
Office Manager: Jane Noonan (509/623-4285; e-mail: jnoonan)
Get Lit! Administrator: Kathy Hill (509/623-4262; e-mail: khill)
Young Writers Programs: Marny Lombard (509/623-4284; e-mail: getlitkids)
Editorial Assistants: Erin Dodge (509/623-4284; e-mail: erin_ewu@yahoo.com) (online marketing and publishing, eCommerce and editorial assistance); Marty Malet (509/623-4284; e-mail: martymaley@ponymail.com) (Get Lit! festival and Web designer); Christine Nicolai (509/623-4285; e-mail: ewupress2) (literary prizes and internship program)

Full Member

Established: 1992
Title output 2006: 12
Titles currently in print: 129

Admitted to AAUP: 2005
Title output 2007: 12

Editorial Program

Scholarly books, general interest titles, and original fiction and poetry. Special areas of interest include literary criticism, environmental issues, Southeast Asian studies, world literature in translation, and the history, culture, and public policy of the Inland Northwest and the Northern Rocky Mountain regions. The Press also sponsors two literary prizes (the Blue Lynx Prize for Poetry and the Spokane Prize for Short Fiction) and the annual Get Lit! festival, in addition to offering internships and courses for students interested in publishing.

University Press of Florida

15 N.W. 15th Street
Gainesville, FL 32611-2079

Phone: (352) 392-1351
Acquisitions phone: (352) 392-9190
Fax: (352) 392-7302
E-mail: (user I.D.)@upf.com
Web site: www.upf.com

Orders:
Phone: (800) 226-3822
Fax: (800) 680-1955
Toll free fax: (800) 680-1955

UK Representative:
Eurospan

Canadian Representative:
Scholarly Book Services

Staff

Director: Meredith Morris Babb (ext. 204; e-mail: mb)
  Assistant to the Director: Cindy Laukert (ext. 201; e-mail: cl)
  Associate Director / Director of Development: Andrea Dzavik, (ext. 234; e-mail: ad)
Acquisitions Editorial: John Byram, Associate Director & Editor-in-Chief (national and
  regional trade, natural history, bioarchaeology) (352/392-9190, ext. 223; e-mail: john)
  Senior Acquisitions Editor: Amy Gorelick (Middle East, Latin American studies, literature)
  (352/392-9190, ext. 225; e-mail: ag)
  Acquisitions Editor: Eli Bortz (history, anthropology, archaeology) (352/392-9190, ext.
  221; e-mail: eli)
Editorial, Design & Production: Lynn Werts, Associate Director & EDP Manager
  (ext. 222; e-mail: lw)
  Assistant Director & Managing Editor: Gillian Hillis (ext. 212; e-mail: gh)
  Project Editors: Susan Albury (ext. 213; e-mail: sa); Jacqueline Kinghorn Brown (ext. 217;
  e-mail: jb); Michele Fiyak-Burkley (ext. 216; e-mail: mf)
  Editorial Assistant: Marthe Walters (e-mail: marthe)
  Design Manager: Larry Leshan (ext. 221; e-mail: LL)
  Production Manager: David Graham (ext. 220; e-mail: dg)
  Designer/Compositor: Robyn Taylor (ext. 219; e-mail: rt)
Marketing: Dennis Lloyd, Associate Director & Marketing Manager (ext. 232; e-mail: dl)
  Publicity and Promotions Manager: Stephanie Williams (ext. 243; e-mail: sw)
  Advertising and Direct Mail Manager: Lisa Neugebauer (ext. 238; e-mail: ln)
  Production Coordinator: Nicole Sorenson (ext. 235; e-mail: ns)
  Exhibits and Awards Coordinator: Elizabeth Ruggieri (ext. 238; e-mail: elizabeth)
Business: Ben Layfield, Associate Director & Business Manager (ext. 209; e-mail: bl)
  Accounting / Order Fulfillment Manager: Sandra Dyson (ext. 210; e-mail: sd)
  Credit Manager: Kim Lake (ext. 211; e-mail: kl)
  Warehouse and Shipping Manager: Charles Hall (352/392-6867; e-mail: charles)
Information Technology: Bryan Lutz, Manager (ext. 215; e-mail: bryan)

Full Member

Established: 1945
Title output 2006: 97
Titles currently in print: 1,513

Admitted to AAUP: 1950
Title output 2007: 106

Editorial Program

Floridiana; new world archaeology; conservation biology; Latin American studies; Caribbean studies; Middle East studies; African American studies; Southern history and culture; Native American studies; dance; natural history; humanities; maritime studies. Submissions are not invited in prose fiction or poetry.

Fordham University Press

Street Address:
Canisius Hall
2546 Belmont Avenue
Bronx, NY 10458-5172

Mailing Address:
University Box L
Bronx, NY 10458-5172

Phone: (718) 817-4795
Fax: (718) 817-4785
E-mail: (user I.D.)@fordham.edu
Web site: www.fordhampress.com

Distribution Address:
New York University Press
838 Broadway, Third Floor
New York, NY 10003
Phone: (800) 996-6987
Fax: (212) 995-4798
E-mail: orders@nyupress.org

European Representative:
Eurospan

Canadian Representative:
Lexa Publishers' Representatives

Staff

Director: Robert Oppedisano (718/817-4789; e-mail: roppedisano)
  Assistant to the Director: Mary Lou Peña (718/817-4781; e-mail: pena)
Editorial Director: Helen Tartar (718/817-4787; e-mail: tartar)
  Editor-at-Large: Saverio Procario (718/817-4790; e-mail: procario)
Managing Editor: Nick Frankovich (718-817-4784; e-mail: frankvoich)
Production Editor: Loomis Mayer (718/817-4788; e-mail: lmayer)
  Publishing Assistant: Kathleen A. Sweeney (718/817-4791; e-mail: kasweeney)
Marketing Manager: Kate O'Brien (718/817-4782; e-mail: bkaobrien)
Business Manager: Margaret M. Noonan (718/817-4780; e-mail: mnoonan)
  Assistant Business Manager: Marie Hall (718/817-4783)

Full Member

Established: 1907
Title output 2006: 44
Titles currently in print: 545

Admitted to AAUP: 1938
Title output 2007: 46
Journals published: 3

Editorial Program

Fordham University Press publishes primarily in the humanities and social sciences, with emphasis on the fields of philosophy, religion, theology, history, and literature. Additionally, the Press publishes books focusing on the New York region and books of interest to the general public.

The Press distributes the publications of Creighton University Press; University of San Francisco Press; St. Joseph's University Press; Rockhurst University Press; the Institution for Advanced Study in the Theater Arts (IASTA); The Reconstructionist Press; Little Room Press; Center for Migration Studies; and St. Bede's Publications.

Journals: *Dante Studies; Joyce Studies Annual; Traditio: Studies in Ancient and Medieval History, Thought, and Religion*

Special series, joint imprints, and/or co-publishing programs: Abrahamic Dialogues; American Philosophy Series; Business, Economics, Legal Studies; Hudson Valley Heritage; International Humanitarian Affairs; The Irish in the Civil War; Medieval Studies; Moral Philosophy and Moral Theology; The North's Civil War; People and the Environment; Perspectives in Continental Philosophy; Reconstructing America; Studies in Religion and Literature; World War II

Gallaudet University Press

800 Florida Avenue, N.E.
Washington, DC 20002-3695

Phone: (202) 651-5488
Fax: (202) 651-5489
E-mail: (user I.D.)@gallaudet.edu
Web site: gupress.gallaudet.edu

European Distributor:
Forest Book Services

Orders:
Gallaudet University Press
Chicago Distribution Center
11030 South Langley Avenue
Chicago, IL 60628
Phone: (800) 621-2736
TTY: (888) 630-9347
Fax: (800) 621-8476

Staff

Executive Director: David F. Armstrong (202/651-5488; e-mail: david.armstrong)
Editorial: Ivey Pittle Wallace, Assistant Director and Acquisitions (202/651-5662; e-mail: ivey.wallace)
Managing Editor: Deirdre Mullervy (202/651-5967; e-mail: deirdre.mullervy)
Production: Jill Hendricks Porco, Coordinator (202/651-5025; e-mail: jill.porco)
Marketing: Dan Wallace, Assistant Director (202/651-5661; e-mail: daniel.wallace)
   Marketing Assistant: Valencia Simmons (202/651-5488; e-mail: valencia.simmons)
Business: Frances W. Clark (202/651-5455; e-mail: frances.clark)

Full Member

Established: 1980
Title output 2006: 16
Titles currently in print: 213

Admitted to AAUP: 1983
Title output 2007: 16
Journals published: 2

Editorial Program

Scholarly books and serious nonfiction from all disciplines as they relate to the interests and culture of people who are deaf, hard of hearing, or experiencing hearing loss. Particular areas of emphasis include signed languages, linguistics, deaf culture, deaf history, disability studies, biography and autobiography, parenting, and special education, as well as instructional works and children's literature with sign language or deafness themes.

The Press distributes select titles from Signum Verlag (Hamburg, Germany).

Journals: *American Annals of the Deaf; Sign Language Studies*

Special imprints: Kendall Green Publications (children's works) and Clerc Books (instructional materials)

Special series: Deaf Lives; Gallaudet Classics in Deaf Studies; Interpreter Education; Sociolinguistics in Deaf Communities; Studies in Interpretation

Georgetown University Press

3240 Prospect Street, N.W.
Washington, DC 20007

Phone: (202) 687-5889
Fax: (202) 687-6340
E-mail: (user I.D.)@georgetown.edu
Web site: www.press.georgetown.edu

Orders:
c/o Hopkins Fulfillment Service
PO Box 50370
Baltimore, MD 21211
Phone: (410) 516-6965; (800) 537-5487
Fax: (410) 516-6998

Staff

Director: Richard Brown (202/687-5912; e-mail: reb7)
  Publishing Assistant: Julie Finnegan Stoner (202/687-4462; e-mail: jcf46)
Associate Director and Acquisitions Editor: Gail Grella (202/687-6263; e-mail: grellag1)
  Acquisitions Editor, Political Science and International Affairs: Donald Jacobs (202/687-5218; e-mail: dpj5)
Electronic Editor: Hope LeGro (202/687-4704; e-mail: hjs6)
Editorial and Production Manager: Deborah Weiner (202/687-6251; e-mail: weinerd)
  Editorial and Production Coordinator: Patti Bower (202/687-0159; e-mail: pjb48)
  Designer: TBA
Director of Marketing and Sales: Gina Lindquist (202/687-9856; e-mail: gla2)
  Marketing Coordinator: Maureen Mills (202/687-3671; e-mail: mm634)
  Publicist: TBA
  Intellectual Property Manager: Puja Telikicherla (202/687-7687; e-mail: pt97)
  Marketing Assistant: Uwi Basaninyenzi (202/687-8170; e-mail: ub6)
Business Manager: Ioan Suciu (202/687-5641; e-mail: suciui)
  Accountant: Sulah Kim (202/687-8151; e-mail: slk33)

Full Member

Established: 1964
Title output 2006: 45
Titles currently in print: 665

Admitted to AAUP: 1986
Title output 2007: 36
Journals published: 1

Editorial Program

Disciplines: bioethics; international affairs; languages and linguistics; political science and public policy; and religion and ethics.

Journal: *The Journal of the Society of Christian Ethics*

Special series: Advancing Human Rights; American Governance and Public Policy; Georgetown Classics in Arabic Language and Linguistics; Moral Traditions; Public Management and Change; Religion and Politics

University of Georgia Press

330 Research Drive, Suite B-100
Athens, GA 30602-4901

Phone: (706) 369-6130
Fax: (706) 369-6131
E-mail: books@ugapress.uga.edu
Indiv: (user I.D.)@ugapress.uga.edu
(unless otherwise indicated)
Web site: www.ugapress.org

Distribution Center:
University of Georgia Press
Distribution Center
4435 Atlanta Highway West Dock
Bogart, GA 30622

Orders and Customer Service:
Phone: (800) 266-5842; (706) 369-6163

UK Distributor:
Eurospan

Staff

Director: Nicole Mitchell (706/369-6143; e-mail: mitchell)
  Assistant to the Director and Contracts & Foreign Rights Manager: Jane Kobres (706/369-6140; e-mail: jkobres)
  Development Officer: Lane Stewart (706/369-6049; e-mail: lstewart@uga.edu)
Acquisitions Editorial: Nancy Grayson, Associate Director and Editor-in-Chief (706/369-6139; e-mail: ngrayson)
  Senior Acquisitions Editor: Derek Krissoff (706/369-6488; e-mail: dkrissoff)
  Acquisitions Editors: Judy Purdy (706/369-6132; e-mail: jpurdy); Erika Stevens (706/369-6135; e-mail: estevens)
  Assistant Editor: Regan Huff (706/369-6141; e-mail: rhuff)
The New Georgia Encyclopedia Project: (www.georgiaencyclopedia.org)
  Editor: John Inscoe (706/542-8848; e-mail: jinscoe@uga.edu)
  Project Director & Managing Editor: Kelly Caudle (706/583-0723; e-mail: kcaudle@uga.edu)
  Electronic Editor: Sarah McKee (706/583-8065; e-mail: semckee@uga.edu)
Editorial, Design, and Production: Jennifer L. Reichlin, ED&P Director (706/369-6136; e-mail: jlreichlin)
  Assistant Managing Editor: Jon Davies (706/369-6138; e-mail: jdavies)
  Project Editor: Courtney Denney (706/369-6137; e-mail: cdenney)
  Production Manager and Designer: Kathi Dailey Morgan (706/369-6152; e-mail: kdmorgan)
  Production Specialist and Designer: Walton Harris (706/369-6155; e-mail: wwharris)

Designers and Art Directors: Mindy Hill (706/369-6151; e-mail: mhill); Erin Kirk New (e-mail: ekirknew)

Marketing and Sales: John McLeod, Marketing and Sales Director (706/369-6158; e-mail: jmcleod)

Publicity Manager: Stacey Sharer (706/369-6160; e-mail: ssharer)

Electronic Information Manager and Assistant Marketing Manager: David Des Jardines (706/369-6159; e-mail: ddesjard)

Marketing Designer: Anne Richmond Boston (706/369-6150; e-mail: arb)

Exhibits and Advertising Manager: Pat Allen (706/369-6156; e-mail: pallen)

Business and Order Fulfillment: Phyllis Wells, Assistant Director for Business (706/369-6134; e-mail: pwells)

Accountant: Marena Smith (706/369-6133; e-mail: msmith)

Permissions Manager and Accounts Payable Representative: Stacey Hayes (706/369-6144; e-mail: shayes)

Customer Service Representative: Betty Downer (706/369-6148; e-mail: downer)

Accounts Receivable Representative: Janice Bell (706/369-6149; e-mail: jbell)

IT Specialist: Charles Nicolosi (e-mail: charlesn@uga.edu)

Full Member

Established: 1938

Admitted to AAUP: 1940

Title output 2006: 67

Title output 2007: 76

Titles currently in print: 996

Editorial Program

Humanities and social sciences with particular interests in American and southern history; American and southern literature; African American studies; American studies; international relations; civil rights history; legal history; environmental history; ecology and environmental studies; ecocriticism and nature writing; geography; landscape studies; natural history; Appalachian studies; anthropology; gender studies; popular culture; cinema and media studies; popular music; urban studies; literary nonfiction; and regional trade titles.

Special series and imprints: Brown Thrasher Books; The Chaucer Library; Environmental History in the American South; Geographies of Justice and Social Transformation; The New Southern Studies; Politics and Society in the Twentieth-Century South; Publications of the Southern Texts Society; Race in the Atlantic World, 1700-1900; Southern Anthropological Society Proceedings; Studies in the Legal History of the South; Studies in Security and International Affairs; The United States and the Americas; VQR Poetry Series; The Works of Tobias Smollett; Wormsloe Foundation Nature Books; Wormsloe Foundation Publications

Literary competitions: Flannery O'Connor Award for Short Fiction; The Association of Writers and Writing Programs Award for Creative Nonfiction; Cave Canem Poetry Prize

Lecture series: Mercer University Lamar Memorial Lectures; Georgia Southern University Jack N. and Addie D. Averitt Lectures; George H. Shriver Lecture Series in Religion in American History

Getty Publications

1200 Getty Center Drive
Suite 500
Los Angeles, CA 90049-1682

Phone: (310) 440-7365
Faxes:
Admin. / Marketing: (310) 440-7758
Design and Production: (310) 440-7706
Editorial: (310) 440-7739
E-mail: pubsinfo@getty.edu
Indiv: (user I.D.)@getty.edu
Web site: www.getty.edu/bookstore

Warehouse Address:
Getty Publications Book Dist. Center
PO Box 49659
Los Angeles, CA 90049-0659

Customer Service / Order Fulfillment:
Phone: (310) 440-7333; (800) 223-3431
Fax: (818) 779-0051

US Distributor:
Oxford University Press

UK / European Distributor:
Windsor Books International

Canadian Distributor:
Canadian Manda Group

Staff
Publisher: TBA
   Acting General Manager: Carolyn Simmons (310/440-7130; e-mail: csimmons)
   Rights Manager: Leslie Rollins (310/440-7102; e-mail: lrollins)
Acquisitions Editorial: Mark Greenberg, Editor-in-Chief (310/440-7097;
   e-mail: mgreenberg)
Head of Publications, The Getty Research Institute: Julia Bloomfield (310/440-7446;
   e-mail: jbloomfield)
Manuscript Editorial: Ann Lucke, Managing Editor (310/440-6525; e-mail: alucke)
Design and Production: Deenie Yudell, Design Manager (310/440-6508; e-mail: dyudell)
   Production Manager: Karen Schmidt (310/440-6504; e-mail: kschmidt)
Marketing and Sales: Robert Flynn (310/440-6486; e-mail: rflynn)
Business and Warehouse: Jeff Wiebe, Distribution Center Manager (310/440-6602; e-mail:
   jwiebe)

Associate Member
Established: 1982
Title output 2006: 41
Titles currently in print: 480

Admitted to AAUP: 1989
Title output 2007: 30

Editorial Program
Scholarly and general interest publications on the visual arts; conservation and the history
of art and the humanities; art related titles for children; and areas related to the work of the
Getty Research Institute, the Getty Conservation Institute, and the collections of the Getty
Museum: antiquities, decorative arts, drawings, manuscripts, paintings, photographs, and
sculpture.

Harvard University Press

79 Garden Street
Cambridge, MA 02138-1499

Phone: (617) 495-2600
Faxes: (617) 495-5898 (General)
(617) 496-4677 (Editorial & Dir. Office)
(617) 496-2550 (Marketing)
E-mail: (firstname_lastname)@harvard.edu
Web site: www.hup.harvard.edu

Customer Service / Orders:
Phone: (800) 405-1619 (US & Canada)
(401) 531-2800 (all others)
Faxes: (800) 406-9145 (US & Canada)
(401) 531-2801 (international)

London Office:
Harvard University Press
Fitzroy House
11 Chenies Street
London WC1E 7EY
United Kingdom
Phone: +44 20 73063 0603
Fax: +44 20 7306 0604
E-mail: info@hup-mitpress.co.uk

Staff

Director: William P. Sisler (617/495-2601)
   Director of Intellectual Property: Melinda Koyanis (617/495-2619)
   Subsidiary Rights Manager: Stephanie Vyce (617/495-2603)
Acquisitions Editorial: Michael G. Fisher, Editor-in-Chief (science and medicine)
   (617/495-2674)
   Executive Editors: Lindsay Waters (humanities, esp. literary criticism, philosophy)
   (617/495-2835); Joyce Seltzer (history and contemporary affairs) (212/337-0280; Fax:
   212/337-0259); John Kulka (humanities) (203/227-4706)
   Acquisitions Editors: Michael Aronson (social sciences, esp. law and economics) (617/495-
   1837); Elizabeth Knoll (behavioral science and neuroscience); Kathleen McDermott
   (history) (617/495-4703); Ann Downer-Hazell (science and medicine) (617/496-1311);
   Sharmila Sen (humanities) (617/495-8122)
Manuscript Editorial: Mary Ann Lane, Managing Editor (617/495-1846)
Design and Production: John Walsh, Assistant Director for Design and Production
   (617/495-2623)
   Art Director: Tim Jones (617/495-2669)
Marketing: Paul Adams, Marketing Director (617/496-8170)
   Advertising Director & Web Administrator: Denise Waddington (617/495-4712)
   Promotion Director: Sheila Barrett (617/495-2618)
   Publicity Director: Mary Kate Maco (617/495-4713)
   Publicity: Rose Ann Miller (617/495-4714); Jennifer Redding (617/495-1284); Andy
   Battle (617/495-8589); Camilla Orr (617/496-1340)
Sales: Susan Donnelly, Sales Director (617/495-2606)
   Assistant Sales Director and Internet Retail Sales: Vanessa Vinarub (617/495-2650)
   Exhibits Manager: Justine Pierce (617/384-7515)

Business: William A. Lindsay, Assistant Director & Chief Financial Officer (617/495-2613)
 Accounting: Fred Waters (617/495-4868); Elizabeth Kernan (617/495-3560)
 Director of Operations: Joan O'Donnell (617/495-2661)
 Manager of Distributed Books and Inventory: Sara Davis (617/495-5022)
 Human Resources Manager: Judith Wilburn (617/495-2602)
London Office: Ann Sexsmith, Manager (e-mail: asexsmith@hup-mitpress.co.uk)

Full Member

Established: 1913   Admitted to AAUP: 1937
Title output 2006: 240   Title output 2007: 250
Titles currently in print: 4,500

Editorial Program

Scholarly books and serious works of general interest in the humanities, the social and
behavioral sciences, the natural sciences, and medicine. The Press does not normally publish
poetry, fiction, festschriften, memoirs, symposia, or unrevised doctoral dissertations.

   The Press distributes publications for a number of Harvard University departments and
affiliates: Archaeological Exploration of Sardis, Center for Hellenic Studies, Center for the
Study of World Religions, David Rockefeller Center for Latin American Studies, Department
of Celtic Languages and Literatures, Department of Comparative Literature, Department of
Music, Department of Near Eastern Languages and Civilizations, Department of Sanskrit
and Indian Studies, Department of the Classics, Derek Bok Center, Division of Applied Sci-
ence, Dumbarton Oaks Research Library and Collection, Harvard Center for Middle Eastern
Studies, Harvard College Library, Harvard Divinity School, Harvard East Asian Legal Stud-
ies, Harvard University Asia Center, Harvard University Center for Jewish Studies, Harvard
University Graduate School of Design, Houghton Library of the Harvard College Library,
HU Center for the Environment China Project, Islamic Legal Studies Program, Harvard
Law School, Peabody Museum Press, School of Public Health, and the Ukrainian Research
Institute of Harvard University.

Special imprints: The Belknap Press

Special series, joint imprints, and/or copublishing programs: The Adams Papers; Carl
Newell Jackson Lectures; Charles Eliot Norton Lectures; Cognitive Science Series; Con-
vergences; Developing Child Series; Godkin Lectures; Harvard Armenian Texts and Stud-
ies; Harvard Books in Biophysics; Harvard East Asian Series; Harvard Economic Studies;
Harvard English Studies; Harvard Film Studies; Harvard Historical Monographs; Harvard
Historical Studies; Harvard Judaic Monographs; Harvard Studies in Business History; Inter-
pretations of Asia Series; John Harvard Library; Language and Thought Series; Loeb Classical
Library; Loeb Classical Monographs; Martin Classical Lectures; Oliver Wendell Holmes
Lectures; Paperbacks in Art History; Publications of the Joint Center for Urban Studies;
Questions of Science; Revealing Antiquity Series; Russian Research Center Studies; Studies
in Cultural History; Twentieth Century Fund Books/Reports; W.E.B. DuBois Lectures; William E. Massey Sr. Lectures in the History of American Civilization; William James Lectures

University of Hawai'i Press

2840 Kolowalu Street
Honolulu, HI 96822-1888

Phone: (808) 956-8257
Fax: (808) 988-6052
E-mail: (user I.D.)@hawaii.edu
Web site: www.uhpress.hawaii.edu

Orders:
Phone: (888) UHPRESS; (808) 956-8255
Fax: (800) 650-7811; (808) 988-6052

European Distributor:
Eurospan

Staff

Director: William H. Hamilton (808/956-8257; e-mail: hamilton)
  Secretary to the Director: Agnes Hiramoto (808/956-8257; e-mail: hiramoto)
Acquisitions Editorial: Patricia Crosby, Executive Editor (808/956-6209; e-mail: pcrosby)
  Editors: Pamela Kelley (808/956-6207; e-mail: pkelley); Keith Leber (808/956-6208;
  e-mail: kleber); Masako Ikeda (808/956-8696; e-mail: masakoi)
  Editorial Assistant: Tammy Zielinski (808/956-8694; e-mail: uhpedit)
Manuscript Editorial: Cheri Dunn, Managing Editor (808/956-6210; e-mail: cheri)
  Managing Editor: Ann Ludeman (808/956-8695; e-mail: aludeman)
Design and Production: JoAnn Tenorio, Manager (808/956-8873; e-mail: tenorio)
  Assistant Production Manager: Paul Herr (808/956-8276; e-mail: herr)
  Designer: Santos Barbasa (808/956-8277; e-mail: barbasa)
  Production Editor: Lucille Aono (808/956-6328; e-mail: lucille)
  Fiscal Support Specialist: Terri Miyasato (808/956-8275; e-mail: terrimiy)
Marketing and Sales: Colins Kawai, Manager (808/956-6417; e-mail: ckawai)
  Sales Manager: Royden Muranaka (808/956-8830; e-mail: royden)
  Direct Mail Manager / Copywriter: Stephanie Chun (808/956-6426; e-mail: chuns)
  Product Manager: Steven Hirashima (808/956-8698; e-mail: stevehir)
  Promotion Manager: Carol Abe (808/956-8697; e-mail: abec)
Journals: Joel Bradshaw, Manager (808/956-6790; e-mail: bradshaw)
  Production Editor: Cindy Chun (808/956-8834; e-mail: cindychu)
  Administrative Assistant: Norman Kaneshiro (808/956-8833; e-mail: uhpjourn)
East-West Export Books: Royden Muranaka, International Sales Manager (808/956-8830;
  e-mail: royden)
  Assistant: Kiera Nishimoto (808/956-8830; e-mail: eweb)
Business: Joel Cosseboom, Manager (808/956-6292; e-mail: cosseboo)
  Credit Manager: Elyse Matsumoto (808/956-6228; e-mail: okido)
  Order Processing: Cindy Yen, Danny Li
  Warehouse: Kyle Nakata, Clifford Newalu
Information Systems: Wanda China, Computer Operations Manager (808/956-6227;
  e-mail: wchina)

Full Member

Established: 1947

Title output 2006: 80

Titles currently in print: 1,289

Admitted to AAUP: 1951

Title output 2007: 80

Journals published: 15

Editorial Program

Asian, Pacific, and Asian American studies in history; art; anthropology; architecture; economics; sociology; philosophy and religion; languages and linguistics; law; literature; performing arts; political science; physical and natural sciences; regional studies.

Journals: *Asian Perspectives; Asian Theatre Journal; Biography; Buddhist-Christian Studies; China Review International; The Contemporary Pacific; Journal of World History; Ka Ho'oilina: The Legacy; Korean Studies; Manoa; Oceanic Linguistics; Pacific Science; Philosophy East and West; Yearbook of the Association of Pacific Coast Geographers; Yishu*

Special series, joint imprints, and/or copublishing programs: Asian Interactions and Comparisons (Association for Asian Studies); Center for Southeast Asian Studies (Kyoto University); Dimensions of Asian Spirituality; Extraordinary Lives: The Experience of Hawai'i Nisei; Harold Lyon Arboretum; Hawai'i Studies on Korea (Korean Studies); Intersections: Asian and Pacific American Transcultural Studies; Kolowalu Books; Kuroda Institute Studies in East Asian Buddhism; Latitude 20 Books; Modern Korean Fiction; Nanzan Library for Asian Religion and Culture; Oceanic Linguistics Special Publications; PALI Language Texts; Pacific Islands Monographs; Perspectives on the Global Past; Pure Land Buddhist Studies; Society for Asian and Comparative Philosophy; Southeast Asia: Politics, Meaning, and Memory; Studies in the Buddhist Tradition (University of Michigan); Talanoa: Contemporary Pacific Literature; Topics in Contemporary Buddhism; Writing Past Colonialism

Howard University Press

2225 Georgia Avenue, N.W.

Suite 718

Washington, DC 20059

Phone: (202) 238-2570

Fax: (202) 588-9849

E-mail: howardupress@howard.edu

Web site: www.hupress.howard.edu

Book Distribution Center:

Howard Univ. Press c/o Maple Press Co.

Lebanon Distribution Center

Fredericksburg, PA 17026

Customer service: (800) 537-5487

Fax: (410) 516-6998

Staff

Director: TBA (202/238-2575)

   Assistant to the Director: Anita L. Rice (202/238-2570; e-mail: arice@howard.edu)

Sales and Marketing Manager: TBA (202/238-2571)

Business Manager: Patricia A. Harris (202/238-2572; e-mail: paharris@howard.edu)

Full Member

Established: 1972

Title output 2006: 0

Titles currently in print: 113

Admitted to AAUP: 1979

Title output 2007: 0

Editorial Program

Scholarly research addressing the contributions, conditions, and concerns of African Americans, other people of African descent throughout the Diaspora, and people of color around the world in a broad range of disciplines: politics, economics, the social sciences, history, health and medicine, education, communications, fine arts and photography, science/technology, literature, literary criticism, drama studies, and more.

Special series: Moorland-Spingarn Series

University of Illinois Press

1325 S. Oak Street
Champaign, IL 61820-6903

Phone: (217) 333-0950
Fax: (217) 244-8082
E-mail: uipress@uillinois.edu
Journals: journals@uillinois.edu
Indiv: (user I.D.)@uillinois.edu
Web site: www.press.uillinois.edu

Warehouse Address and Orders:
University of Illinois Press
c/o Chicago Distribution Center
11030 South Langley Avenue
Chicago, IL 60628

Orders:
(Books) (800) 621-2736
orders@press.uchicago.edu
(Journals) (866) 244-0626

UK / European Representative:
Combined Academic Publishers

Canadian Representative:
Scholarly Book Services

Staff

Director: Willis G. Regier (217/244-0728; e-mail: wregier)
    Associate Director and Editor-in-Chief: Joan Catapano (217/265-0490; e-mail: jcatapan)
    Assistant to the Director: Mary Wolfe (217/244-4691; e-mail: mwolfe)
    Rights and Permissions: Kathleen Kornell (217/244-0820; e-mail: uip-rights)
Acquisitions Editorial: Joan Catapano, Editor-in-Chief (history, feminist studies, African American studies, film, anthropology, philosophy, ethnic studies) (217/265-0490; e-mail: jcatapan)
    Acquisitions Editors: Kendra Boileau (Asian American studies, communications, food studies, history, religion) (217/244-4681; e-mail: kboileau); Laurie Matheson (American history, Appalachian studies, labor studies, music, sociology) (217/244-4685; e-mail: lmatheso); Willis G. Regier (classics, literature, religion, translations, sports history, Lincoln studies, Nietzsche studies) (217/244-0728; e-mail: wregier)
    Assistant Editors: Rebecca McNulty Schreiber (criminology) (217/244-5182; e-mail: rmcnulty); Breanne Ertmer (folklore) (217/333-6088; e-mail: ertmer)
Electronic Publisher: Paul Arroyo (217/244-7147; e-mail: parroyo)
    Electronic Publishing Assistant: Ayanna Qadeem (217/244-3908; e-mail: qadeem)
Manuscript Editorial: Rebecca Crist, Managing Editor (217/244-3279; e-mail: rcrist)
    Assistant Managing Editors: Angela Burton (217/244-6579; e-mail: alburton); Jennifer Clark (217/244-8041; e-mail: jsclark1)
Production: Kristine Ding, Production Manager (217/244-4701; e-mail: kding)
    Assistant Production Manager: Barbara Evans (217/244-1311; e-mail: bsevans)
Design: Copenhaver Cumpston, Art Director (217/333-9227; e-mail: cumpston)
    Designer: Dennis Roberts (217/244-0392; e-mail: droberts); Kelly Gray (217/244-4706; e-mail: TBA)

Marketing: Lisa Bayer, Marketing Director (217/244-4683; e-mail: lbayer)
  Assistant Marketing Director / Web and Direct Mail Promotions: Barbara Horne
  (217/244-4686; e-mail: bhorne)
  Publicity Manager: Michael Roux (217/244-4689; e-mail: mroux)
  Sales Manager: Lynda Schuh (217/333-9071; e-mail: lschuh)
  Assistant Sales Manager: Susie Dueringer (217/244-4703; e-mail: sdueringer)
  Exhibits and Awards Manager: Margo Chaney (217/244-6491; e-mail: mechaney)
  Advertising Manager: Denise Peeler (217/244-4690; e-mail: dpeeler)
Journals: Clydette Wantland, Journals Manager (217/244-6496; e-mail: cwantlan)
  Journals Production Editors: Heather Munson (217/244-6488; e-mail: hmunson); Lisa
  Savage (217/244-8870; e-mail: lasavage); Rohn Koester (217/244-9179; e-mail: rkoester)
  Journals Circulation Manager: Cheryl Jestis (866/244-0626; e-mail: jestis)
  Circulation Specialist: Jennifer Stowe (217/244-1564; e-mail: jwolfers@uiuc.edu)
  Journals Marketing and Advertising Manager: Jeff McArdle (217/244-0381; e-mail:
  jmcardle)
Chief Financial Officer: Lisa Emerson (217/244-0091; e-mail: lemerson)
  Assistant to CFO: Kathy O'Neill (217/244-6479; e-mail: oneill2)
Network Administrator: Louis W. Mesker (217/244-8025; e-mail: lmesker)

Full Member

Established: 1918	Admitted to AAUP: 1937
Title output 2006: 132	Title output 2007: 134
Titles currently in print: 1,700	Journals published: 31

Editorial Program

Scholarly books and serious nonfiction, with special interests in American history; American literature (especially twentieth century); critical theory; American music; African American history and literature; sport history; religious studies; cultural studies; communications; cinema studies; law and society; regional photography and art; philosophy; architectural history; environmental studies; sociology; western history; women's studies; working-class history; and poetry.

Journals: *American Journal of Psychology; American Literary Realism; American Music; American Philosophical Quarterly; Black Music Research Journal; Black Women, Gender, and Families; Dance Research Journal; Ethnomusicology; Feminist Teacher; History of Philosophy Quarterly; Journal of the Abraham Lincoln Association; Journal of Aesthetic Education; Journal of American Ethnic History; Journal of American Folklore; Journal of Criminal Law and Criminology; Journal of Education Finance; Journal of English and Germanic Philology; Journal of Film & Video; Journal of Seventeenth-Century Music; Law and History Review; Music and Moving Image; National Association of Laboratory Schools Journal; Northwestern Journal of International Law & Business; Northwestern University Law Review; The Pluralist; Perspectives on Work; Public Affairs Quarterly; Radical Teacher; State Politics and Policy Quarterly; William James Studies; World History Connected*

The University of Illinois Press is a founder and manager of the History Cooperative, an online journals consortium representing twenty history journals and their sponsoring societies, www.historycooperative.org/home.html

Special series, joint imprints, and/or copublishing programs: The Asian American Experience; Bach Perspectives; Blacks in the New World; Contemporary Film Directors; The Environment and the Human Condition; Folklore and Society; The Food Series; Great Arguments in the Supreme Court; Hispanisms; The History of Communication; International Nietzsche Studies; Music in American Life; Sport and Society; Statue of Liberty-Ellis Island Centennial Series; Theodore Dreiser Edition; Women in American History; Working Class in American History

Indiana Historical Society Press

Indiana Historical Society
450 West Ohio Street
Indianapolis, IN 46202-3269

Orders:
Phone: (317) 234-0026; (800) 447-1830

Phone: (317) 232-6546
Fax: (317) 233-0857
E-mail: (user I.D.)@indianahistory.org
Web site: www.indianahistory.org/ihs_press

Staff

Senior Director: Paula Corpuz (317/232-6545; e-mail: pcorpuz)
Senior Editor: Ray Boomhower (317/232-1877; e-mail: rboomhower)
Editor, Family History Publications: Teresa Baer (317/234-0071; e-mail: tbaer)
    Editorial Assistant, Family History Publications: Geniel Breeze (317/234-2716;
    e-mail: gbreeze)
Editor: Kathy Breen (317/232-1884; e-mail: kbreen)
    Editorial Assistant: Rachel Popma (317/233-3156; e-mail: rpopma)

Associate Member

Established: 1830
Title output 2006: 13
Titles currently in print: 118

Admitted to AAUP: 2005
Title output 2007: 8
Journals published: 2

Editorial Program

The Indiana Historical Society Press promotes the understanding of Indiana and its people, including involvements beyond the borders of the state, through a varied publications program. The IHS Press seeks publishable material for its books (for adults and children), its popular history quarterly (*Traces of Indiana* and *Midwestern History*), and its family history quarterly (*The Hoosier Geneologist*). The IHS Press seeks publications about Indiana and the Midwest on topics such as (but not limited to) biography, personal narrative, cultural heritage, the visual arts, folklore, geography, and history in its many varieties—architectural, agricultural, economic, ethnic, family, immigration, industrial, literary, medical, military, musical, political, sports, transportation, and women's history.
Special series: Indiana Biography Series, Youth Biography Series

Indiana University Press

601 North Morton Street
Bloomington, IN 47404-3797

Phone: (812) 855-8817
Fax: (812) 855-8507
E-mail: iupress@indiana.edu
Indiv: (user I.D.)@indiana.edu
Web site: iupress.indiana.edu

Warehouse Address:
802 E. 13th Street
Bloomington, IN 47408-2101
Phone: (812) 855-4362

Orders:
Phone: (800) 842-6796
Fax: (812) 855-7931
E-mail: iuporder@indiana.edu

Canadian Representative:
Lexa Publishers' Representative

UK / European Representative:
Combined Academic Publishers

Staff

Director: Janet Rabinowitch (812/855-4773; e-mail: jrabinow) (Russian, East European, and Jewish and Holocaust studies)

Assistant to the Director and Rights Manager: Anne Roecklein (812/855-6314; e-mail: paroeckl)

Acquisitions Editorial: Robert Sloan, Editorial Director (African American studies, bioethics, American history, military, paleontology, philanthropy) (812/855-7561; e-mail: rjsloan)

Sponsoring Editors: Dee Mortensen (Africa, philosophy, religion) (812/855-0268; e-mail: mortense); Jane Behnken (music, film/media/cultural studies) (812/855-5261; e-mail: jquinet); Linda Oblack (regional, Quarry books, railroads) (812/855-2175; e-mail: loblack); Rebecca Tolen (anthropology, Asia, Middle East, international studies) (812/855-2756; e-mail: retolen)

Assistant Sponsoring Editors: Anne Teillard-Clemmer (Assistant to the Editorial Director) (812/855-5262; e-mail: ateillar); Laura MacLeod (812/856-0097; e-mail: lmacleod); Katie Baber (Assistant Music Editor) (812/855-5063; e-mail: iupmusic); Peter Froehlich (812/855-1744; e-mail: pfroehli)

Manuscript Editorial: Miki Bird, Managing Editor (812/855-9686; e-mail: msbird)

Project Managers: June Silay (812/856-4645; e-mail: jsilay); Brian Herrmann (812/855-5428; e-mail: bherrman); Marvin Keenan (812/855-5064; e-mail: mwkeenan); Neil Ragsdale (812/856-5428; e-mail: nearagsd)

Production and Design: Bernadette Zoss, Production Director (812/855-5563; e-mail: bzoss)

Senior Artists and Book Designers: Pam Rude (812/855-0264; e-mail: psrude); Matt Williamson (812/855-8778; e-mail: mswillia)

Production Coordinator: Dan Pyle (812/855-6777; e-mail: dapyle)

Publishing Services Coordinator: Tony Brewer (812/855-9444; e-mail: tbrewer)

Production Assistant: Sarah Jacobi (812/855-6777; e-mail: sajacob)

Marketing and Sales: Patricia Hoefling, Marketing and Sales Director (812/855-6553; e-mail: phoeflin)

Publicist: Valerie McClanahan (812/855-5429; e-mail: vmcclana)

Direct Marketing Manager: Deborah Rush (812/855-4415; e-mail: drush)

Electronic Marketing Manager: Laura Baich (812/855-8287; e-mail: lbaich)

Advertising and Exhibit Manager: Mandy Clarke (812/855-4522; e-mail: alstahl)

Publicity Coordinator: Theresa Halter (812/855-8054; e-mail: thalter)
Sales: Mary Beth Haas, Sales Manager (812/855-9440; e-mail: mbhaas)
Assistant Sales Manager: Kate Matthen (812/855-5366; e-mail: kmatthen)
Sales and Marketing Assistant: Rhonda Van Der Dussen (812/855-6657; e-mail: rdussen)
Journals, Electronic, and Serials Publishing: Kathryn Caras, Director of Electronic and Serials
    Publishing (812/855-3830; e-mail: kcaras)
    Electronic and Serials Manager: Joy Andreakis (812/856-5218; e-mail: jandreak)
    Journals Marketing Manager: TBA
    Journals Production Coordinator: Judith Caldwell (812/856-0582; e-mail: jucaldwe)
Business and Operations: Jan Jenkins, Director of Operations (812/855-4901;
    e-mail: janjenki)
    Senior Accounting Coordinator: Kathy Whaley (812/855-2726; e-mail: kwhaley)
    Assistant Business Manager for Network Systems and Order Processing: Janie Pearson
    (812/855-1588; e-mail: cjfender)
    Assistant Business Manager for Accounts Receivable & Customer Service: Kim Childers
    (812/855-4134; e-mail: kchilder)
    Senior Customer Service Representative: Mary Lou Shelly (812/855-8818;
    e-mail: mlshelly)
    Customer Service Representative: Jessica Thompson (812/855-1519; e-mail: thompsjr)
    Warehouse Manager: Mark Kelly (812/855-4362; e-mail: markkell)
Information Technology: Ted Boardman, Technology Director for Publishing Operations
    (812/855-6468; e-mail: tboardma)
    IT Manager: Rich Pierce (812/856-0210; e-mail: ripierce)

Full Member

Established: 1950	Admitted to AAUP: 1952
Title output 2006: 144	Title output 2007: 145
Titles currently in print: 2,000	Journals published: 27

Editorial Program

African studies; African American studies; anthropology; Asian and South Asian studies; bio-ethics; cultural studies; film and media studies; folklore; history; international studies; Jewish and Holocaust studies; Middle East studies; military history; music; paleontology; philanthropy; philosophy; railroad history; religion; Russian and East European studies; state and regional studies; women's and gender studies.

Journals: *Africa Today; Aleph: Studies In Judaism; Bridges: A Jewish Feminist Journal; e-Service Journal; Ethics & the Environment; Film History; History & Memory; Hypatia: A Journal of Feminist Philosophy; Indiana Journal of Global Legal Studies; Israel Studies; Jewish Social Studies; Journal of Early Modern Cultural Studies; Journal of Feminist Studies in Religion; Journal of Folklore Research; Journal of Modern Literature; JMEWS: Journal of Middle East Women's Studies; Meridians: feminism, race, transnationalism; Nashim: A Journal of Jewish Women's & Gender Issues; Native Plants Journal; NWSA Journal; Philosophy of Music Education Review; Prooftexts: A Journal of Jewish Literary History; Research in African Literatures; Small Axe: A Journal of Caribbean Studies; Textual Cultures; Transactions of the Charles S. Peirce Society: A Quarterly Journal in American Philosophy; Victorian Studies*

Special series: African Expressive Cultures; African Issues; African Systems of Thought; American Philosophy; American West in the Twentieth Century; Bioethics and the Humanities (formerly Medical Ethics); Blacks in the Diaspora; Chinese in Context Language Learning Series; Contemporary Indian Studies (sponsored by the American Institute of Indian

Studies); Counterpoints: Music and Education; The Early Music Institute; Excavations at Ancient Halieis; Excavations at Franchthi Cave, Greece; The Helen and Martin Schwartz Lectures in Jewish Studies; A History of the Trans-Appalachian Frontier; Hypatia Books; India Today; Indiana Masterpiece Editions; Indiana Repertoire Guides; Indiana Series in Middle East Studies; Indiana Series in the Philosophy of Religion; Indiana Studies in Biblical Literature; Indiana-Michigan Series in Russian and East European Studies; Interdisciplinary Studies in History; Jewish Literature and Culture; Kinsey Institute Series; Library of Indiana Classics; Life of the Past; Material Culture; Midwestern History and Culture; The Modern Jewish Experience; Musical Meaning and Interpretation; New Anthropologies of Europe; Perspectives; Philanthropic and Nonprofit Studies; Profiles in Popular Music; Railroads Past and Present; Readings in…; Religion in North America; Russian Music Studies; Studies in Ancient Folklore and Popular Culture; Studies in Continental Thought; Tracking Globalization; Traditional Arts of Africa; Twentieth-Century Battles; United Nations Intellectual History Project; The Variorum Edition of the Poetry of John Donne

University of Iowa Press

Editorial Office:
119 West Park Road
100 Kuhl House
Iowa City, IA 52242-1000

Phone: (319) 335-2000
Fax: (319) 335-2055
E-mail: (user I.D.)@uiowa.edu
Web site: www.uiowapress.org

Order Fulfillment:
University of Iowa Press
c/o Chicago Distribution Center
11030 South Langley Avenue
Chicago, IL 60628
Phone: (800) 621-2736
Fax: (800) 621-8476

UK / European Representative:
Eurospan

Staff

Director: Holly Carver (319/335-2013; e-mail: holly-carver)
　Assistant to the Director/Rights and Permissions: Rhonda Wetjen (319/335-3424; e-mail: rhonda-wetjen)
Editorial: Holly Carver (natural history, regional history, anthropology/archaeology)
　Acquisitions Editor: Joseph Parsons (literary criticism and history, creative nonfiction, letters and diaries) (319/335-3440; e-mail: joseph-parsons)
Managing Editor: Charlotte Wright (319/335-2011; e-mail: charlotte-wright)
Design and Production: Karen Copp, Associate Director and Design and Production Manager (319/335-2014; e-mail: karen-copp)
Marketing: Jim McCoy, Marketing and Sales Director (319/335-2008; e-mail: james-mccoy)
　Associate Marketing Manager: Allison Thomas (319/335-2015; e-mail: allison-thomas)

Full Member
Established: 1969
Title output 2006: 41
Titles currently in print: 600

Admitted to AAUP: 1982
Title output 2007: 40

American literary criticism and history, particularly children's literature, biography, and women's studies; letters, diaries, and memoirs; short fiction (award winners only); poetry (single-author titles and anthologies); creative nonfiction; regional studies; regional natural history; archaeology/anthropology; theatre history; American studies; medicine; and literature.

Special series: American Land and Life Series; Bur Oak Books and Bur Oak Guides; Contemporary North American Poetry; Iowa Poetry Prize; Iowa Short Fiction Award and John Simmons Short Fiction Award; Iowa Szathmáry Culinary Arts Series; Iowa Whitman Series; Kuhl House Poets; Sightline Books: The Iowa Series in Literary Nonfiction; Studies in Theatre History and Culture; Writers in Their Own Time

Island Press

Editorial/Administration:
1718 Connecticut Avenue, N.W., Suite 300
Washington, DC 20009-1148

Phone: (202) 232-7933
Fax: (202) 234-1328
E-mail: (firstinitial)(lastname)@islandpress.org
Web site: www.islandpress.org

Order Fulfillment:
Chicago Distribution Center
11030 South Langley Avenue
Chicago, IL 60628
Phone: (800) 621-2736
Fax: (800) 621-8476

UK / European Representative:
Eurospan

Canadian Representative:
Broadview Press

Staff
President: Charles C. Savitt
Assistant to the President: Karen Lomax (ext. 27)
VP & Chief Financial Officer: Ken Hartzell (301/576-6221)
VP of Programs and Communications: George Abar (ext. 28)
VP of Development: Krishna Roy (ext. 25)
Permissions: Angela Osborn, Fulfillment and Rights Manager (ext. 35)
Acquisitions / Editorial: Todd Baldwin, VP & Associate Publisher (ext. 14)
Design and Production: Maureen Gately, Director of Production and Design (ext. 49)
Marketing / Sales / Advertising / Publicity: Brian Weese, Director of Marketing
   and Sales (ext. 32)
IT: Trevor Angel, IT Manager (ext. 48)

Associate Member
Established: 1984
Title output 2006: 40
Titles currently in print: 700

Admitted to AAUP: 1999
Title output 2007: 40

Editorial Program
Scholarly and professional titles in environmental studies and natural resource management; nonfiction literary trade titles (through Shearwater Books imprint) on nature and the environment; electronic publishing on environmental topics and news (through Web site). Subject areas include ecosystems management, protection of biodiversity and human health, environmentally responsible land use planning, sustainable design, marine science and policy, climate and energy, and economics and policy.

The Press's full name is Island Press—Center for Resource Economics.
Special series, joint imprints and/or copublishing programs: Case Studies in Land and Community Design (with the Landscape Architecture Foundation); Ecoregions of the World: A Conservation Assessment (with The World Wildlife Fund); Foundations of Contemporary Environmental Studies; The Millennium Ecosystem Assessment; The Science and Practice of Ecological Restoration (with the Society for Ecological Restoration International); SCOPE Monograph Series (with The Scientific Committee on Problems of the Environment); State of the Wild (with Wildlife Conservation Society); The World's Water (with The Pacific Institute for Studies in Development, Environment, and Security)

The Jewish Publication Society

2100 Arch Street, 2nd Floor
Philadelphia, PA 19103

Phone: (215) 832-0600
Fax: (215) 568-2017
E-mail: (user I.D.)@jewishpub.org
Web site: www.jewishpub.org

Orders:
Phone: (800) 355-1165

UK Representative:
Eurospan

Canadian Representative:
Scholarly Book Services

Staff
Director: Ellen Frankel (215/832-0607; e-mail: efrankel)
COO and Publishing Director: Carol Hupping (215/832-0605; e-mail: chupping)
Acquisitions: Rena Potok (215/832-0604; e-mail: rpotok)
Production: Robin Norman (215/832-0606; e-mail: rnorman)
Sales and Marketing: Laurie Schlesinger (215/832-0613; e-mail: lschlesinger)
Finance: Nyles Cole (215/832-0602; e-mail: ncole)

Associate Member
Established: 1888

Title output 2006: 13
Titles currently in print: 200

Admitted to AAUP: 2004
(Former membership: 1993-2001)
Title output 2007: 16

Editorial Program
Nonfiction trade titles and serious works of nonfiction, all with Jewish content, particularly in Bible studies, Jewish ethics, contemporary issues, philosophy, midrash and folktales, history, holidays and customs, women's studies, theology, biography, classic texts, and reference. JPS publishes the NJPS Bible and Bible commentaries, as well as children's story collections and young adult novels.
Special series: JPS Bible Commentaries and JPS Guides

The Johns Hopkins University Press

2715 N. Charles Street
Baltimore, MD 21218-4363

Phone: (410) 516-6900
Fax: (410) 516-6998/6968
E-mail: (user I.D.)@press.jhu.edu
Web site: www.press.jhu.edu

Distribution Center:
704 Legionaire Drive
Fredericksburg, PA 17026

Orders and Customer Service:
(800) 537-5487

UK Representative:
Yale Representation, Ltd.

Staff

Director: Kathleen Keane (410/516-6971; e-mail: kk)
  Assistant to the Director: Karen Reider (410/516-6971; e-mail: kar)
  Rights and Permissions: John Lane (410/516-6063; e-mail: jl)
  Office and Facilities Coordinator: Nora Reedy (410/516-7035; e-mail: ncr)
  Director, Finance and Administration: Catherine Millar (410/516-6941; e-mail: cam)
  Director of Development: Jack Holmes (410/516-6928; e-mail: jmh)
Acquisitions Editorial: Trevor Lipscombe, Editor-in-Chief (mathematics, physics) (410/516-6919; e-mail: tcl)
  Executive Editors: Henry Y. K. Tom (European history, political science) (410/516-6908; e-mail: hyt); Jacqueline C. Wehmueller (consumer health, history of medicine) (410/516-6904; e-mail: jcw)
  Senior Editors: Robert J. Brugger (American history, history of science and technology, regional books) (410/516-6909; e-mail: rjb); Vincent Burke (life sciences) (410/516-6999; e-mail: vjb); Wendy Harris (psychiatry, gerontology, bioethics, public health) (410/516-6907; e-mail: wah)
  Editors: Michael Lonegro (humanities, classics, ancient Near Eastern studies) (410/516-6903; e-mail: mbl); Ashleigh McKown (higher education) (410/516-6997; e-mail: aem)
Project MUSE: Mary Rose Muccie, Director (410/516-6981; e-mail mrm)
  Business Manager: Harry A. Dean (410/516-6510; e-mail: had)
  Marketing and Sales Manager: Melanie B. Schaffner (410/516-3846; e-mail: mbs)
  International Sales Coordinator: Ann Snoeyenbos (410/516-6992; e-mail: aps)
  Subscription Support Specialist: Lora Czarnowsky (410/516-6989; e-mail: llc)
  Electronic Publishing Technologies Manager: Wendy Queen (410/516-3845; e-mail: wjq)
  Manager, User Services: Elizabeth W. Brown (410/516-6834; e-mail: ewb)
  Authorities Librarian: William Kulp (410/516-8968; e-mail: wak)
  Authorities Librarian / Indexer: Elisa Tan (410/516-6496; e-mail: eit)
Manuscript Editorial: Juliana M. McCarthy, Managing Editor (410/516-6912; e-mail: jmm)
  Assistant Managing Editor: Linda E. Forlifer (410/516-6911; e-mail: lef)
  Manuscript Editor: Anne M. Whitmore (410/516-6916; e-mail: amw)
  Production Editors: Andre M. Barnett (410/516-6995; e-mail: amb); Courtney Bond (410/516-6901; e-mail: cmb); Kimberly F. Johnson (410/516-6915; e-mail: kfj); Carol Zimmerman (410/516-6914; e-mail: clz)
Design and Production: John Cronin, Production Manager (410/516-6922; e-mail: jgc)
  Art Director: Martha Sewall (410/516-6921; e-mail: mds)

Senior Book Designers: Glen Burris (410/516-6924; e-mail: gmb); Wilma Rosenberger (410/516-6925; e-mail: wer)
Production Coordinators: Robert Schreur (410/516-3855; e-mail: rjs); Carol Eckhart (410/516-3862; e-mail: cle); Linda West (410/516-6920; e-mail: lmw)
Marketing: Becky Brasington Clark, Director (410/516-6931; e-mail: rbc)
Sales Director: Tom Lovett (410/516-6936; e-mail: tjl)
Promotion Manager: Karen Willmes (410/516-6932; e-mail: klw)
Publicity Manager: Kathy Alexander (410/516-4162; e-mail: ka)
Exhibits Manager: Brendan Coyne (410/516-6937; e-mail: bcc)
Electronic Promotion Coordinator: Colleen Condon (410/516-6972; e-mail: cmc)
Journals: William M. Breichner, Publisher (410/516-6985; e-mail: wmb)
Journals Fulfillment Systems Project Manager: Matt Brook (410/516-6899; e-mail: mb)
Journals Marketing Manager: Loliza Klose (410/516-6689; e-mail: llk)
Journals Production Manager: Carol Hamblen (410/516-6986; e-mail: crh)
Journals Subscription Manager: Alta Anthony (410/516-6938; e-mail: aha)
Journals Advertising Coordinator: Ashley Patton (410/516-7096; e-mail: ajp)
Business: Beth Corrigan, Accounting Manager (410/516-6974; e-mail: mec)
Fulfillment: William F. Bishop, Manager, Fulfillment Operations (410/516-6961; e-mail: wfb)
Credit & Collections: Edris Spence (410/516-3854; e-mail: ems)
Information Systems: Stacey L. Armstead, Manager (410/516-6979; e-mail: sla)
Database Administrator/Programmer: Robert Oeste (410/516-6933; e-mail: rto)

Full Member

Established: 1878   Admitted to AAUP: 1937
Title output 2006: 216   Title output 2007: 246
Titles currently in print: 2,560   Journals published: 62

Editorial Program

History (American, European, ancient, history of science, technology, and medicine); humanities (literary and cultural studies, classics); medicine and health (consumer health, public health, gerontology and geriatrics, clinical psychology and psychiatry); bioethics; science (biology, physics, and natural history); mathematics; political science; economics; higher education; reference books; and regional books.

The Press is publisher for the International Food Policy Research Institute and copublisher with the Woodrow Wilson Center Press.

The Press, through Hopkins Fulfillment Service handles book order processing and distribution for: Baylor University Press, Brookings Institution Press, Catholic University of America Press, Center for Talented Youth, Georgetown University Press, Health Publications Business Group, Howard University Press, Johns Hopkins University Press, University of Massachusetts Press, University of Pennsylvania Press, University of Pennsylvania Museum Publications, Resources for the Future, University of Washington Press, Urban Institute Press, and World Resources Institute.

The Press, in cooperation with the Johns Hopkins University's Milton S. Eisenhower Library and the participating publishers, manages Project MUSE®: Scholarly Journals Online (http://muse.jhu.edu). Project MUSE provides electronic subscription access to full-text, current periodical content from some 350 titles published by more than 70 not-for-profit publishers in the humanities and the social sciences. Other online publishing initiatives include electronic versions of *The Johns Hopkins Guide to Literary Theory and Criticism, The Papers of Dwight David Eisenhower*, the *Encyclopedia of American Studies*, and the *World Shakespeare Bibliography*.

Journals: *American Imago; American Jewish History; American Journal of Mathematics; American Journal of Philology; American Quarterly; Arethusa; The Bulletin of the Center for Children's Books; Bulletin of the History of Medicine; Callaloo; Children's Literature; Children's Literature Association Quarterly; Comparative Technology Transfer and Society; Configurations; diacritics; Double Take/Points of Entry; Eighteenth-Century Studies; Encyclopedia of American Studies; The Emily Dickinson Journal; ELH: English Literary History; The Henry James Review; Human Rights Quarterly; ICSID Review; Journal of Asian American Studies; Journal of College Student Development; Journal of Colonialism and Colonial History; Journal of Democracy; Journal of Early Christian Studies; Journal of Health Care for the Poor and Underserved; Journal of Modern Greek Studies; Journal of the History of Philosophy; Journal of Women's History; Kennedy Institute of Ethics Journal; Late Imperial China; L'Esprit Créateur; Library Trends; The Lion and the Unicorn; Literature and Medicine; MLN; Modern Fiction Studies; Modernism/Modernity; New Literary History; Partial Answers: Journal of Literature and the History of Ideas; Perspectives in Biology & Medicine; Philosophy and Literature; Philosophy, Psychiatry, and Psychology; portal: Libraries and the Academy; Postmodern Culture; Reviews in American History; Progress In Community Health Partnerships: Research, Education, and Action; Reviews in Higher Education; SAIS Review; Sewanee Review; Shakespeare Bulletin; Shakespeare Quarterly; Sirena; South Central Review; Spiritus: A Journal of Christian Spirituality; Studies in English Literature; Technology & Culture; Theatre Journal; Theatre Topics; Theory and Event; Transactions of the American Philological Association; World Politics; World Shakespeare Bibliography Online.*

Online-only journals: *Journal of Colonialism and Colonial History; Postmodern Culture; Theory and Event*

The Press also handles subscription fulfillment for Princeton University Press's journal, *Annals of Mathematics*, for journals published by Penn State University Press, and for *Imagine*, a publication of the Center for Talented Youth of The Johns Hopkins University.

Special series, joint imprints, and/or copublishing programs: The Complete Poetry of Percy Bysshe Shelley; Documentary History of the First Federal Congress; Johns Hopkins: Poetry and Fiction; The Johns Hopkins Studies in the History of Technology; The Johns Hopkins University Studies in History and Political Science; The Papers of Dwight David Eisenhower; The Papers of George Catlett Marshall; The Papers of Frederick Law Olmsted; The Papers of Thomas A. Edison; Parallax: Re-visions of Culture and Society; New Series in NASA History

University Press of Kansas

2502 Westbrooke Circle
Lawrence, KS 66045-4444

Phone: (785) 864-4154
Fax: (785) 864-4586
E-mail: upress@ku.edu
Indiv: (user I.D.)@ku.edu
Web site: www.kansaspress.ku.edu

UK / European Representative:
Eurospan

Warehouse Address:
2445 Westbrooke Circle
Lawrence, KS 66045-4440
Phone: (785) 864-4156

Orders:
Phone: (785) 864-4155
E-mail: upkorders@ku.edu

Canadian Representative:
Scholarly Book Services

Staff
Director: Fred Woodward (785/864-4667; e-mail: fwoodward)
  Assistant Director: Susan Schott (785/864-9165; e-mail: sschott)
  Assistant to the Director: Sara Henderson White (785/864-9125; e-mail: shwhite)
Editorial: Michael Briggs, Editor-in-Chief (political science, military history, law) (785/864-9162; e-mail: mbriggs)
  Acquisitions Editors: Kalyani Fernando (American history, American studies, Native American studies, women's studies) (785/864-9160; e-mail: kfernando); Fred Woodward (political science, presidential studies, US political history, American political thought, regional studies) (785/864-4667; e-mail: fwoodward)
  Editorial Assistant: Nicole Ishikawa (785/864-9161; e-mail: edassist)
Manuscript Editorial, Design and Production: Susan McRory, Senior Production Editor (785/864-9185; e-mail: smcrory)
  Production Editor: Larisa Martin (785/864-9169; e-mail: lmartin)
  Production Specialist: TBA (785/864-9123)
  Production Assistant: Kelly Chrisman (785/864-9186; e-mail: prodassist)
Marketing: Susan Schott, Assistant Director and Marketing Manager (785/864-9165; e-mail: sschott)
  Publicity Manager: Ranjit Arab (785/864-9170; e-mail: rarab)
  Direct Mail & Exhibits Manager: Debra Diehl (785/864-9166; e-mail: ddiehl)
  Advertising Coordinator/Marketing Designer: Karl Janssen (785/864-9164; e-mail: kjanssen)
  Marketing Assistant: Suzanne Galle (785/864-9167; e-mail: sgalle)
Business: Conrad Roberts, Business Manager (785/864-9158; e-mail: ceroberts)
  Accounting Manager: Britt DeTienne (785/864-9159; e-mail: bdetienne)
  Warehouse Manager: Kyle Ostrom (785/864-4156)

Full Member
Established: 1946
Title output 2006: 51
Titles currently in print: 773

Admitted to AAUP: 1946
Title output 2007: 55

Editorial Program

American history; military and intelligence studies; Western history and Native American studies; American government and public policy; presidential studies; constitutional and legal studies; ethics and political philosophy; environmental studies; American studies; women's studies; Kansas, the Great Plains, and the Midwest. The Press does not consider fiction, poetry, or festschriften for publication.

The Press distributes a series of natural history handbooks for the University of Kansas Natural History Museum.

Special series, joint imprints, and/or copublishing programs: American Political Thought; American Presidential Elections; American Presidency; CultureAmerica; Kansas Nature Guides; Landmark Law Cases and American Society; Modern First Ladies; Modern War Studies; Studies in Government and Public Policy; US Army War College Guides to Civil War Battles

The Kent State University Press

Street Address:
307 Lowry Hall
Kent State University
Kent, OH 44242-0001

Mailing Address:
PO Box 5190
Kent, OH 44242-0001

Phone: (330) 672-7913
Fax: (330) 672-3104
E-mail: (user I.D.)@kent.edu
Web site: www.kentstateuniversitypress.com

Orders:
Phone: (419) 281-1802
Fax: (419) 281-6883

UK / European Representative:
Eurospan

Canadian Representative:
Scholarly Book Services

Staff

Director: Will Underwood (330/672-8094; e-mail: wunderwo)
Acquisitions: Joanna Hildebrand Craig, Assistant Director and Editor-in-Chief (330/672-8099; e-mail: jhildebr)
Editorial: Mary D. Young (330/672-8101; e-mail: mdyoung)
  Manuscript Editor: Rebekah Cotton (330/672-8095); e-mail: rcotton2)
Design and Production: Christine A. Brooks, Manager (330/672-8092; e-mail: cbrooks)
  Assistant Design and Production Manager: Darryl M. Crosby (330/672-8091; e-mail: dcrosby)
Marketing: Susan L. Cash, Manager (330/672-8097; e-mail: scash)
  Marketing Assistant: Brett J. Neff (330/672-8098; e-mail: bjneff)
Journals Circulation/Secretary: Sandra D. Clark (330/672-8090; e-mail: sclark1)
Bookkeeper: Norma E. Hubbell (330/672-8096; e-mail: nhubbell)

Full Member

Established: 1966
Title output 2006: 36
Titles currently in print: 425

Admitted to AAUP: 1970
Title output 2007: 36
Journals published: 2

Editorial Program

History: Civil War era; US military, cultural/social, diplomatic, true crime; Ohio/Midwestern studies; fashion/costume; material culture. Literature: US (to ca. 1950); regional/Midwestern. Regional literary nonfiction; poetry only through Wick Poetry Center; no fiction.

Journals: *Civil War History; Ohio History*

Special series: Civil War in the North; Cleveland Theater; Literature and Medicine; New Studies in US Foreign Relations; Reading Hemingway; Sacred Landmarks; Teaching Hemingway; Translation Studies; True Crime History; Violence Prevention, Intervention, and Policy; Voices of Diversity; Narratives of the Immigrant Experience; Writing Sports; Wick Poetry

Imprint: Black Squirrel Books (Ohio reprints)

The University Press of Kentucky

663 South Limestone Street
Lexington, KY 40508-4008

Phone: (859) 257-8761
Fax: (859) 257-7975
E-mail: (user I.D.)@uky.edu
Web site: www.kentuckypress.com

Warehouse Address:
Maple Press Lebanon Distribution Center
704 Legionaire Drive
Fredericksburg, PA 17026

Orders:
Phone: (859) 257-8400;
(800) 839-6855
Fax: (859) 257-8481

UK / European Representative:
Eurospan

Canadian Representative:
Scholarly Book Services

Staff

Director: Stephen M. Wrinn (859/257-8432; e-mail: smwrin2)
    Assistant to the Director & Editorial Assistant: Anne Dean Watkins (e-mail: adwatk0)
Acquisitions Editors: Stephen M. Wrinn (American and Southern history, American studies, world history, Civil War, military history, political science, political theory, public policy, international studies, African American studies); Laura Sutton (Kentuckiana, regional studies, Appalachian studies, folklore) (859/257-8150; e-mail: lsutton); Leila Salisbury (film studies, popular culture) (859/257-8442; e-mail: leilas)
    Editorial Assistant: Ann Malcolm (859/257-9492; e-mail: ann.malcolm)
Editing, Design & Production: Melinda Wirkus, Director of Editing, Design & Production (859/257-8438)
    Production Manager: Richard E. Farkas (859/257-8435; e-mail: rfark1)
    Assistant Production Manager: Pat Gonzales (859/257-4669; e-mail: pagonz0)
    Editing Supervisors: David Cobb (859/257-4252; e-mail: dlcobb2); Ila McEntire (859/257-8433; e-mail: ila.mcentire)
Marketing: Leila Salisbury, Marketing Director (859/257-8442; e-mail: leilas)
    Sales Manager: John P. Hussey (859/257-4249; e-mail: jphuss2)
    Advertising, Direct Mail & Website Manager: Allison Webster (859/257-2817; e-mail: abwebs0)

Publicity Manager: Mack McCormick (859/257-5200; e-mail: permissions)
Exhibits & Rights Manager: Hap Houlihan (859/257-6855; e-mail: hap.houlihan)
Finance and Administration: Craig R. Wilkie, Assistant Director / Director of Finance & Administration (859/257-8436; e-mail: crwilk00)
Database Administrator and Technology Support: Tim Elam (859/257-8761; e-mail: taelam2)
Order Fulfillment Manager: Teresa W. Collins (859/257-8405; e-mail: twell1)
Credit Manager: Scot Skidmore (859/257-8445; e-mail: jsskid2)
Customer Service Representative: Robert Brandon (859/257-8400, 800/839-6855; e-mail: rbrandon)

Full Member

Established: 1943
Title output 2006: 61
Titles currently in print: 985

Admitted to AAUP: 1947
Title output 2007: 54

Editorial Program

Scholarly books in the fields of American history; military history; film studies; political science; international studies; folklore and material culture; African American studies; serious nonfiction of general interest. Regionally, the Press maintains an interest in Kentucky and the Ohio Valley, Appalachia, and the upper South. Submissions are not invited in fiction, drama, or poetry.

Special series: Asia in the New Millennium; Civil Rights and the Struggle for Black Equality in America; The Civil War and Society; Culture of the Land: A Series in the New Agrarianism; The Essential Television Reader Series; Kentucky Remembered: An Oral History Series; Kentucky Voices; Material Worlds; New Books for New Readers; New Directions in Southern History; The Ohio River Valley; The Philosophy of Popular Culture; Political Companions to Great American Authors; Provocations: Political Thought and Contemporary Issues; Public Papers of the Governors of Kentucky; Religion in the South; Screen Classics; Topics in Kentucky History; Virginia at War; Witnesses to the Civil War

Leuven University Press / Universitaire Pers Leuven

Minderbroedersstraat 4 - bus 5602
B-3000 Leuven
Belgium

Phone: +32 16 32 53 45
Fax: +32 16 32 53 52
E-mail: info@upers.kuleuven.be
Indiv. (user I.D.)@upers.kuleuven.be
Web site: www.lup.be

US Representative:
Cornell University Press Services
P.O. Box 6525
750 Cascadilla Street
Ithaca, NY 14851-6525 USA
E-mail: orderbook@cupserv.org
Web site: www.cornellpress.cornell.edu

Staff

Director and Acquisitions Editorial: Marike Schipper (+32 16 32 53 47; e-mail: marike.schipper)
Assistant to the Director: Vera Mans (+32 16 32 53 45; e-mail: vera.mans)
Manuscript Editorial: Beatrice Van Eeghem (+32 16 32 53 40; e-mail: beatrice.vaneeghem)

Production: Patricia di Costanzo (+32 16 32 53 53; e-mail: patricia.dicostanzo)
Marketing: Nienke van Schaverbeke (+32 16 32 53 51; e-mail: nienke.vanschaverbeke)
Customer Service and Order Processing: Régine Vanswijgenhoven (+32 16 32 53 50; e-mail:
   regine.vanswijgenhoven)

International Member

Established: 1971
Title output 2006: 35
Titles currently in print: 990

Admitted to AAUP: 2005
Title output 2007: 40
Journals published: 1

Editorial Program

Scholarly publications with emphasis on philosophy, religion, history, archaeology, literature,
linguistics, musicology, psychology, pedagogics, anthropology, economics, law and medicine.
Journal: *Humanistica Lovaniensia: A Journal of Neo-Latin Studies*
Special series: Aardkundige Mededelingen; Acta Archaeologica Lovanienisa-Monograph-
iae; Acta Biomedica Lovaniensia; Ancient and Medieval Philosophy Series 1; Ancient and
Medieval Philosophy Series 2: Henrici de Gandavo Opera Omnia; Avisos de Flandes; Col-
lected Writings of the Orpheus-Institute; Corpus Latinum Commentariorum in Aristotelem
Graecorum; Egyptian Prehistory Monographs; Figures of the Unconscious; Gaston Eyskens
Lectures; Italian Studies; Kadoc-Artes; Kadoc-Studies on Religion, Culture and Society;
Leuven Chinese Studies; Leuven Law Series; Leuven Notes in Mathematical and Theoretical
Physics; Louvain Philosophical Studies; Mediaevalia Lovaniensia; Sociology Today; Symbolae
Facultatis Litterarum Lovaniensis; Studia Psychologica; Studia Paedagogica; Studia Anthro-
pologica; Supplementa Humanistica Lovaniensia; Studies in Social and Economic History;
Surgical Oncology
Copublishing programs: Peeters and Brepols.

Louisiana State University Press

3990 W. Lakeshore Drive
Baton Rouge, LA 70808

Phone: (225) 578-6294
E-mail: lsupress@lsu.edu
Indiv: (user I.D.)@lsu.edu
Web site: www.lsu.edu/lsupress

UK Distributor:
TBA

Warehouse, Orders and Cust. Service:
Longleaf Services
PO Box 8895
Chapel Hill, NC 27515-8895
Phone: (800) 848-6224
Fax: (800) 272-6817
E-mail: longleaf@unc.edu

Canadian Distributor:
Scholarly Book Services

Staff

Director: MaryKatherine Callaway (225/578-6295; e-mail: mkc)
   Assistant to the Director and Fundraising Coordinator: Erica Bossier (e-mail: ebossie)
Acquisitions Editorial: John Easterly, Executive Editor (literary studies) (225/578-6618;
   e-mail: jeaster)

Acquiring Editors: Rand Dotson (history) (e-mail: pdotso1); Margaret Hart (trade) (e-mail: mhart); Alisa Plant (European history) (e-mail: aplant); Joseph Powell (environmental studies and geography) (e-mail: jpowell)

Manuscript Editorial: Lee Sioles, Managing Editor (225/578-6467; e-mail: lsioles)
  Senior Editor: George Roupe (e-mail: groupe1)

Design and Production: Laura Gleason, Assistant Director and Production Manager (225/578-5912; e-mail: lgleasn)
  Assistant Production Manager: Amanda Scallan (e-mail: amandas)

Marketing: Barbara Outland, Manager (225/578-6666; e-mail: boutlan)
  Sales Manager: Rod Mills (e-mail: rmills)

Senior Publicist: Amanda Atkins (e-mail: aatkins)
  Direct Marketing and Electronic Promotions: Robert Keane (e-mail: rkeane)
  Advertising and Copy Coordinator: Jessica McDonald (e-mail: jessmcdo)

Accounting and Fulfillment: William Bossier, Associate Director and CFO (225/578-6482; e-mail: wbossie)
  Fulfillment Operations Manager: Rebekah Brown (rbrown1)
  Permissions: Debra Langlois (e-mail: dlanglo)

Subsidiary Rights: McIntosh & Otis, Inc., 353 Lexington Ave., New York, NY 10016 (212/687-7400)

Full Member

Established: 1935	Admitted to AAUP: unknown
Title output 2006: 89	Title output 2007: 83
Titles currently in print: 1,374	

Editorial Program

Humanities and social sciences, with special emphasis on Southern history and literature; European history in the Atlantic world; geography and environmental studies; poetry; and jazz. **Special series, joint imprints and/or copublishing programs:** Antislavery, Abolition, and the Atlantic World; Conflicting Worlds; Environmental History/Urban Studies; Lectures in Southern History; Making the Modern South; Papers of Jefferson Davis; Political Traditions in Foreign Policy; politics@media; Southern Biography; Southern Literary Studies; Southern Messenger Poets; Voices of the South; W.L. Fleming Lectures in Southern History; Walt Whitman Award of the Academy of American Poets; Yellow Shoe Fiction
  The Press also distributes the Lena-Miles Weaver Todd Poetry Series

McGill-Queen's University Press

Montreal Office:
3430 McTavish Street
Montreal, QC H3A 1X9
Canada

Phone: (514) 398-3750
Fax: (514) 398-4333
E-mail: mqup@mqup.ca
Indiv: (user I.D.)@mcgill.ca
Web site: www.mqup.ca

Kingston Office:
Queen's University
Kingston, ON K7L 3N6
Canada

Phone: (613) 533-2155
Fax: (613) 533-6822
E-mail: mqup@post.queensu.ca

Canadian Distributor:
Georgetown Terminal Warehouses
34 Armstrong Avenue
Georgetown, ON L7G 4R9
Canada
Phone: (905) 873-9781
Fax: (905) 873-6170
E-mail: orders@gtwcanada.com

US Distributor:
CUP Services
PO Box 6525
Ithaca, NY 14851-6525
Phone: (800) 666-2211
Fax: (800) 688-2877
E-mail: orderbook@cupserv.org

UK / European Distributor:
Marston Books Services

Staff

Executive Director: Philip J. Cercone (Montreal, 514/398-2910; e-mail: philip.cercone)
Editor-in-Chief: Philip J. Cercone
Editorial, Montreal Office: John Zucchi, Deputy Senior Editor (514/398-3750; e-mail: john.zucchi)
   Editor: Jonathan Crago (514/398-7480; e-mail: jonathan.crago)
   Manuscript Editor: Joan V. McGilvray (514/398-3922; e-mail: joan.mcgilvray)
   Editorial Assistants: Joanne Pisano (514/398-2068; e-mail: joanne.pisano); Brenda Prince (514/398-3279; e-mail: brenda.prince)
Editorial, Kingston Office: Donald H. Akenson, Senior Editor (613/533-2155; e-mail: mqup@post.queensu.ca)
   Deputy Senior Editor: Kyla Madden (613/533-2155; e-mail: 6kmm3@post.queensu.ca)
   Editors: Joan Harcourt (613/533-2155; e-mail: bjh@post.queensu.ca); Roger Martin (613/533-2155; e-mail: mqup@post.queensu.ca)
Production Manager: Susanne McAdam (514/398-6996; e-mail: susanne.mcadam)
   Production Coordinator: Elena Goranescu (514/398-7395; e-mail: elena.goranescu)
   Production Assistant: Karen Biskin (514/398-1342; e-mail: production.mqup)
Marketing Manager: Susan McIntosh (514/398-6306; e-mail: susan.mcintosh)
   Sales Manager: Jeff Dalziel (514/398-5165; e-mail: jeff.dalziel)
   Educational Sales Administrator: Roy Ward (514/398-7177; e-mail: roy.ward)
   Direct Mail & Exhibits Coordinator: Filomena Falocco (514/398-2912; e-mail: filomena.falocco)

Electronic Marketing Coordinator: Sylvie O'Halloran (514/398-1343;
e-mail: sylvie.ohalloran)
Marketing Assistant: Sasha Laing (514/398-2914; e-mail: marketing.mqup)
Publicist: Jacqueline Davis (514/398-2555; e-mail: jacqueline.davis)
Business Manager: Linda Whittaker (514/398-5336; e-mail: linda.whittaker)
Administrative Coordinator: Dorothy Beaven (514/398-2911; e-mail: dorothy.beaven)
Administrative Clerk: Carol Cardinal (514/398-2056; e-mail: carol.cardinal)
Clerk/Receptionist: Carmie Vacca (514/398-3750; e-mail: carmie.vacca)

Full Member
Established: 1969 as a joint press
Admitted to AAUP: 1963 (as McGill University Press)
Title output 2006: 115   Title output 2007: 124
Titles currently in print: c. 2,350

Editorial Program

Scholarly books and well-researched studies of general interest in the humanities and social sciences, including anthropology, especially North American native peoples; architecture; Arctic and northern studies; art history; Canadian studies; Canadian literature; classics; communication and media studies; cultural studies; economics; education; environmental studies; ethnic studies; film studies; folklore and material culture; geography; health and society; history; Irish and Gaelic studies; law; linguistics; literary criticism; medieval and renaissance studies; military history; native studies; philosophy; poetry; photography; political economy; political science; public administration; Quebec studies; religious studies; Slavic and Eastern European studies; sociology; theatre; and women's studies.

Special series: Arts Insights; CHORA, Intervals in the Philosophy of Architecture; Canada Among Nations; Canada: The State of the Federation; Canadian Association of Geographers Series in Canadian Geography; Canadian Public Administration; Carleton Library; Central Problems of Philosophy; Central Works of Philosophy; Centre for Editing Early Canadian Texts; Challenge and Change for the Military; Comparative Charting of Social Change; Continental European Philosophy; Critical Perspectives on Public Affairs; Culture of Cities; Fontanus Monograph; Footprints; Foreign Policy, Security and Strategic Studies; Fundamentals of Philosophy; Global Dialogue on Federalism; Global Dialogue on Federalism Booklet; Governance and Public Management; Harbinger Poetry; How Ottawa Spends; Hugh MacLennan Poetry; Innovation, Science, Environment; International Social Survey Programme; McGill-Queen's Native and Northern; McGill-Queen's Studies in Ethnic History; McGill-Queen's Studies in the History of Ideas; McGill-Queen's Studies in the History of Religion; McGill-Queen's/Associated Medical Services Studies in the History of Medicine, Health, and Society; Nordic Voices; Philosophy Now; Public Policy; Queen's Policy Studies; Rupert's Land Record Society; Social Union; Studies in Nationalism and Ethnic Conflict; Studies on the History of Quebec / Études d'histoire du Québec; Understanding Movements in Modern Thought; War and European Society

Marquette University Press

1415 West Wisconsin Avenue
Box 3141
Milwaukee, WI 53201-3141

Warehouse Address:
30 Amberwood Parkway, PO Box 388
Ashland, OH 44805

Phone: (414) 288-1564
Fax: (414) 288-7813
E-mail: (user I.D.)@marquette.edu
Web site: marquette.edu/mupress/

Orders and Customer Service:
Phone: (800) 247-6553; (419) 281-1802
Fax: (419) 281-6883

Canadian Representative:
Scholarly Book Services

Staff
Director: Andrew Tallon (414/288-1564; e-mail: andrew.tallon)
Editorial, Marketing, Design and Production: Andrew Tallon
Business: Maureen Kondrick (414/288-1564; e-mail: maureen.kondrick)
Journals: Andrew Tallon
   Journals Marketing: Pamela K. Swope (800/444-2419, ext. 1; e-mail: pkswope@pdcnet.org)

Full Member
Established: 1916
Title output 2006: 17
Titles currently in print: 350

Admitted to AAUP: 1998
Title output 2007: 22
Journals published: 1

Editorial Program
Philosophy; theology; history; urban studies; journalism; education; and mediæval history.
Journal: *Philosophy & Theology*
Philosophy series: Aquinas Lecture; Marquette Studies in Philosophy; Mediæval Philosophical Texts in Translation
Theology series: Marquette Studies in Theology; Père Marquette Lecture; Reformation Texts with Translation: Series 1, Biblical Studies; Series 2, Women in the Reformation; Series 3, Late Reformation
History series: Klement Lecture (Civil War); Marquette Studies in History (Modern);Urban Studies Series

University of Massachusetts Press

Street Address:
671 North Pleasant Street
Amherst, MA 01003

Mailing Address:
PO Box 429
Amherst, MA 01004

Phone: (413) 545-2217
Fax: (413) 545-1226
E-mail: (user I.D.)@umpress.umass.edu
(unless otherwise indicated)
Web site: www.umass.edu/umpress

Orders:
c/o Hopkins Fulfillment Services
PO Box 50370
Baltimore, MD 21211
Phone: (800) 537-5487
Fax: (410) 516-6998

Canadian Representative:
Scholarly Book Services

UK / European Representative:
Eurospan

Staff
Director: Bruce Wilcox (413/545-4990; e-mail: wilcox)
Acquisitions Editorial: Clark Dougan, Senior Editor (413/545-4989; e-mail: cdougan)
Manuscript Editorial: Carol Betsch, Managing Editor (413/545-4991; e-mail: betsch)
Design and Production: Jack Harrison, Manager (413/545-4998; e-mail: harrison)
   Designer & Associate Production Manager: Sally Nichols (413/545-4997; e-mail: snichols)
Business and Marketing: Richard Lozier, Business Manager (413/545-4994; e-mail: rlozier)
   Web and Promotion Manager: Carla Potts (413/545-2217; e-mail: potts)

Full Member
Established: 1963
Title output 2006: 37
Titles currently in print: 950

Admitted to AAUP: 1966
Title output 2007: 39

Editorial Program
Scholarly books and serious nonfiction, with special interests in African American studies; American studies, history, and literature; architecture and landscape design; biography; environmental studies; ethnic studies; history of the book; intellectual history; women's and gender studies; and books of regional interest.
Special series, joint imprints and/or copublishing programs: American Popular Music; Ancient China in Context; AWP Award Series in Short Fiction; Culture, Politics, and the Cold War; Juniper Prizes (poetry and fiction); Library of American Landscape History; Massachusetts Studies in Early Modern Culture; Native Americans of the Northeast; Public History in Historical Perspective; Studies in Print Culture and the History of the Book

The MIT Press

55 Hayward Street
Cambridge, MA 02142-1315

Phone: (617) 253-5646 (main)
(617) 253-5641 (marketing)
Fax: (617) 258-6779
E-mail: (user I.D.)@mit.edu
Web site: mitpress.mit.edu

Journals:
238 Main St., Suite 500
Cambridge, MA 02142
Phone: (617) 253-2889
Fax: (617) 577-1545

London Office:
The MIT Press, Ltd.
Fitzroy House
11 Chenies Street
London WC1E 7EY
United Kingdom
Phone: +44 (20) 7306 0603
Fax: +44 (20) 7306 0604
E-mail: info@hup-mitpress.co.uk

Book Orders:
Phone: (800) 405-1619 (US/Can);
(401) 531-2800 (International)
Fax: (800) 406-9145 (US/Can);
(401) 531-2801 (International)
E-mail: mitpress-orders@mit.edu

Customer Service:
Phone: (401) 658-4226
E-mail: mitpress-order-inq@mit.edu

Warehouse Address:
Triliteral
100 Maple Ridge Drive
Cumberland, RI 02864
E-mail: sheila.lilja@triliteral.org

Staff

Director: Ellen Faran (617/253-4078; e-mail: ewfaran)
　Assistant to the Director: Mary Frances Gydus (617/253-5255; e-mail: mfgydus)
　Director of Finance and Operations: Rebecca Schrader (617/253-5250; e-mail: recs)
Acquisitions Editorial: Ellen Faran, Director (617/253-4078; e-mail: ewfaran)
　Editors: Margy Avery (science, technology, and society) (617/253-1653; e-mail: mavery); Roger Conover (art, architecture, design, photography, cultural studies, critical theory) (617/253-1677; e-mail: conover); John S. Covell (economics, business & finance) (617/253-3757; e-mail: jcovell); Jane Macdonald (economics, business & finance) (617/253-1605; e-mail: janem); Clay Morgan (environmental sciences & bioethics) (617/253-4113; e-mail: claym); Robert Prior (computer science & biology) (617/253-1584; e-mail: prior); Doug Sery (computer science) (617/253-5187; e-mail: dsery); Tom Stone (cognitive neuroscience, psychology & linguistics) (617/252-1636; e-mail: tstone)
Manuscript Editorial: Michael Sims, Managing Editor (617/253-2080; e-mail: msims)
Design: Yasuyo Iguchi, Design Manager (617/253-8034; e-mail: iguchi)
Production: Terry Lamoureux, Production Manager (617/253-2881; e-mail: terryl)
Marketing and Sales: Gita Manaktala, Director of Marketing (617/253-3172; e-mail: manak)

Domestic Sales & Marketing Manager: Anne Bunn (617/253-8838; e-mail: annebunn)
International Sales & Marketing Manager: Tom Clerkin (617/253-2887; e-mail: clerkin)
Subsidiary Rights Manager: Cristina Sanmartín (617/253-0629; e-mail: csan)
Publicity Manager: Colleen Lanick (617/253-2874; e-mail: colleenl)
Electronic Marketing Manager: Jake Furbush (617/258-0583; e-mail: jfurbush)
Promotions Manager: Astrid Baehrecke (617/253-7297; e-mail: baehreck)
Advertising Manager: Vinnie Scorziello (617/253-3516; e-mail: gigivida)
Textbook Manager: Michelle Pullano (617/253-3620; e-mail: mpullano)
Exhibits Manager: John Costello (617/258-5764; e-mail: jcostell)
Journals: Rebecca McLeod, Journals Manager (617/258-0596; e-mail: mcleod)
 Journals Business Manager: June McCaull (617/258-0593; e-mail: jmccaull)
 Journals Circulation Manager: Abbie Hiscox (617/452-3765; e-mail: hiscox)
 Journals Editorial & Production Manager: Rachel Besen (617/258-0585; e-mail: rbesen)
 Journals Marketing Manager: Laura Esterly (617/258-0594; e-mail: lesterly)
 Journals Subsidiary Rights Manager: Christina Ellas (617/258-0591; e-mail: cellas)
Warehouse: Sheila Lilja, General Manager (e-mail: shiela.lilja@triliteral.org)
 Customer Service Manager: Cathy Morrone (401/531-2800; e-mail: cathy.
 morrone@triliteral.org)
Information Systems: Tony Irarragorri, IT Manager (617/258-6783; e-mail: tonyi)

Full Member

Established: 1961

Title output 2006: 296

Titles currently in print: 3,400

Admitted to AAUP: 1961

Title output 2007: 259

Journals published: 34

Editorial Program

Contemporary art; architecture/design arts; photography; computer science and artificial intelligence; new media studies; cognitive science; neuroscience; psychology; philosophy; linguistics; economics, finance and business; environmental studies; quantitative biology; science, technology, and society (STS); natural history; security studies; social and political theory.

 Copublishing and distribution programs: AAAI Press; Afterall Books; Alphabet Series; Canadian Centre for Architecture; Perspecta; Semiotext(e); Whitechapel Documents of Contemporary Art; Zone Books.

Journals: *African Arts; Artificial Life; Asian Economic Papers; Biological Theory; Computational Linguistics; Computer Music Journal; Daedalus; Design Issues; Education Finance and Policy; Evolutionary Computation; Global Environmental Politics; Grey Room; Information Technologies and International Development; Innovations; International Security; Journal of Cognitive Neuroscience; Journal of Cold War Studies; Journal of the European Economic Association; Journal of Industrial Ecology; Journal of Interdisciplinary History; Leonardo; Leonardo Music Journal; Linguistic Inquiry; Neural Computation; The New England Quarterly; October; PAJ: A Journal of Performance and Art; Perspectives on Science; Presence: Teleoperators and Virtual Environments; Quarterly Journal of Economics; The Review of Economics and Statistics; TDR: The Drama Review; The Washington Quarterly; World Policy Journal*

Special series: Acting with Technology; Adaptive Computation and Machine Learning; American Academy Studies in Global Security; American and Comparative Environmental Policy; Arne Ryde Memorial Lectures; Artificial Intelligence; Basic Bioethics; BCSIA Studies in International Security; Boston Review; Bradford Books; Cairoli Lectures; Cellular and Molecular Neuroscience; CESifo Book Series; CESifo Seminar Series; Cognitive Neuroscience; Computational Molecular Biology; Computational Models of Cognition and Perception; Computational Neuroscience; Contemporary Philosophical Monographs; Cooperative Information Systems; Current Studies in Linguistics; Dahlem Workshop Reports; Dibner Institute Studies in the History of Science and Technology; Economic Learning and Social Evolution; Electronic Culture; Food, Health, and the Environment; Frontiers in Health Policy Research; Global Environmental Accord: Strategies for Sustainability and Institutional Innovation; Graham Foundation Books; History of Computing; Information Revolution and Global Politics; Information Systems; Innovation Policy and the Economy; Inside Technology; Intelligent Robotics and Autonomous Agents; Issues in Clinical and Cognitive Neuropsychology; Jean Nicod Series; Language, Speech, and Communication; Learning, Development and Conceptual Change; Lemelson Center Studies in Invention and Innovation; Leonardo Books; Life and Mind; Linguistic Inquiry Monographs; Mediawork pamphlet series; MIT Readers in Contemporary Philosophy; Munich Lectures; NBER Macroeconomics Annual; Neural Information Processing; Neural Network Modeling and Connectionism; October Books; October Files; Ohlin Lectures; Organization Studies; Philosophical Psychopathology: Disorders in Mind; Politics, Science, and the Environment; Publications of the Burndy Library; Representation and Mind; Scientific and Engineering Computation; Short Circuits; Social Neuroscience; Studies in Contemporary German Social Thought; Studies in Dynamical Economic Science; Tax Policy and the Economy; Technical Communication, Multimedia, and Information Systems; Transformations: Studies in the History of Science and Technology; Urban and Industrial Environments; Vienna Series in Theoretical Biology; Walras-Pareto Lectures; Writing Architecture; Writing Art; Yrjo Jahnsson Lectures Series; Zeuthen Lecture Series

Mercer University Press

1400 Coleman Avenue
Macon, GA 31207

Phone: (478) 301-2880
Fax: (478) 301-2585
E-mail: (user I.D.)@mercer.edu
Web site: www.mupress.org

Orders:
Phone: (800) 637-2378, ext. 2880
Georgia orders: (800) 342-0841, ext. 2880
E-mail: mupressorders@mercer.edu

UK Representative:
Gracewing Publishing

Staff

Director and Acquisitions: Marc A. Jolley (e-mail: jolley_ma)
   Acquisitions Editorial: Edd Rowell, Senior Editor (e-mail: rowell_el)
Manuscript Editorial: Kevin Manus, Associate Editor (e-mail: manus_kc)
Production: Marsha Luttrell, Publishing Assistant (e-mail: luttrell_mm)
Marketing: Barbara Keene, Director of Marketing and Sales (e-mail: keene_b)
   Marketing Assistant: Niccole Rowe (e-mail: rowe_an)
Business: Regenia (Jenny) Toole, Business Office (e-mail: toole_rw)
   Customer Service: Dana Dotherow (e-mail: dotherow_dg)

Full Member

Established: 1979
Title output 2006: 43
Titles currently in print: 841

Admitted to AAUP: 2000
Title output 2007: 44

Editorial Program

Regional trade titles and serious works of nonfiction in history, particularly in the history of the United States (with an emphasis on the American South), the history of religion, and the history of literature; Southern regional studies; literature and literary criticism; Southern literary fiction; African American studies; political science; philosophy of religion; theology and biblical studies; Jewish studies; art and art criticism; natural history.

Special series: Baptists; Civil War Georgia; the International Kierkegaard Commentary; Mercer Classics in Biblical Studies; the Mercer Commentary on the Bible; the Melungeons; Mercer Paul Tillich Series; Mercer Flannery O'Connor Series; Music and the American South; Sports and Religion; Voices of the African Diaspora

The University of Michigan Press

839 Greene Street
Ann Arbor, MI 48104-3209

Phone: (734) 764-4388
Fax: (734) 615-1540
E-mail: um.press@umich.edu
Indiv: (user I.D.)@umich.edu
Web site: www.press.umich.edu

Orders:
University of Michigan Press
c/o Client Distribution Services
1094 Flex Drive
Jackson, TN 38301
Phone: (800) 343-4499 (US customers)
ESL Helpline: (877) 364-2942
Faxes: (800) 351-5073

UK Representative:
Eurospan

Staff

Director: Philip Pochoda (734/936-0452; e-mail: pochoda)
  Associate Director: Mary Erwin (734/763-4134; e-mail: merwin)
  Assistant to the Director / Permissions: Deb Shafer (734/615-6478; e-mail: dshafer)
Acquisitions Editorial:
  Editors: Chris Hebert (music, fiction, classical studies) (734/615-6479; e-mail: hebertc); Mary Erwin (regional, medical) (734/763-4134; e-mail: merwin); Kelly Sippell (ESL, applied linguistics) (734/764-4447; e-mail: ksippell); Alison Mackeen (media studies, humanities) (734/936-4922; e-mail: amackeen); Philip Pochoda (American history) (734/936-0452; e-mail: pochoda)
  Editorial Assistants: Catherine Cassel (734/647-2463; e-mail: cscassel); Sara Remington (734/936-2841; e-mail: sremingt); Christine Byks (734/936-8932; e-mail: cbyks)
English as a Second Language: Kelly Sippell, Director (734/764-4447; e-mail: ksippell)
  Exhibits / Catalog Coordinator: Lauren Naimola (734/763-3237; e-mail: lnaimola)
  Editorial Assistant: Lindsay Devine (e-mail: lsdevine)
  Senior Copyediting Coordinator: Deborah Kopka (e-mail: dkopka)
  Assistant Marketing Manager: Jason Contrucci (734/936-0459; e-mail: contrucc)
Manuscript Editorial: Christina Milton, Managing Editor (734/764-4390; e-mail: cmilton)
  Senior Copyediting Coordinators: Marcia LaBrenz (734/647-4480; e-mail: mlabrenz);

Kevin Rennells (734/763-1526; e-mail: rennells)

Copyediting Coordinator: Mary Hashman (734/936-0461; e-mail: mhashman)

Manuscript Editors: Andrea Olson (734/936-0394; e-mail: ajolson); Ellen McCarthy (e-mail: emcc)

Assistant Editor: Rosemary Bush (734/763-0170; e-mail: rabush)

Design and Production: John Grucelski, Production Manager (734/764-4391; e-mail: jgrucel)

Senior Production Coordinators: Mary Sexton (734/763-1525; e-mail: sextonm); Jillian Downey (734/615-8114; e-mail: jilliand); Paula Newcomb (734/763-6417; e-mail: newcombp)

Designer: Heidi Dailey (734/764-4128; e-mail: hdailey)

Marketing and Sales: Michael Kehoe, Marketing and Sales Director (734/936-0388; e-mail: mkehoe)

Trade Marketing Manager: Mary Bisbee-Beek (734/764-0163; e-mail: bisbeeb)

Trade Marketing Assistant: Stephanie Grohoski (734/763-6737; e-mail: sgrolosk)

Advertising / Marketing Coordinator and Copywriter: Joe Mooney (734/615-9939; e-mail: jfmooney)

Marketing Manager—Social Sciences: TBA (734/763-0163)

Marketing Manager—Humanities: Giles Brown (734/764-4330; e-mail: agbrown)

Web Designer: Melissa Baker-Young (734/764-6802; e-mail: mbakeryo)

Business: Gabriela Beres, Business Manager (734/936-2227; e-mail: gsberes)

Accountant: Karyn McIntire (734/763-0146; e-mail: klydic)

Accounts Payable: Linda Rowley (734/647-9083; e-mail: lrowley)

Facilities: Larry Gable (734/764-2468; e-mail: lgable)

Mail: Will Lovick (e-mail: willski)

Systems Administrator: Kerri Kijewski (734/936-3636; e-mail: kijewski)

Full Member

Established: 1930   Admitted to AAUP: 1963

Title output 2006: 160   Title output 2007: 156

Titles currently in print: 2,698

Editorial Program

Scholarly and trade works in African American studies; American studies; American history; anthropology; cultural studies; disability studies; economics; English as a second language; environmental studies; gay and lesbian studies; German studies; law; literature; literary criticism and theory; media studies and film; Michigan and Great Lakes; music; Native American studies; political science; theater and performance; women and gender studies; fiction; sports.

The Press distributes works of Pluto Press, the Center for Chinese Studies, and the Center for South and Southeast Asian Studies.

Special series: Advances in Heterodox Economics; Analytical Perspectives on Politics; Ann Arbor Paperbacks; Bibliotheca Teubneriana; The Comparative Studies in Society and History Book; Conversations in Medicine and Society; Corporealities: Discourses of Disability; Critical Perspectives on Women and Gender; Development and Inequality in the Market Economy; Economics, Cognition, and Society; Economics of Education; Editorial Theory and Literary Criticism; English for Academic & Professional Purposes; Evolving Values for a Capitalist World; Great Lakes Environment; Human-Environment Interaction; Intensive Course in English; Interests, Identities and Institutions in Comparative Politics; International Series on the Research of Learning and Instruction of Writing; Jazz Perspectives; Kelsey Museum Studies; Law, Meaning, and Violence; The Memoirs of the American Academy in Rome; Michigan Series in English for Academic and Professional Purposes; The Michigan Series on Teaching Multilingual Writers; Michigan Studies in International Political Economy; Michigan Studies in Political Analysis; Middle English Dictionary; Monumenta Chartae Papyraceae; The Paper and Monographs of the American Academy in Rome; Pew Studies in Economics and Security; Poets on Poetry; Political Analysis; The Politics of Race and Ethnicity; Recentiores: Later Latin Texts and Contexts; Selected Tanner Lectures in Human Values; Social History, Popular Culture, and Politics in Germany; Studies in International Economics; Studies in International Trade Policy; Studies in Literature and Science; Stylus: Supplements to the Memoirs of the American Academy in Rome; Sweetwater Fiction; TEXT: An Interdisciplinary Annual of Textual Studies; The Thackeray Edition; Theater: Theory/Text/Performance; Thomas Spencer Jerome Lectures; Triangulations: Lesbian/Gay/Queer/Theater/Drama/Performance; Under Discussion

Michigan State University Press

1405 South Harrison Road, Suite 25
East Lansing, MI 48823-5245

Phone: (517) 355-9543
Director's Office Fax: (517) 353-6766
E-mail: msupress@msu.edu
Indiv: (user I.D.)@msu.edu
Web site and online catalog: msupress.msu.edu

Customer Service:
Phone: (517) 355-9543, ext. 100
Fax: (517) 432-2611;
(800) 678-2120

UK / European Distributor:
Eurospan

Canadian Distributor:
University of British Columbia

Staff

Director: Gabriel Dotto (ext. 117; e-mail: dotto@msu.edu)
Development Director: TBA (ext. 127)
Editorial: Julie L. Loehr, Editor-in-Chief / Assistant Director (ext. 103; e-mail: loehr)
  Acquisitions Editor: Martha A. Bates (ext. 104; e-mail: batesmar)
  Production: Annette Tanner, Manager (ext. 114; e-mail: tanneran)
  Editor: Kristine Blakslee (ext. 131; e-mail: blakes17)
Marketing & Sales: Julie Reaume (ext. 109; e-mail: reaumej)
  Web Site Coordinator: Dawn Martin (ext. 108; e-mail: marti778)
Journals: Margot Landa Kielhorn, Managing Editor (ext. 102; e-mail: kielhorn)
  Production Editor: Sharon Caldwell (ext. 111; e-mail: smcald)
Business Manager: Laura Carantza (ext. 116; e-mail: carantza)
  Fulfillment Manager: Julie Wrzesinski (ext. 101; e-mail: wrzesin2)
  Warehouse Coordinator: Brett Robinson (ext. 105)
Information Systems: Jesse Howard, Manager (ext. 106; e-mail: howard10)
  IT Administrator: Peter Cole (ext. 124; e-mail: colepet)

Full Member
Established: 1947

Admitted to AAUP: 1992
(Previous membership, 1951-1972)

Title output 2006: 27
Titles currently in print: 598

Title output 2007: 28
Journals published: 11

Editorial Program
Scholarly books and general nonfiction with areas of special interest in African studies; African American studies; Agricultural Science; American studies; American Indian studies; Canadian studies; creative nonfiction; Great Lakes regional studies; politics and the global economy; books relating to the state of Michigan; poetry; the social and environmental sciences; US history; urban studies; women's studies.

The Press distributes publications for African Books Collective; University of Alberta Press; Blue Griffin Records; University of Calgary Press; University of Manitoba Press; Colleagues Press; Grand Valley State University; Kresge Art Museum; Mackinac Island Historic Parks; Michigan State University African Studies Center; the Michigan State University Museum; Verdehr Trio Musical Scores.

Journals: *Contagion: Journal of Violence, Mimesis, and Culture; Esoterica; Fourth Genre; French Colonial History; Journal for the Study of Radicalism; Italian Culture; CR: The New Centennial Review; Northeast African Studies; Real Analysis Exchange; Red Cedar Review; Rhetoric & Public Affairs*

Special series: African Diaspora Research Project; American Indian Series; Black American and Diasporic Studies Environmental Research Series; Discovering the Peoples of Michigan; Eurasian Political Economy and Public Policy Series; Julian Samora Research Institute Occasional Papers; Rhetoric and Public Affairs Series; Rhetorical History of the United States; the Schomburg Studies on the Black Experience; Schoolcraft Series

Minnesota Historical Society Press

345 Kellogg Blvd. West
Saint Paul, MN 55102

Orders:
Phone: (800) 621-2736

Phone: (651) 259-3200
Fax: (651) 297-1345
E-mail: (user I.D.)@mnhs.org
Web site: www.mhspress.org

Staff
Director: Gregory M. Britton (651/259-3210; e-mail: greg.britton)
Acquisitions: Gregory M. Britton, Ann Regan
Editor: Ann Regan (651/259-3206; e-mail: ann.regan)
Design and Production: Will Powers (651/259-3209; e-mail: william.powers)
Marketing: Alison Vandenberg (651/259-3203; e-mail: alison.vandenberg)
Sales: Mary Poggione (651/259-3204; e-mail: mary.poggione)
Rights and Permissions: Monica Collins (651/259-3200; e-mail: monica.collins)
Journals: Anne Kaplan (651/259-3207; e-mail: anne.kaplan)

Associate Member

Established: 1859
Title output 2006: 25
Titles currently in print: 322

Admitted to AAUP: 2001
Title output 2007: 31
Journals published: 1

Editorial Program
The Minnesota Historical Society Press publishes books on the cultural heritage of the Upper Midwest. Specific list strengths include history, regional studies, memoir and literary nonfiction, ethnic studies, travel and adventure, military history, African American history, Native American studies, architectural history, and photography.
Journal: *Minnesota History*
Special series: Minnesota Byways; Native Voices; People of Minnesota
Imprint: Borealis Books

University of Minnesota Press

111 Third Avenue South
Suite 290
Minneapolis, MN 55401-2552

Phone: (612) 627-1970
Fax: (612) 627-1980
E-mail: (user I.D.)@umn.edu
Web site: www.upress.umn.edu

Orders:
University of Minnesota Press
Chicago Distribution Center
11030 South Langley Avenue
Chicago, IL 60628
Phone: (800) 621-2736; (773) 568-1550
Fax: (800) 621-8476; (773) 660-2235

UK Distributor:
NBN Plymbridge

UK Representative:
University Presses Marketing

Staff
Director: Douglas Armato (612/627-1972; e-mail: armat001)
  Associate Director and Test Division Manager: Beverly Kaemmer (612/627-1963; e-mail: kaemm002)
  External Relations Administrator: Susan Doerr (612/627-1967; e-mail: doer0012)
  Rights and Permissions: Jeffery Moen (612/627-1978; e-mail: moenx017)
Acquisitions Editorial: Richard Morrison, Executive Editor (literary and cultural studies, art and visual studies, anthropology) (612/627-1974; e-mail: morri094)
  Senior Editor: Todd Orjala (regional) (612/627-1973; e-mail: t-orja)
  Editors: Pieter Martin (architecture, political science, urban studies) (612/627-1976; e-mail: marti190); Jason Weidemann (cinema, media, geography, sociology) (612/627-1975; e-mail: weide007)
Managing Editor: Laura Westlund (612/627-1985; e-mail: westl003)
Design and Production: Daniel Ochsner, Manager (612/627-1981; e-mail: ochsn013)
Marketing: Emily Hamilton, Manager (612/627-1936; e-mail: eph)
  Direct Response and Scholarly Promotions: Stacy Zellmann (612/627-1934; e-mail: zellm003)
  Trade Advertising: Emily Hamilton (612/627-1936; e-mail: eph)
  Publicist: Heather Skinner (612/627-1932; e-mail: skinn077)
Sales: Bo Sherman, Sales Director (612/627-1931; e-mail: sherm184)
  Exhibits and Sales Assistant: Anne Klingbeil (612/627-1938; e-mail: klin0207)

Journals: Susan Doerr, Manager (612/627-1967; e-mail: doer0012)
Business: TBA, Chief Financial Officer (612/627-1941)
Computer Operations: Robin Moir, IT Manager (612/627-1944; e-mail: moirx001)

Full Member

Established: 1925	Admitted to AAUP: 1937
Title output 2006: 94	Title output 2007: 102
Titles currently in print: 1,373	Journals published: 5

Editorial Program

Literary and cultural studies; social and political theory; cinema and media studies; art and visual studies; digital culture; feminist studies; gay and lesbian studies; anthropology; architecture; geography; international relations; Native American studies; personality assessment, clinical psychology and psychiatry; philosophy; and Upper Midwest studies.

Journals: (* available online) *Buildings & Landscapes** (formerly called Perspectives in Vernacular Architecture); Cultural Critique*; Future Anterior*; The Moving Image*; Wicazo Sa Review**

Special series, joint imprints, and/or copublishing programs: Borderlines; Contradictions of Modernity; Critical American Studies; Cultural Studies of the Americas; Electronic Mediations; Fesler-Lampert Minnesota Heritage Book Series; Globalization and Community; Indigenous Americas; Minnesota Studies in the Philosophy of Science; MMPI-2 Monographs; MMPI-A Monographs; Posthumanities; Public Worlds; Social Movements, Protest, and Contention; Theory and History of Literature; Visible Evidence

University Press of Mississippi

3825 Ridgewood Road
Jackson, MS 39211-6492

Phone: (601) 432-6205
Fax: (601) 432-6217
E-mail: press@ihl.state.ms.us
Indiv: (user I.D)@ihl.state.ms.us
Web site: www.upress.state.ms.us

Warehouse Address:
Maple -Vail Book Mfg. Group
Lebanon Distribution Center
704 Legionaire Drive
Fredericksburg, PA 17026

Orders:
(800) 737-7788; (601) 432-6205

Canadian Representative:
Scholarly Book Services

UK Representative:
Roundhouse Publishing

Staff

Director: Seetha Srinivasan (601/432-6275; e-mail: ssrinivasan)
   Administrative Assistant/Rights and Permissions: Cynthia Foster (601/432-6205;
   e-mail: cfoster)
   Development Assistant: Rosie Swanson (601/432-6246; e-mail: bookfriends)
Acquisitions Editorial: Craig Gill, Assistant Director / Editor-in-Chief (601/432-6371;
   e-mail: cgill)
   Editor: Walter Biggins (601/432-6102; e-mail: wbiggins)

Manuscript Editorial: Anne Stascavage, Managing Editor (601/432-6249; e-mail: astascavage)
  Editorial Assistant: Valerie Jones (601/432-6206; e-mail: vjones)
Design and Production: John A. Langston, Assistant Director / Art Director (601/432-6554; e-mail: jlangston)
  Assistant Production Manager / Designer / Electronic Projects Manager: Todd Lape (601/432-6274; e-mail: tlape)
  Senior Production Editor: Shane Gong (601/432-6795; e-mail: sgong)
  Designer: Pete Halverson (601/432-6274; e-mail: phalverson)
Marketing and Sales: Steve Yates, Assistant Director / Marketing Director (601/432-6695; e-mail: syates)
  Assistant Marketing Manager / Direct Mail Manager: Ginger Tucker (601/432-6424; e-mail: gtucker)
  Advertising and Marketing Services Manager: Kathy Burgess (601/432-6105; e-mail: kburgess)
  Publicist: Clint Kimberling (601/432-6459; e-mail: ckimberling)
  Marketing Assistant: Emily Hubbard (601/432-6206; e-mail: ehubbard)
Business: Isabel Metz, Assistant Director / Business Manager (601/432-6551; e-mail: imetz)
  Customer Service and Order Supervisor: Sandy Alexander (601/432-6272; e-mail: salexander)

Full Member

Established: 1970

Title output 2006: 81

Titles currently in print: 965

Admitted to AAUP: 1976

Title output 2007: 96

Editorial Program

Scholarly and trade titles in African American studies, American studies, literature, history, and culture; art and architecture; ethnic studies; folklife; health; music; natural sciences; photography; popular culture; serious nonfiction of general interest; Southern studies; women's studies; other liberal arts.

Special series: American Made Music; Chancellor Porter L. Fortune Symposium in Southern History; Conversations with Comic Artists; Conversations with Filmmakers; Faulkner and Yoknapatawpha; Great Comic Artists; Hollywood Legends; Literary Conversations; Margaret Walker Alexander Series in African American Studies; Southern Icons; Studies in Popular Culture; Understanding Health and Sickness; Willie Morris Books in Memoir and Biography

University of Missouri Press

2910 LeMone Boulevard
Columbia, MO 65201-8227

Phone: (573) 882-7641
Fax: (573) 884-4498
Indiv: (user I.D.)@umsystem.edu
Web site: press.umsystem.edu

Orders:
Phone: (800) 828-1894
E-mail: orders@umsystem.edu

UK Representative:
Eurospan

Canadian Representative:
Scholarly Book Service

Staff

Director: Beverly Jarrett (e-mail: jarrettb)
  Associate Director: Linda Frech (e-mail: frechl)
  Executive Staff Assistant: Maria Oropallo (e-mail: oropallom)
  Editorial Assistant: Lori Hall Jones (e-mail: halljonesl)
Acquisitions Editorial: Beverly Jarrett, Editor-in-Chief
  Acquisitions Editors: Clair Willcox (e-mail: willcoxc); Gary Kass (e-mail: kassg)
Manuscript Editorial: Jane Lago, Managing Editor (e-mail: lagoj)
  Manuscript Editors: John Brenner (e-mail: brennerj); Julie Schroeder (e-mail: schroederjm); Sara Davis (e-mail: davissd)
Design and Production: Dwight Browne, Assistant Director and Production Manager (e-mail: browned)
  Assistant Production Manager: Nikki Waltz (e-mail: waltzn)
  Senior Designers: Kristie Lee (e-mail: leek); Jenny Cropp (e-mail: croppj)
Marketing: Karen Renner, Marketing Manager (e-mail: rennerk)
  Publicity / Exhibits Manager: Beth Chandler (e-mail: chandlerb)
  Advertising, Exhibits, and Direct Mail Manager: Eve Kidd Crawford (e-mail: kidde)
  Marketing Designer: Aaron Leuders (e-mail: leudersa)
  Publicity and Sales Assistant: Jennifer Gravley (e-mail: gravleyj)
Business: Linda Frech, Associate Director and Chief Financial Officer (e-mail: frechl)
  Business Manager: Tracy Martinez (e-mail: martinezt)
  Order Fulfillment Supervisor: Debbie Guilford (e-mail: guilfordd)
  Order Entry Clerk: Lyn Smith (e-mail: smithls)
  Warehouse Clerk: Vicky Ridgeway

Full Member

Established: 1958
Title output 2006: 61
Title currently in print: 748

Admitted to AAUP: 1960
Title output 2007: 67

Editorial Program

American and European history, including intellectual history and biography; African American studies; women's studies; American and British literary criticism; journalism; political science, including foreign relations; political philosophy and ethics; regional studies of Missouri, the Midwest, and South Central United States; and creative non-fiction.

Special series: Afro-Romance Writers; Eric Voegelin Institute in Political Philosophy; Give 'Em Hell Harry; Mark Twain and His Circle; Missouri Biography; Missouri Heritage Readers; New Directions in the History of the Southern Economy; Shades of Blue and Gray; Southern Women; Sports and American Culture

Modern Language Association of America

26 Broadway, 3rd floor
New York, NY 10004-1789

Phone: (646) 576-5000
Fax: (646) 458-0030
E-mail: info@mla.org
Indiv: (firstinitial)(lastname)@mla.org
Web site: www.mla.org

Book Orders:
Phone: (646) 576-5161
Fax: (646) 576-5160
E-mail: bookorders@mla.org

Staff

Executive Director: Rosemary G. Feal (646/576-5102)
Director of Book Publications: David G. Nicholls (646/576-5040)
  Assistant Director of Book Publications: Sonia Kane (646/576-5043)
  Associate Acquisitions Editor: James E. Hatch (646/576-5044)
  Permissions and Contracts Manager: Marcia E. Henry (646/576-5042)
Manuscript Editorial (includes journals): Director of Publishing Operations and Managing Editor of MLA Publications: Judy Goulding (646/576-5015)
  Associate Managing Editor for Book Publications: Elizabeth Holland (646/576-5020)
Production Director and Supervisor of Electronic Production Services: Judith Altreuter (646/576-5010)
Marketing and Sales Director: Kathleen Hansen (646/576-5018)
Member and Customer Services Manager: Leonard J. Moreton (646/576-5146)
Information Technology Center Manager: Kinglen Wang (646/576-5200)

Associate Member

Established: 1883
Title output 2006: 16
Titles currently in print: 294

Admitted to AAUP: 1992
Title output 2007: 15
Journals published: 4

Editorial Program

Scholarly, pedagogical, and professional books on language and literature.
Journals: *ADE* and *ADFL Bulletins*; *MLA International Bibliography*; *MLA Newsletter*; *PMLA*; *Profession*
Book series: Approaches to Teaching World Literature; New Variorum Edition of Shakespeare; Options for Teaching; Teaching Languages, Literatures, and Cultures; Text and Translations; World Literatures Reimagined

The National Academies Press

500 Fifth Street, N.W.
Washington, DC 20001

Bookstore phone: (202) 334-2612
Fax: (202) 334-2793
E-mail: (user I.D.)@nas.edu
Web site: www.nap.edu

Orders (US and Canada):
Phone: (800) 624-6242; (202) 334-3313
Fax: (202) 334-2451
E-mail: zjones@nas.edu

UK Distributor:
Marston Book Services

Staff

Executive Director: Barbara Kline Pope (202/334-3328; e-mail: bkline)
  Executive Assistant to the Director: Olive Schwarzschild (202/334-3038; e-mail: oschwarz)
  Director of Operations: Sandy Adams (202/334-3157; e-mail: sadams)
Executive Editor: Stephen M. Mautner (202/334-3336; e-mail: smautner)
Production Manager: Dorothy Lewis (202/334-2409; e-mail: dlewis)
Director, Composition, Graphics and Design: Jim Gormley (202/334-3325; e-mail: jgormley)
Director of Outreach and Marketing: Ann Merchant (202/334-3117; e-mail: amerchan)
  Sales and Marketing Manager: Virginia Bryant (202/334-3037; e-mail: vbryant)
  Sales Representatives: Natalie Jones (London) (2082 924400; e-mail: nj@njonesbooks.co.uk); David Smith (South East & East Anglia) (1279-437979; e-mail: djsmith@aptresource.free-online.co.uk); Barbara Martin (South West, West Midlands & Buckinghamshire) (1908 660560; e-mail: representation@barbaramartin.plus.com)
Permissions Editor: Luci Nielsen (202/334-3180; e-mail: lnielsen)
Business Manager: Rachel Levy (202/334-3329; e-mail: rlevy)
  Customer Service: Zina Jones (202/334-3116; e-mail: zjones)
  Warehouse: Tim Murphy (202/334-2625; e-mail: tmurphy)
Director of Strategic Web Communications: Michael Jensen (202/334-2403; e-mail: mjensen)
  Director of Digital Operations and Internet Technologies: Alphonse MacDonald (202/334 3625; e-mail: amacdonald)

Associate Member

Established: 1864
Title output 2006: 186
Titles currently in print: 3,014

Admitted to AAUP: 1988
Title output 2007: 200

Editorial Program

Primarily professional-level, policy-oriented titles in agricultural sciences; behavioral and social sciences; biology; chemistry; computer sciences; earth sciences; economics; education; energy; engineering; environmental issues; industry; international issues; materials science; medicine; natural resources; nutrition; physical sciences; public policy issues; statistics; transportation; and urban and rural development.

National Gallery of Art

Street Address:
Sixth Street and Constitution Avenue NW
Washington, DC

Mailing Address:
2000B South Club Drive
Landover, MD 20785

Publishing Office:
Phone: (202) 842-6200
Fax: (202) 408-8530
E-mail: (user I.D.)@nga.gov
Web site: www.nga.gov

Customer Service / Order Fulfillment:
Phone: (202) 842-6465

Staff

Deputy Director: Alan Shestack
Editor-in-Chief: Judy Metro (202/842-6205; e-mail: j-metro)
Production Manager and Deputy Publisher: Chris Vogel (202/842-6209; e-mail: c-vogel)
Chief of Web and New Media: Joanna Champagne (202/842-6207; e-mail: j-champagne)
Design Manager: Wendy Schleicher (202/789-4601; e-mail: w-schleicher)
Senior Editor and Manager of Systematic Catalogues: Karen Sagstetter (202/842-6208;
   e-mail: k-sagstetter)
Managing Editor of CASVA Publications: Cynthia Ware (202/842-6204; e-mail: c-ware)
Senior Editors: Tam Bryfogle (202/842-6498; e-mail: t-bryfogle); Julie Warnement
   (202/842-6136; e-mail: j-warnement)
   Associate Senior Editor: Ulrike Mills (202/842-6613; e-mail: u-mills)
Permissions Coordinator: Sara Sanders-Buell (202/842-6719; e-mail: s-sanders-buell)
Budget Coordinator: Josseline de Saint Just (202/842-6452; e-mail: j-desaintjust)
Production Assistant and Designer: Rio DeNaro (202/842-6697; e-mail: r-denaro)
Production Editor: Mariah Shay (202/842-6758; e-mail: m-shay)
   Editorial Assistants: Magda Nakassis (202/842-6203; e-mail: m-nakassis); Amanda Sparrow
   (202/842-6032; e-mail: a-sparrow)
   Staff and Editorial Assistant: Jennifer Bates (202/842-6200; e-mail: j-bates)
Web Site Team
   Manager: John Gordy (202/842-6872; e-mail: j-gordy)
   Designers: Guillermo Saenz (202/789-4987; e-mail: g-saenz); Suzanne Sarraf (202/842-
   6841; e-mail: s-sarraf)
   Production Assistant: Carlos Gomez (202/842-6423; e-mail: c-gomez)

Associate Member

Established: 1941
Title output 2006: 6
Titles currently in print: 112

Admitted to AAUP: 1992
Title output 2007: 10

Editorial Program

The National Gallery publishes exhibition catalogues on all subjects and permanent collection catalogues (including Western art of the early Renaissance through the contemporary
era); a symposium series; Studies in the History of Art, in conjunction with the Center for
Advanced Study in the Visual Arts; educational online programs and catalogues; exhibition
brochures and wall texts; online features for permanent collection and special exhibitions;
scholarly and popular publications based on objects in the museum's collections; scholarly

publications on conservation; educational materials and guides for use by the public and by teachers and schools; and the calendar of events, film and music programs, bulletins, and all Gallery ephemera. Unsolicited manuscripts are not invited at this time.

Naval Institute Press

291 Wood Road
Annapolis MD 21402-5034

Orders:
Phone: (800) 233-8764

Phone: (410) 268-6110
Fax: (410) 295-1084/5
E-mail: (firstinitial)(lastname)@usni.org
Web site: www.usni.org

Staff
Director: Richard A. Russell (410/295-1031)
  Business Manager: Prospero Hernandez (410/295-1046)
  Editorial Production Assistant: Carol Parkinson (410/295-1030)
Senior Acquisitions Editor: Thomas J. Cutler (410/295-1038)
  Subsidiary Rights & Acquisitions / Imports: Susan Todd Brook (410/295-1037)
  Acquisitions Editor: Laura D. Johnston (410/295-1080)
  Assistant Editor: Elizabeth Bauman (410/295-1039)
Production Manager / Creative Director: Christine Onrubia (410/295-1040)
  Editorial Manager: Susan Corrado (410/295-1032)
  Production Editor: Marla Traweek (410/295-1020)
Director of Sales and Marketing: George Keating (410/295-1025)
  Publicist: Judy Heise (410/295-1028)
  Exhibits and Special Sales Manager: Brian Walker (410/295-1082)
Journals, U.S. Naval Institute:
  Proceedings, Editor-in-Chief: Robert Timberg (410/295-1078)
  Naval History, Editor-in-Chief: Richard Latture (410/295-1076)
Publisher, U.S. Naval Institute: William M. Miller (410/295-1068)
Chief Financial Officer, U.S. Naval Institute: Robert Johnson (410/295-1707)

Full Member
Established: 1899
Title output 2006: 73
Titles currently in print: 650

Admitted to AAUP: 1949
Title output 2007: 58
Journals published: 2

Editorial Program
Joint and general military subjects; military biography; naval history and literature; naval and military reference; oceanography; navigation; military law; naval science textbooks; sea power; shipbuilding; professional guides; nautical arts and lore; technical guides; fiction.
Journals: *Proceedings*; *Naval History*
Special series: Bluejacket Books (paperback series); Classics of Naval Literature; Classics of Sea Power; Fundamentals of Naval Science; Library of Naval Biography; Naval Institute Special Warfare; Blue and Gold Professional Library

University of Nebraska Press

1111 Lincoln Mall
Lincoln, NE 68588-0630

Phone: (402) 472-3581
Fax: (402) 472-0308 (Editorial)
E-mail: (user I.D.)@unl.edu
Web site: www.nebraskapress.unl.edu; bisonbooks.com

Orders:
Phone: (402) 472-3581; (800) 755-1105
Fax: (402) 472-6214; (800) 526-2617

UK Distributor:
Combined Academic Publishers

Staff

Director: TBA

Assistant Director for Business / CFO: Tera Beermann (402/472-0011; e-mail: tbeermann2)

Rights and Permissions: Elaine Maruhn (402/472-7702; e-mail: emaruhn1)

Acquisitions Editorial: Ladette Randolph, Associate Director & Humanities Editor (402/472-2861; e-mail: lrandolph1)

Editor-in-Chief and History Editor: Heather Lundine (402/472-0645; e-mail: hlundine2)

Sports Editor: Rob Taylor (402/472-0325; e-mail: rtaylor6)

Bison Books Manager: Tom Swanson (402/472-5945; e-mail: tswanson3)

Manuscript Editorial:

Project Editors: Joeth Zucco (402/472-0199; e-mail: jzucco2); Ann Baker (402/472-0095; e-mail: abaker2); Sara Springsteen (402/472-4008; e-mail: sspringsteen1)

Design and Production: Alison Rold, Production Manager (402/472-7706; e-mail: arold1)

Assistant Production Manager: Carolyn Einspahr (402/472-7704; e-mail: ceinspahr1)

Designers: Andrea Shahan (402/472-7718; e-mail: ashahan1); Raymond Boeche (402/472-0318; e-mail: rboeche1); Roger Buchholz (402/472-7713; e-mail: rbuchholz1)

Marketing and Sales: Margie Rine, Marketing Manager (402/472-7946; e-mail: mrine3)

Sales Coordinator: Rob Buchanan (402/472-0160; e-mail: rbuchanan1)

Publicity Coordinator: Kate Salem (402/472-5938; e-mail: ksalem2)

Direct Mail Manager: Tish Fobben (402/472-4627; e-mail: pfobben2)

Events, Exhibits & Awards Coordinator: Wendi Foster (402/472-2759; e-mail: wfoster3)

Advertising & Design Coordinator: Kim Rutledge (402/472-5514; e-mail: krutledge2)

Blog Coordinator: DeMisty Bellinger (402/472-7710; e-mail: dbelling@unlnotes.unl.edu)

E-Commerce Coordinator: Erica Corwin (402/472-9313; e-mail: ecorwin1)

Accelerated Publishing and Management: Manjit Kaur, Manager (402/472-7703; e-mail: mkaur2)

Project Supervisor: Melissa Slocum (402/472-2292; e-mail: mslocum)

Marketing and Fulfillment Manager: Joyce Gettman (402/472-8330; e-mail: jgettman2)

Coordinator: Stacia Fleegal (402/472-8536; e-mail: sfleegal2)

Desktop Compositor: Shirley Thornton (402/472-5028; e-mail: sthorton3)

Business Services: Debra Turner, Assistant Director for Operations (402/472-5944; e-mail: dturner1)

Senior Accountant: Deborah Kohl (402/472-9202; e-mail: dkohl2)

Customer Service: Bob Widhalm, Supervisor (402/472-5947; e-mail: rwidhalm1)
Shipping & Warehouse: Fred Urdiales, Supervisor (402/472-6128; e-mail: furdiales1)
Technology: Jana Faust, Electronic Projects Manager (402/472-0171; e-mail: jfaust2)

Full Member

Established: 1941   Admitted to AAUP: Unknown
Title output 2006: 163   Title output 2007: 168
Titles currently in print: 2,184   Journals published: 12
                                          Journals distributed: 1

Editorial Program

African American studies; American literature; American studies; the American West; anthropology and ethnology; creative nonfiction; environmental studies; history; the Great Plains; Jewish studies and Judaica; Latin American studies; military history; Native Americans and First Nations; natural history; Nebraskiana; philosophy and religion; photography; science fiction; sports history; translations; women's studies. Submissions are not invited in original poetry or fiction.

The Press distributes for the Buros Institute of Mental Measurement, Dalkey Archive Press, Gordian Knot Books, the Kentucky Quilt Project, Lewis and Clark College, the Society for American Baseball Research, and Whale and Star Press.

Journals: *American Indian Quarterly; Cather Studies; Collaborative Anthropologies; French Forum; Frontiers: A Journal of Women's Studies; Histories of Anthropology; Journal of Sports Media; Legacy: A Journal of American Women Writers; NINE: A Journal of Baseball History & Culture; Nineteenth-Century French Studies; River Teeth: A Journal of Nonfiction Narrative; Studies in American Indian Literatures; Studies in Jewish Civilization; symploke: A Journal for the Intermingling of Literary, Cultural, and Theoretical Scholarship; Women and Music: A Journal of Gender and Culture; Women in German Yearbook*

Imprints: Bison Books

Book series: American Lives; American Indian Lives; At Table; Beyond Armageddon; Bison Frontiers of Imagination; Cather Studies; Complete Letters of Henry James; Critical Studies in the History of Anthropology; Engendering Latin America; European Women Writers; Extraordinary Worlds; France Overseas; French Modernist Library; Frontiers of Narrative; Great Campaigns of the Civil War; Histories of Scandinavian Literature; History of the American West; Indians of the Southeast; Indigenous Education; Iroquoians and Their World; Jerry Malloy Book Prize; Journals of the Lewis and Clark Expedition; Key Issues of the Civil War Era; Latin American Women Writers; Law in the American West; North American Indian Prose Award; Our Sustainable Future; Politics and Governments of the American States; Post-Western Horizons; Sources of American Indian Oral Literature; Stages; Studies in Jewish Civilization (for Creighton University Press); Studies in the Anthropology of North American Indians; Studies in the Native Languages of the Americas; Studies in War, Society, and the Military; Texts and Contexts; This Hallowed Ground: Guides to Civil War Battlefields; Willa Cather Scholarly Edition; Women in German Yearbook; Women in the West

University of Nevada Press

Morrill Hall, Mail Stop 0166
Reno, NV 89557-0166

Phone: (775) 784-6573
Fax: (775) 784-6200
E-mail: (user I.D.)@unpress.nevada.edu
Web site: www.unpress.nevada.edu

Orders:
Phone: (877) NVBOOKS

Warehouse Address:
5625 Fox Avenue, Rm. 120
Reno, NV 89506

Canadian Representative:
Scholarly Book Services

UK Representative:
Eurospan

Staff

Director: Joanne O'Hare (775/682-7389; e-mail: johare)
Acquisitions Editors: Charlotte Dihoff (775/682-7390; e-mail: cdihoff); Margaret F. Dalrymple (775/682-7393; e-mail: mdalrymple); Joanne O'Hare
Managing Editor: Sara Vélez Mallea (775/682-7386; e-mail: svelez-mallea)
Design & Production Manager: Kathleen Szawiola (775/682-7395; e-mail: kszawiola)
Marketing & Sales Manager: Victoria Davies (775/682-7391; e-mail: vdavies)
    Marketing Assistant: Monica Robertson (775/682-7386; e-mail: mrobertson)
Business Manager: Sheryl Laguna (775/682-7387; e-mail: slaguna)
    Customer Service/Office Manager: Charlotte Eberhard Heatherly (775/682-7385; e-mail: cheatherly)
    Warehouse Manager: Michael Jackson (775/682-8564; e-mail: mjackson)

Full Member

Established: 1961
Title output 2006: 19
Titles currently in print: 323

Admitted to AAUP: 1982
Title output 2007: 21

Editorial Program

Scholarly books and serious fiction and nonfiction, with special interests in the history, literature, biography, anthropology, and natural history of Nevada, the Great Basin, and the West, and books dealing with the Basque peoples of Europe and the Americas. Additional interests include Native American studies; geography, natural resources, ethnic studies, and gambling.

The Press distributes titles from Companion Press and from the University of Nevada Reno's Center for Basque Studies.

Special series: Basque Studies; Gambling Studies; Great Basin Natural History; The Urban West; Western Literature; Wilbur S. Shepperson Series in Nevada History

University Press of New England

1 Court Street, Suite 250
Lebanon, NH 03766-1358

Phone: (603) 448-1533
Fax: (603) 448-7006
E-mail: university.press@dartmouth.edu
Indiv: (firstname.lastname)@dartmouth.edu
Web site: www.upne.com

Canadian Representative:
University of British Columbia Press /
Unipresses

Customer Service / Order Fulfillment:
Phone: (800) 421-1561

Warehouse:
UPNE Fulfillment Center
c/o Maple Press Lebanon
Distribution Centre
704 Legionaire Drive
Fredricksburg, PA 17026
Phone: (603) 643-5585
Fax: (603) 643-1540

European Representative:
Eurospan

Staff

Director: Michael Burton (603/448-1533, ext. 241)
   Assistant to the Director, Permissions Manager: Sarah N. Slater (603/448-1533, ext. 201)
   Associate Director, Operations: Thomas Johnson (603/643-5585, ext. 202)
   Systems Administrator: David Bellows (603/643-5585, ext. 101)
Editor-in-Chief: Phyllis Deutsch (603/448-1533, ext. 222)
   Senior Acquisitions Editor: Ellen Wicklum (603/448-1533, ext. 225)
   Acquisitions Editor: Richard Pult (603/448-1533, ext. 226)
   Editorial Assistant: Lori Miller (603/448-1533, ext. 221)
Manuscript Editorial: Mary Crittendon, Managing Editor (603/448-1533, ext. 243)
   Production Editors: Ann Brash (603/448-1533, ext. 244); Elizabeth Rawitsch (603/448-1533, ext. 235)
Design and Production: Michael Burton, Associate Director and Director of Design and Production (603/448-1533, ext. 241)
   Designer: Katherine B. Kimball (603/448-1533, ext. 246)
   Production Coordinator: Douglas Tifft (603/448-1533, ext. 245)
Marketing: Sarah L. Welsch, Assistant Director for Marketing & Sales (603/643-5585, ext. 203, or 603/448-1533, ext. 234)
   Sales and Trade Exhibits Manager: Sherri Strickland (603/643-5585, ext. 106)
   Sales and Trade Exhibits Assistant: Deborah Forward (603/643-5585, ext. 105)
   Publicity and Subsidiary Rights Manager: Barbara Briggs (603/448-1533, ext. 233)
   Direct Marketing, Design and Advertising Associate: Christine Hauck (603/448-1533, ext. 232)
   Publicity Assistant: Kristina Garcia (603/448-1533, ext. 231)
   Marketing Assistant and Academic Exhibits Coordinator: TBA (603/448-1533, ext. 231)
Business: Thomas Johnson, Associate Director, Operations (603/643-5585, ext. 202)
   Accounting Supervisor: Donna Youngman (603/643-5585, ext. 201)
   Accounting Associate: Timothy Semple (603/643-5585, ext. 102)
   Customer Service Representatives: Barbara Benson (603/643-5585, ext. 103); Barbara McBeth (603/643-5585, ext. 104)

Full Member

Established: 1970
Title output 2006: 82
Titles currently in print: 900

Admitted to AAUP: 1975
Title output 2007: 79

Publishes books under the consortium member imprints of Brandeis University Press, Dartmouth College Press, University of New Hampshire Press, Tufts University Press, University of Vermont Press, Northeastern University Press, and University Press of New England.

<u>Editorial Program</u>
General trade, scholarly, instructional, and reference works for scholars, teachers, students, and the public. The Press concentrates in American studies, literature, history, religion, and cultural studies; art, architecture, photography, and material culture; ethics; ethnic studies (including African American, Jewish, Native American, and Shaker studies); interdisciplinary studies; folklore, music, and popular culture; languages; nature and the environment; natural sciences; New England studies; social issues/social sciences; and Trans-Atlantic and cross-cultural studies. Special series feature such topics as civil society, modernism, and visual culture.

The Press, through UPNE Distribution Services handles book order processing and distribution for: Wesleyan University Press; New England College Press, Fence Books; Four Way Books; Sheep Meadow Press; Saturnalia Books; CavanKerry Press; and Harvest Hill Books.
Special series: Becoming Modern: New Nineteenth-Century Studies; Brandeis Series in American Jewish History, Culture and Life; HBI Series on Jewish Women; Civil Society: Historical and Contemporary Perspectives; Collected Writings of Rousseau; Hardscrabble Books: Fiction of New England; Interfaces: Studies in Visual Culture; Menahem Stern Jerusalem Lectures: Brandeis University/Historical Society of Israel; The Northeastern Library of Black Literature; The Northeastern Series on Gender, Crime, and Law; Reencounters with Colonialism: New Perspectives on the Americas; Revisiting New England: The New Regionalism; the Northeastern Series on Democratization and Political Development, The Samuel French Morse Poetry Prize; Tauber Institute for the Study of European Jewry Series; Understanding Science and Technology; Vermont Folklife Center's Children's Book Series

---

University of New Mexico Press

MSCO4 2820
1312 Basehart Rd. SE.
Albuquerque, NM 87106-4363

Phone: (505) 277-2346
Fax: (505) 272-7141
E-mail: unmpress@unm.edu
Web site: www.unmpress.com

<u>Customer Service and Warehouse:</u>
1312 Basehart Rd. SE
Albuquerque, NM 87106-4363
Phone: (505) 272-7777; (800) 249-7737
Fax: (505) 272-7778
(800) 622-8667 (orders)

<u>UK / European Representative:</u>
Eurospan

<u>Canadian Representative:</u>
CODASAT

Staff
Director: Luther Wilson (e-mail: lwilson@unm.edu)
  Assistant to the Director: Kristen Ferris (505/272-7186; e-mail: kferris@upress.unm.edu)

Rights and Permissions: Judy Kepler (e-mail: jkepler@upress.unm.edu)
Editor-in-Chief: Clark Whitehorn (e-mail: clarkw@upress.unm.edu)
  Acquisitions Editors: Luther Wilson (e-mail: lwilson); Lisa Pacheco
  (e-mail: lisap@upress.unm.edu)
Managing Editor: Maya Allen-Gallegos (505/272-7014; e-mail: mayag@upress.unm.edu)
Senior Graphic Designers: Melissa Tandysh (505/272-7192;
  e-mail: melissat@unm.edu);
  Mina Yamashita (505/272-7196; e-mail: minay@upress.unm.edu);
  Kathy Sparkes (505/272-7189; e-mail: kathys@upress.unm.edu);
  Damien Shay (505/272-7188; e-mail: damiens@upress.unm.edu)
Sales and Marketing: Glenda Madden, Manager (505/272-7178;
  e-mail: gmadden@unm.edu)
  Advertising and Exhibits: Christina Frain (505/272-7183; e-mail: cfrain@upress.unm.edu)
  Direct Mail and Website: Nancy Woodard (505/272-7195; e-mail: nwoodard@unm.edu)
  Publicist: Amanda Sutton (505/272-7190; e-mail: amanda@upress unm.edu)
  Events Coordinator: Katherine MacGilvray (505/272-7177;
   e-mail: katm@upress.unm.edu)
  Sales Representatives: Kay Marcotte (505/272-7181; e-mail: kaym@upress.unm.edu);
  Sheri Hozier (e-mail: sherih@unm.edu)
Associate Director for Operations: Richard Schuetz (505/272-7187;
  e-mail: rschuetz@upress.unm.edu)
  Manager, Business Services: Ernest Earick (e-mail: earick@unm.edu)
  Accounting: Lyudmila Markova (e-mail: milam@unm.edu); Irina Kumyzbaeva (e-mail:
  Irinak@upress.unm.edu)
  Customer Service and Credit Manager: Stewart Marshall (e-mail: smarshal@unm.edu)
  Customer Service Assistants: Susan Hoffman; Jim Langley; Joyce Perz (e-mail;
  joycep@upress.unm.edu)
  Warehouse Manager: Susan Coatney (505/272-7770; e-mail: susanc@upress.unm.edu)
Technical Support: Kevin Lowrie (e-mail: klowrie@upress.unm.edu)

Full Member

Established: 1929   Admitted to AAUP: 1937
Title output 2006: 96   Title output 2007: 98
Titles currently in print: 975

Editorial Program

Scholarly books, fiction, poetry, and nonfiction, with special interests in social and cultural anthropology; ethnic studies; Southwest and Mesoamerican archaeology; Religions of the Americas; American frontier history; Western American literature; Latin American history; history of photography; art and photography; and books that deal with important aspects of Southwest or Rocky Mountain states, including natural history and land grant studies.

Special series, joint imprints and/or copublishing programs: Calvin P. Horn Lectures in Western History and Culture; Dialogos Series; Histories of the American Frontier; The Journals of Don Diego de Vargas; New American West; New Mexico Land Grant series; Pasó por Aquí Series on the Nuevomexicano Literary Heritage; School of American Research Southwest Indian Arts; Tamarind Papers; University of Arizona Southwest Center, Religions of the Americas

New York University Press

838 Broadway, 3rd Floor
New York, NY 10003-4812

Phone: (212) 998-2575
Fax: (212) 995-3833
E-mail: orders@nyupress.edu
Indiv: (firstname.lastname)@nyu.edu
Web site: www.nyupress.org

UK / European Representative:
Eurospan

Orders and Customer Service:
Phone: (800) 996-6987
Fax: (212) 995-4798

Warehouse:
The Maple Press
Lebanon Distribution Center
704 Legionaire Drive
Fredricksburg, PA 17026

Staff

Director: Steve Maikowski (212/998-2573)
  Assistant to the Director and Subsidiary Rights Coordinator: Michael B. Richards
  (212/998-2571)
Acquisitions Editorial: Eric Zinner, Editor-in-Chief (cultural and literary studies, American
  studies, twentieth-century American history) (212/998-2544)
  Executive Editor: Ilene Kalish (sociology, criminology, politics) (212/998-2556)
  Senior Editor: Deborah Gershenowitz (American history, military history, law)
  (212/998-2570)
  Editor: Jennifer Hammer (religion, Jewish studies, psychology, anthropology)
  (212/998-2491)
  Assistant Editor: Emily Park (film and media studies) (212/998-2426)
  Editorial Assistant: Gabrielle Begue (212/992-9995)
Program Officer for Digital Scholarly Publishing: Monica McCormick
Manuscript Editorial / Design and Production: Despina P. Gimbel, Managing Editor
  (212/998-2572)
  Production Manager: Charles Hames (212/998-2628)
  Production Coordinator: Tom Helleberg (212/998-2578)
  Production Assistant / Permissions Coordinator: TBA (212/992-9998)
Marketing and Sales: Fredric Nachbaur, Marketing and Sales Director (212/998-2588)
  Direct Mail Coordinator: Brandon Kelley (212/998-2558)
  Publicist: Betsy Steve (212/992-9991)
  Exhibits Coordinator / Sales Assistant: Stephanie O'Cain (212/998-2547)
  E-marketing and Sales Coordinator: Shilpi Suneja (212/998-2591)
Business: Carline Yup, Business and Operations Director (212/998-2569)
  Accounts Receivable Supervisor: Nadine Rached (212/992-9987)
  Sales and Print on Demand Coordinator: Jesse Henderson (212/998-2546)
Computer and Information Systems: Brett Hopp, Information Systems Manager
  (212/998-2536)

Full Member

Established: 1916
Title output 2006: 125
Titles currently in print: 1,850

Admitted to AAUP: 1937
Title output 2007: 127

Editorial Program

History; law; sociology; Asian American studies; African American studies; Latino/a studies, political science; criminology; psychology; gender studies; cultural and literary studies; media, film, and communications; urban studies; Jewish studies; anthropology; religion; reference; American business and finance; New York regional interest.

NYU Press is the exclusive North American distributor for Monthly Review Press and Fordham University Press.

Special series: Alternative Criminology; American History and Culture; Clay Sanskrit Library Series; Cultural Front; Culture, Labor, and History; Ex Machina: Law, Technology, and Society; The History of Disability; Intersections: Transdisciplinary Perspectives on Genders and Sexualities; Nation of Newcomers: Immigrant History as American History; New and Alternative Religions; New Perspectives on Crime, Deviance, and Law; Psychology of Law; Qualitative Studies in Psychology; Religion, Race, and Ethnicity; Qualitative Studies in Religion; Sexual Cultures

The University of North Carolina Press

116 South Boundary Street
Chapel Hill, NC 27514-3808

Phone: (919) 966-3561
Fax: (919) 966-3829
E-mail: uncpress@unc.edu
Indiv: (user I.D.)@unc.edu
Web site: www.uncpress.unc.edu

Warehouse:
Maple Press Company
Lebanon Distribution Center
704 Legionaire Drive
Fredericksburg, PA 17026

Orders:
Longleaf Services
Phone: (800) 848-6224
Fax: (800) 272-6817

UK / European Representative:
Eurospan

Canadian Representative:
Scholarly Book Services

Staff

Director: Kate Douglas Torrey (919/962-3748; e-mail: Kate_Torrey)
   Advancement Coordinator and Assistant to the Director: Beth Lassiter (919/962-0358; e-mail: Beth_Lassiter)
   Director of Development: Joanna Ruth Marsland (919/962-0924; e-mail: Joanna_Ruth_Marsland)
Acquisitions Editorial: David Perry, Assistant Director and Editor-in-Chief (regional trade, Civil War and military history) (919/962-0482; e-mail: David_Perry)
   Assistant to the Editor-in-Chief: Zachary Read (919/962-0536; e-mail: Zachary_Read)
   Assistant Director and Senior Editor: Charles Grench (history) (919/962-0481; e-mail: Charles_Grench)
   Senior Editors: Elaine Maisner (religious studies, Latin American studies, regional trade) (919/962-0810; e-mail: Elaine_Maisner); Sian Hunter (literary studies, American studies, social medicine, gender studies) (919/962-0486; e-mail: Sian_Hunter)

Editor: Mark Simpson-Vos (special projects, regional reference, Native American studies, electronic projects) (919/962-0535; e-mail: Mark_Simpson-Vos)
   Assistant Editor: Katy O'Brien (919/962-0538; e-mail: Katy_OBrien)
   Editorial Assistant: Nathan McCamic (919/962-0390; e-mail: Nathan_McCamic)
Manuscript Editorial: Ron Maner, Assistant Director and Managing Editor (919/962-0540; e-mail: Ron_Maner)
   Associate Managing Editor: Paula Wald (919/962-0544; e-mail: Paula_Wald)
   Assistant Managing Editor: Paul Betz (919/962-0530; e-mail: Paul_Betz)
   Manuscript Editors: Mary Caviness (919/962-0545; e-mail: Mary_Caviness); Stephanie Wenzel (919/962-0366; e-mail: Stephanie_Wenzel); Jay Mazzocchi (919/962-0546; e-mail: Jay_Mazzocchi)
   Assistant Editor: Ian Burton-Oakes (919/962-0549; e-mail: Ian_Burton-Oakes)
Design and Production: Heidi Perov, Design and Production Manager (919/962-0572; e-mail: Heidi_Perov)
   Design Director and Assistant Production Manager: Kim Bryant (919/962-0571; e-mail: Kim_Bryant)
   Reprints Controller: Jackie Johnson (919/962-0569; e-mail: Jackie_Johnson)
   Designer/Typographer: Eric Brooks (919/962-0575; e-mail: Eric_Brooks)
   Production Assistant: Michelle Coppedge (919/962-0577; e-mail: Michelle_Coppedge)
Marketing: Dino Battista, Assistant Director and Marketing Manager (919/962-0579; e-mail: Dino_Battista)
   Sales Director: Michael Donatelli (919/962-0475; e-mail: Michael_Donatelli)
   Director of Publicity: Gina Mahalek (919/962-0581; e-mail: Gina_Mahalek)
   Chief Copywriter and Catalog Coordinator: Ellen Bush (919/962-0583; e-mail: Ellen_Bush)
   Director of Advertising and Electronic Marketing: Christine Egan (919/962-0582; e-mail: Chris_Egan)
   Direct Marketing and Reprints Manager and Restocks Coordinator: Laura Gribbin (919/962-0585; e-mail: Laura_Gribbin)
   Exhibits Manager and Awards Coordinator: Ivis Bohlen (919/962-0594; e-mail: Ivis_Bohlen)
   Assistant Publicity Manager: Meagan Bonnell (919/962-0591; e-mail: Meagan_Bonnell)
   Sales Assistant: Luke Miller (919/962-1250; e-mail: Luke_Miller)
   Marketing Designer: Catherine Brutvan (919/962-0590; e-mail: Cat_Brutvan)
Journals: Suzi Waters, Journals Manager (919/962-4201; e-mail: Suzi_Waters)
Business: Robbie Dircks, Associate Director & CFO (919/962-1400; e-mail: Robbie_Dircks)
   Rights & Contracts Manager: Vicky Wells (919/962-0369; e-mail: Vicky_Wells)
   Accounting Manager: Roy Alexander (919/962-4203; e-mail: Roy_Alexander)
   Operations Manager for Longleaf Services: BJ Smith (919/962-1230; BJ_Smith)
   Customer Service Manager: Teresa Thomas (919/962-1231; e-mail: Teresa_Thomas)
   Credit Manager: Terry Miles (919/962-1263; e-mail: Terry_Miles)
   Office Manager: Alison Kieber (919/966-3561; e-mail: Alison_Kieber)
Information Systems: Tom Franklin, Information Technology Manager (919/962-4196); e-mail: Tom_Franklin)
   Electronic Projects Coordinator: Marjorie Fowler (919/962-0471; e-mail: Marjorie_Fowler)

Full Member

Established: 1922

Title output 2006: 100

Titles currently in print: 1,381

Admitted to AAUP: 1937

Title output 2007: 107

Journals published: 9

Editorial Program

American and European history; American literature; American studies; African American studies; Southern studies; religious studies; popular culture; legal history; classics; gender studies; Native American studies; maritime studies; urban studies; public policy; Latin American studies; business and economic history; social medicine; sports; regional trade; and North Caroliniana. Submissions are not invited in fiction, poetry, or drama.

The Press distributes titles published by the Thomas Jefferson Foundation.

Journals: *Appalachian Heritage, The Comparatist; Early American Literature; The High School Journal; Social Forces; Southern Cultures; Southern Literary Journal; Studies in Philology; Southeastern Geographer*

Special series: Bettie Allison Rand Lectures in Art History; Chapel Hill Books; Civil War America; Cultural Studies of the United States; Dental Laboratory Technology Manuals; Dental Assisting Manuals; Envisioning Cuba; The Fred W. Morrison Series in Southern Studies; Gender and American Culture; Islamic Civilization and Muslim Networks; The John Hope Franklin Series in African American History and Culture; Latin America in Translation/en Traducción/em Traducão; Luther H. Hodges Series in Business, Society, and the State; Military Campaigns of the Civil War; The New Cold War History; New Directions in Southern Studies; Richard Hampton Jenrette Series in Architecture and the Decorative Arts; The Steven and Janice Brose Lectures in the Civil War Era; Studies in Legal History; Studies in Rural Culture; Studies in Social Medicine; Studies in the History of Greece and Rome; Studies in the Romance Languages and Literatures; Thornton H. Brooks Series in American Law and Society

Joint imprints: Omohundro Institute of Early American History and Culture, sponsored by Colonial Williamsburg and the College of William and Mary

The University of North Texas Press

Street Address:

1820 Highland Street

Bain Hall 101

Denton, TX 76201

Mailing Address:

PO Box 311336

Denton, TX 76203

Phone: (940) 565-2142

Fax: (940) 565-4590

E-mail: (user I.D.)@unt.edu

Web site: www.unt.edu/untpress

Orders:

Phone: (800) 826-8911

UK Representative:

Eurospan

Staff

Director: Ron Chrisman (e-mail: rchrisman)
  Assistant to the Director: Mary Young (e-mail: myoung)
Managing Editor: Karen DeVinney (e-mail: kdevinney)
Marketing Manager: Paula Oates (e-mail: poates)

Full Member

Established: 1988
Title output 2006: 17
Titles currently in print: 317

Admitted to AAUP: 2003
Title output 2007: 15
Journals published: 1

Editorial Program

Humanities and social sciences, with special emphasis on Texas history and culture, military history, western history, criminal justice, folklore, multicultural topics, music, nature writing, natural and environmental history, culinary history, and women's studies. Submissions in poetry and fiction are invited only through the Vassar Miller and Katherine Anne Porter Prize competition.

Journal: *Theoria*

Special series: A. C. Greene; Al Filo: Mexican American Studies; Contemporary Issues and Debates; Evelyn Oppenheimer; Frances B. Vick; Great American Cooking; Katherine Anne Porter Prize in Short Fiction; North Texas Crime and Criminal Justice; North Texas Lives of Musicians; North Texas Military Biography and Memoir; Philosophy and the Environment; Practical Guide; Publications of the Texas Folklore Society; Southwestern Nature Writing Series; Temple Big Thicket; Texas Poets; Texas Writers; Vassar Miller Prize in Poetry; War and the Southwest; and Western Life

Northern Illinois University Press

2280 Bethany Road
DeKalb, IL 60115

Phone: (815) 753-1826
Fax: (815) 753-1845
E-mail: (user I.D.)@niu.edu
Web site: www.niupress.niu.edu

UK Distributor:
Eurospan

Customer Service:
Phone: (815) 753-1826

Order Fulfillment:
Phone: (815) 753-1075

Staff

Director: J. Alex Schwartz (815/753-1826; e-mail: aschwartz)
Acquisitions Editorial: Melody Herr (815/753-9907; e-mail: mherr)
Manuscript Editorial: Susan Bean, Managing Editor (815/753-9908; e-mail: sbean)
Design and Production Manager: Julia Fauci (815/753-9904; e-mail: jfauci)
Marketing and Sales: Linda Manning, Marketing Manager (815/753-9905;
  e-mail: lmanning2)
Business and Warehouse: Barbara Berg, Business Manager (815/753-1826; e-mail: bberg)
  Order Processing: Pat Yenerich (815/753-1075; e-mail: pyenerich)

Full Member

Established: 1964   Admitted to AAUP: 1972
Title output 2006: 20   Title output 2007: 15
Titles currently in print: 350

Editorial Program

US history; US Civil War; European history; Russian history and culture; politics and political theory; American literature and culture; history of religion; anthropology; transportation
history; urban studies; women's studies; studies on alcohol and substance abuse, regional
studies on Chicago and the Midwest.
Special series: Railroads in America; Russian Studies

Northwestern University Press

629 Noyes Street   Orders:
Evanston, IL 60208-4210   Northwestern University Press
                                                  Chicago Distribution Center
Phone: (847) 491-2046   11030 South Langley Avenue
Fax: (847) 491-8150   Chicago, IL 60628
E-mail: nupress@northwestern.edu   Phone: (800) 621-2736; (773) 568-1550
Indiv: (user I.D.)@northwestern.edu   Fax: (800) 621-8476; (773) 660-2235
Web site: www.nupress.northwestern.edu

UK Distributor: Canadian Distributor:
Eurospan   Scholarly Book Service

Staff

Director: Donna Shear (847/491-8111; e-mail: d-shear)
Senior Editor: Henry Carrigan (847/491-8112; e-mail: h-carrigan)
   Acquisitions Editor: Mike Levine (847/491-7384; e-mail: mike-levine)
   Assistant Acquisitions Editor: Mairead Case (847/467-1279; e-mail: mairead-case)
Managing Editor: Anne Gendler (847/491-3844; e-mail: a-gendler)
   Senior Project Editors: Serena Brommel (847/491-2458; e-mail: s-brommel); Jessica
   Paumier (847/467-7362; e-mail: j-paumier)
Art Director: Marianne Jankowski (847/467-5368; e-mail: ma-jankowski)
Production Manager: A. C. Racette (847/491-8113; e-mail: a-racette)
   Production Coordinator: Jason Stauter (847/467-3392; e-mail: j-stauter)
Sales and Subsidiary Rights Manager: Parneshia Jones (847/491-7420; e-mail: p-jones3)
   Publicity Manager: Sara Hoerdeman (847/491-5315; e-mail: s-hoerdeman)
   Marketing and Sales Coordinator: Nora Gorman (847/467-0319; e-mail: n-gorman)
   Sales Representatives: Blake Delodder (301/322-4509; e-mail: bdelodder@press.uchi-
   cago.edu); Gary Hart (323/663-3529; e-mail: ghart@press.uchicago.edu); Bailey Walsh
   (608/218-1669; e-mail: bwalsh@press.uchicago.edu); George Carroll (425/922.1045;
   e-mail: george@redsides.com); Henry Hubert (303/422-8640; e-mail: hjhubert@earthlink.
   net); Don Morrison (800/446-4095; 615/269-8977; e-mail: msgbooks@aol.com); Bill
   Verner (919/286-4839; e-mail: vermin@mindspring.com); Arthur Viders (813/886-4868;
   e-mail: aviders@tampabay.rr.com)

TriQuarterly Editor: Susan Firestone Hahn (847/491-8314)
  Associate Editor: Ian Morris (847/467-7351; e-mail: i-morris)
Business Manager: Kirstie Felland (847/491-8310; e-mail: kfelland)

Full Member

Established: 1959   Admitted to AAUP: 1988
Title output 2006: 57   Title output 2007: 50
Titles currently in print: 1,100   Journals published: 2

Editorial Program
The Press publishes in drama/performance studies; Chicago region; fiction; poetry; Latino fiction and biography; literary criticism; literature in translation; law; philosophy; Slavic studies.
Distributed Presses: FC2; Glas; Talonbooks; Tia Chucha Press
Imprints: Hydra Books; TriQuarterly Books; The Marlboro Press; Latino Voices
Journals: *TriQuarterly; Renaissance Drama*
Special series: Avant-Garde and Modernism Studies; European Classics; European Drama Classics; European Poetry Classics; Jewish Lives; Law-in-Context; Marlboro Travel; Medill School of Journalism's Visions of the American Press; the Northwestern-Newberry Edition of the Writings of Herman Melville; Rethinking Theory; Studies in Phenomenology and Existential Philosophy; Studies in Russian Literature and Theory; Topics in Historical Philosophy; Writings from an Unbound Europe

University of Notre Dame Press

310 Flanner Hall
Notre Dame, IN 46556

Phone: (574) 631-6346
Fax: (574) 631-8148
E-mail: nd.undpress.1@nd.edu
Indiv: (user I.D.)@nd.edu
Web site: www.undpress.nd.edu

UK / European Representative:
Eurospan

Orders:
University of Notre Dame Press
Chicago Distribution Center
11030 South Langley Avenue
Chicago, IL 60628
Phone: (800) 621-2736
Fax: (800) 621-8476

Staff
Director: Barbara Hanrahan (574/631-3265; e-mail: hanrahan.4)
Senior Acquisitions Editor: Charles Van Hof (574/631-4912; e-mail: cvanhof)
  Assistant Editor: Lowell Francis (574/631-4913; e-mail: francis.24)
  Secretary: Gina Bixler (574/631-6346; e-mail: bixler.1)
Manuscript Editorial: Rebecca DeBoer, Managing Editor (574/631-4908; e-mail: deboer.8)
  Manuscript Editor: Matthew Dowd (574/631-4914; e-mail: mdowd1)
  Assistant Editor: Katie Lehman (574/631-4911; e-mail: mlehman.2)
Design and Production: Wendy McMillen, Manager (574/631-4907; e-mail: mcmillen.3)
  Assistant Production Manager: Jennifer Driver (574/631-3266; e-mail: jdriver)
  Art Director and Web Administrator: Margaret Gloster (574/631-4906; e-mail: gloster.1)
Marketing: Kathryn Pitts, Manager (574/631-3267; e-mail: pitts.5)

Electronic Marketing Manager: Emily McKnight (574/631-4909; e-mail: mcknight.3)
Assistant Manager: Ann Bromley (574/631-4910; e-mail: bromley.1)
Exhibits Coordinator: Susan Roberts (574/631-4905; e-mail: srobert3)
Business: Diane Schaut, Manager (574/631-4904; e-mail: schaut.1)

Full Member
Established: 1949   Admitted to AAUP: 1959
Title output 2006: 54   Title output 2007: 56
Titles currently in print: 900

Editorial Program
Religion; theology; philosophy; ethics; political science; medieval and early modern studies;
classics; Catholic studies; business ethics; American history; European history; Latin American studies; religion and literature; Irish studies; history and philosophy of science; international relations; peace studies; patristics; political theory. Submissions are not invited in the
hard sciences, mathematics, psychology, or novel-length fiction.

Special series, joint imprints, and/or copublishing programs: African American Intel-
lectual Heritage; Andrés Montoya Poetry Prize; Christianity and Judaism in Antiquity; The
Collected Works of Jacques Maritain; Contemporary European Politics and Society; Conway
Lectures; Erasmus Institute Publications; Ernest Sandeen Prize in Poetry; Faith and Rea-
son; History, Languages, and Cultures of the Spanish and Portuguese Worlds; The Irish in
America; Kellogg Institute for International Studies; Latino Perspectives; The Medieval Book;
Publications in Medieval Studies; Notre Dame Studies in Ethics and Culture; Notre Dame
Studies In Medical Ethics; Notre Dame Texts in Medieval Culture; Poetics of Orality and
Literacy; Richard Sullivan Prize in Short Fiction; Studies in Spirituality and Theology; Trans-
Reformation Studies; Ward-Phillips Lectures in English Language and Literature; William
and Katherine Devers Series in Dante Studies; The Collected Works of Cardinal Newman

Ohio University Press

19 Circle Drive, The Ridges   Orders:
Athens, OH 45701-2979   Ohio University Press
                                          Chicago Distribution Center
Phone: (740) 593-1155   11030 South Langley Avenue
Fax: (740) 593-4536   Chicago, IL 60628
E-mail: (user I.D.)@ohio.edu   Phone: (800) 621-2736
Web site: www.ohio.edu/oupress   Fax: (800) 621-8476

UK / European Representative:
Eurospan

Staff
Director: David Sanders (740/593-1157; e-mail: dsanders1)
Senior Editor: Gillian Berchowitz (740/593-1159; e-mail: berchowi)
Managing Editor: Nancy Basmajian (740/593-1161; e-mail: basmajia)

Project Editors: John Morris (740/597-1592; e-mail: morrisj4);
   Rick Huard (740/597-1941; e-mail: huard)
Production Manager: Beth Pratt (740/593-1162; e-mail: prattb)
Marketing and Sales: Jean Cunningham, Marketing Manager (740/593-1160;
   e-mail: cunningh)
   Publicity Manager: Jeff Kallet (740/593-1158; e-mail: kallet)
   Marketing Associate: Carolyn King (740/597-2998; e-mail: kingc3)
Business: Bonnie Rand, Chief Financial Officer (740/593-1156; e-mail: rand)
   Assistant Business Manager: Kristi Goldsberry (740/593-2309; e-mail: goldsbek)
   Customer Service Manager: Judy Wilson (740/593-1154; e-mail: wilson1)

Full Member

Established: 1964   Admitted to AAUP: 1966
Title output 2006: 50   Title output 2007: 50
Titles currently in print: 875

Editorial Program

Special series, joint imprints, and/or copublishing programs: African Series; The Collected Letters of George Gissing; The Complete Works of Robert Browning; The Complete
Works of William Howard Taft; Eastern African Series; Gender and Ethnicity in Appalachia;
Global and Comparative Studies; Latin America Series; Law, Society, and Politics in the Midwest; Ohio Bicentennial; Perspectives on the History of Congress and Perspectives on the Art
and Architecture of the United States Capitol (for the US Capitol Historical Society); Polish
and Polish-American Studies Series; Research in International Studies; Series in Continental
Thought; Series in Ecology and History; Southeast Asia Series; Western African Series; White
Coat Pocket Guide

University of Oklahoma Press

2800 Venture Drive   Orders:
Norman, OK 73069   Phone: (800) 627-7377
                                            Fax: (405) 364-5798; (800) 735-0476
Phone: (405) 325-2000
Faxes: (405) 325-4000 (director/rights/acquisitions/marketing);
(405) 307-9048 (manuscript editing/production/finance)
E-mail: (user I.D.)@ou.edu
Web site: www.oupress.com

UK Representative: Canadian Representative:
Aldington Books   Hargreaves, Fuller & Co.

Staff

Director: B. Byron Price (405/325-5666; e-mail: b_byron_price)
Senior Associate Director / Publisher: John Drayton (405/325-3189; e-mail: jdrayton)
   Assistant to the Director: Astrud Reed (405/325-3189; e-mail: astrud)
   Rights, Permissions, and Contracts: Angelika Tietz (405/325-5326; e-mail: atietz)
Editorial: Charles E. (Chuck) Rankin, Associate Director and Editor-in-Chief (405/325-
   5609; e-mail: cerankin)
   Acquisitions Editors: Kirk Bjornsgaard (regional studies) (405/325-9658; e-mail: kirkb);

Matt Bokovoy (Chicana/Chicano literature, contemporary American West, natural history, political science) (405/325-2916; e-mail: mbokovoy); John Drayton (classical studies, literature) (405/325-3189; e-mail: jdrayton); Alessandra Jacobi Tamulevich (native studies: North, Central, and South America) (405/325-2365; e-mail: jacobi); Charles E. (Chuck) Rankin (American West, military history) (405/325-5609; e-mail: cerankin)

Manuscript Editing: Alice Stanton, Managing Editor (405/325-4922; e-mail: astanton)
  Associate Editors: Steven Baker (405/325-1325; e-mail: steven.b.baker); Julie Shilling (405/325-3268; e-mail: jshilling)

Production: Emmy Ezzell, Production Manager (405/325-3186; e-mail: eezzell)
  Assistant Production Manager: Connie Arnold (405/325-3185; e-mail: carnold)
  Production Editor: Susan Garrett (405/325-2408; e-mail: sgarrett)

Marketing and Sales: Dale Bennie, Associate Director / Sales and Marketing Manager (405/325-3207; e-mail: dbennie)
  Publicity Manager: Sandy See (405/325-3200; e-mail: ssee)
  Sales Manager: Mandy Berry (405/325-3202; e-mail: maberry)
  Promotions Manager: Christi Madden (405/325-6462; e-mail: christimadden)
  Exhibits, Awards, and Sales Coordinator: Tara Malone (405/325-3328; e-mail: tmalone)
  Designer: Tony Roberts (405/325-4283; e-mail: tonyroberts)

Business: Diane Cotts, Assistant Director and Chief Financial Officer (405/325-3276; e-mail: dcotts)
  Distribution and Operations Manager: Rick Stinchcomb (405/325-2013; e-mail: rstinchcomb)
  Customer Service: Kathy Benson (405/325-2287; e-mail: kbenson)
  Accounts Receivable: Diane Cannon (405/325-2326; e-mail: dcannon)

Full Member

Established: 1928   Admitted to AAUP: 1937
Title output 2006: 69   Title output 2007: 69
Titles currently in print: 1,200

Editorial Program

Scholarly books, general nonfiction, and fiction with special interests in the American West, Classical Studies, Native Studies (North, Central, and South America), Natural History, Political Science, and Regional Studies.

Special series: American Exploration and Travel; American Indian Law and Policy; American Indian Literature and Critical Studies; Animal Natural History; Campaigns and Commanders; Chicana and Chicano Visions of the Americas; Civilization of the American Indian; Congressional Studies; Gilcrease-Oklahoma Series on Western Art and Artists; International and Security Affairs Series; Julian J. Rothbaum Distinguished Lecture Series; Oklahoma Native American Series; Oklahoma Series in Classical Culture; Oklahoma Stories and Storytellers; Oklahoma Western Biographies; Race and Culture in the American West; Sam Noble Oklahoma Museum of Natural History Publications; Variorum Chaucer; Western Frontier Library

Oregon State University Press

121 The Valley Library
Corvallis, OR 97331-4501

Phone: (541) 737-3166
Fax: (541) 737-3170
E-mail: osu.press@oregonstate.edu
Indiv: (user I.D.)@oregonstate.edu
Web site: oregonstate.edu/dept/press/

Order Fulfillment & Distribution:
The University of Arizona Press
330 S. Toole, Suite 200
Tucson, AZ 85701
Phone: (800) 426-3797;
(520) 626-4218 (in Arizona &
outside continental US)

Canadian Distributor:
University of British Columbia Press

Staff

Director: Karyle Butcher (541/737-3411; e-mail: karyle.butcher)
Associate Director: Tom Booth (503/796-0547; fax 503/796-0549; e-mail: thomas.booth)
Acquisitions Editor: Mary Elizabeth Braun (541/737-3873; e-mail: mary.braun)
Managing Editor & Production Manager: Jo Alexander (541/737-3864; e-mail: jo.alexander)
Editorial & Marketing Assistant: Abby Phillips Metzger (541/737-3166; e-mail:
  philliab@onid.orst.edu)

Full Member

Established: 1961
Title output 2006: 14
Titles currently in print: 190

Admitted to AAUP: 1991
Title output 2007: 11

Editorial Program

The Oregon State University Press primarily publishes books dealing with the history, natural history, cultures, and literature of the Pacific Northwest, as well as natural resources, natural resource management, and environmental history.

University of Ottawa Press / Les Presses de l'Université d'Ottawa

542 King Edward Avenue
Ottawa, ON K1N 6N5
Canada

Phone: (613) 562-5246
Fax: (613) 562-5247
Web site: www.uopress.uottawa.ca

Canadian / US Orders (English titles):
UTP Distribution
5201 Dufferin Street
North York ON M3H 5T8
Canada
Phone: (800) 565-9523; (416) 667-7791
Fax: (416) 667-7832; (800) 221-9985
E-mail: utpbooks@utpress.utoronto.ca

Canadian Orders (French titles):
UNIVERS
845, rue Marie-Victorin,
Saint-Nicolas QC G7A 3S8 Canada
Phone: (800)-859-7474; (418) 831-7474;
Fax: (418) 831-4021
E-mail: univers@distribution-univers.qc.ca

International Orders (French titles):
Exportlivre
289 Desaulniers Boulevard
Saint-Lambert QC J4P 1M8 Canada

Phone: (450) 671-3888
Fax: (450) 671-2121
E-mail: order@exportlivre.com

UK / European Distributor (English titles):
NBN International

Staff
Director: TBA (e-mail: press@uottawa.ca)
Editor: Eric Nelson (e-mail: enelson@uottawa.ca)
Managing Editor: Marie Clausén (e-mail: msec@uottawa.ca)
Marketing Coordinator: Jessica Clark (e-mail: promote@uottawa.ca)
Journals: *Francophonie d'Amérique* (e-mail: crccf@uottawa.ca); *Journal of Prisoners on Prisons* (e-mail: jpp@uottawa.ca)

Full Member
Established: 1936
Title output 2006: 14
Titles currently in print: 250

Admitted to AAUP: 2005
Title output 2007: 30
Journals published: 2

Editorial Program
Canadian studies, Canadian literature, Canadian History, criminology, cultural transfers, education, French America, health science, international development and globalization, governance, philosophy, religion, translation, language, women's studies.
Journals: *Francophonies D'Amérique*; *Journal of Prisoners on Prisons*
Imprint: Harvest House

Oxford University Press

Editorial Offices:
198 Madison Avenue
New York, NY 10016
Phone: (212) 726-6000
Fax: (212) 726-6440
E-mail: (firstname.lastname)@oup.com
Web site: www.oup.com

Canadian Office:
70 Wynford Drive
Don Mills, ON M3C 1J9
Canada
Phone: (416) 441-2941
Fax: (416) 441-0345

Customer Service:
Orders/Prices: (800) 451-7556
Inquiries: (800) 445-9714
ELT: (800) 441-5445
Journals: (800) 852-7323
Music Retail: (800) 292-0639
Fax: (919) 677-1303

Distribution Center &
Journals Office:
2001 Evans Road
Cary, NC 27513
Phone: (919) 677-0977
Dist. Fax: (919) 677-8877
Journals Fax: (919) 677-1714

UK Office:
Great Clarendon Street
Oxford OX2 6DP
United Kingdom
Phone: +44 1865 556767
Fax: +44 1865 556646

English Language Teaching:
Phone: (212) 726-6300
Fax: (212) 726-6388

Staff

President OUP-USA: Tim Barton
  Assistant to the President: Arlene Jacks
  Senior Vice President Administration and CFO Finance, Legal, Distribution, Accounting: Ellen Taus
  Vice President and Publisher of the Higher Education Group: John Challice
  Vice President and Publisher of Reference and School: Casper Grathwohl
  Vice President and Publisher of Trade and Academic: Niko Pfund
  Vice President and Director of Technology: Corey Podolsky
  Vice President and Publisher Brain Sciences, Medicine and Social Work: Joan Bossert
  Vice President, Business Development and Rights, Academic & US Divisions: Evan Schnittman
  Vice President Sales and Marketing: Colleen Scollans
  Vice President of Human Resources: Marilyn Okrent
  Vice President of Operations: Tom Shannon
  Vice President and Director, US EDP: Michael Weinstein
  Vice President Publisher, Law: Shelly Albaum
  President, American English Language Teaching & Asia: Barbara Rifkind
  General Counsel: Barbara Cohen
Trade and Academic
Publisher: Niko Pfund
Editorial: Terry Vaughn (economics and finance); Tim Bent (trade, history and politics); Susan Ferber (history); Peter Prescott (life sciences); Jeremy Lewis (chemistry); Shannon

McLachlan (literature and film); Peter Ohlin (philosophy and linguistics,); Cynthia Read (religion); Theo Calderara (religion); Suzanne Ryan (music); Stefan Vranka (classics); David McBride (politics); Nancy Toff (history); Linda Robbins (paperbacks); Donald Kraus (Bibles); Michael Penn (math)

Professional

Publisher: Joan Bossert

Editorial: Catharine Carlin (cognitive psychology, developmental psychology, cognitive neuroscience, ophthalmology); Mariclaire Cloutier (clinical psychology, forensic psychology); Lori Handelman (social psychology, Oxford Library of Psychology); Craig Panner (neurology, neuroscience); Marion Osmun (psychiatry, trade books); Shelley Reinhardt (neuropsychology, palliative medicine); Maura Roessner (social work)

Reference and Online

Publisher: Casper Grathwohl

Director, Online Product Development: Lisa Nachtigall

Editorial: Kim Robinson (reference); Stephen Wagley (content and editorial); Christine Kuan (art); Laura Macy (music); Benjamin Keene (trade reference, culinary history); Eric Stannard (content); Tanya LaPlante (content); Amber Fischer (research); Christine Lindberg (dictionary program); Ben Zimmer (English language dictionaries); Orion Montoya (technology); Damon Zucca (acquisitions editorial)

Higher Education

Publisher: John Challice

Editorial: Jennifer Carpenter (politics); Robert Miller (philosophy, religion & classics); Sherith Pankratz (sociology and criminal justice); Janet Beatty (English / art / anthropology / music); Jason Noe (life sciences / chemistry); Patrick Lynch (brain sciences); Lori Wood (law); Brian Wheel (history)

Marketing: Adam Glazer; Kim Rimmer

Law

Publisher: Shelly Albaum

Editorial: Christopher Collins (academic & scholarly law); Matt Gallaway (intellectual property, media & communications law); Olivia Lane (commercial, insolvency, investment/finance law); Larry Selby (arbitration, litigation, corporate, international trade and all other practice areas)

Medical

Editorial Director: Catherine Barnes

Editorial: Yvonne Honigsberg (medical libraries, pain medicine); Andrea Seils (American handbooks, radiology); Bill Lamsback (public health & epidemiology, clinical genetics)

Music

Head of Music Publishing: David Blackwell

US Music: Louis Fifer

Copyrights and Licensing: Brian Hill

EDP / Manufacturing

Director UK/US EDP: Catherine Pearce

VP and Director US EDP: Michael Weinstein

Director UK/US Stock Planning: Paul Major

Director Stock Planning US: Gigi Brienza

Production Managers: Steven Cestaro, Nancy Hoagland, Lynda Castillo, Diem Bloom
Creative Director: Amy Rosen
Business Development and Rights
Vice President of Business Development and Rights: Evan Schnittman
  Assistant to Vice President: Kathryn Nelson
Sales and Marketing
Vice President Sales and Marketing: Colleen Scollans
Marketing Directors: Kim Craven (academic and trade); Greg Bussy (medicine and brain sciences); Rebecca Seger (reference); Sarah Ultsch (law)
Publicity Director: Christian Purdy
Director of Key Accounts: BJ Gabriel
Associate Director of Field and Inside Sales: Lenny Allen
Director of Library Sales: Richard Hopper
Operations
Operations: Tom Shannon
Human Resources: Marilyn Okrent
EDP: Michael Weinstein
Office Services: Terese Dickerson
Finance
Senior Vice President and Chief Financial Officer: Ellen Taus
Director Finance: Stephen Nussbaum
English Language Teaching Division
President, American English Language Teaching & Asia: Barbara Rifkind
Editorial Director: Sally Yagan
Publishers: Laura Pearson (international); Stephanie Karras (adult)
Marketing and Sales: Myndee Males
Production: Shanta Persaud
Design: Robert Carangelo
Journals (North Carolina)
US Subscriber Services: Charlotte Brabants
Marketing Manager: Tricia Hudson
Production: Elizabeth Gardner
Distribution Center (North Carolina)
Inventory Planning / Control: Kenneth Guerin
Credit and Collection: Banks Honeycutt
Customer Service: Donna Jones
Warehouse Operations: Cameron Shaw
Accounting Services: Dottie Warlick
Cary Facilities: Daniel Wingard
Technology
Business Technology Services: Corey Podolsky
  Assistant to Vice President: Anita Kolenovic

Full Member

Established: 1895

Title output 2006: 1,600

Titles currently in print: 19,876

Admitted to AAUP: 1950

Title output 2007: 2,100

Journals published (US only): 38

Editorial Program
Scholarly monographs; general nonfiction; Bibles; college textbooks; medical books; music; reference books; journals; children's books; English language teaching. Submissions are not invited in the area of fiction.

Journals published in the US: *American Journal of Epidemiology; American Law and Economics Review; American Literary History; Behavioral Ecology; Brief Treatment and Crisis Intervention; Biostatistics; Chemical Senses; Contemporary Economic Policy; Economic Inquiry; Enterprise & Society: The International Journal of Business History; Epidemiologic Reviews; Glycobiology; Holocaust and Genocide Studies; Integrative and Comparative Biology; Journal of Deaf Studies and Deaf Education; Journal of Financial Econometrics; Journal of Heredity; Journal of Law, Economics, & Organization; Journal of Pediatric Psychology; Journal of Public Administration Research and Theory; Journal of the American Academy of Religion; Journal of the History of Medicine and Allied Sciences; Journal of the National Cancer Institute; Modern Judaism; Molecular Biology and Evolution; The Musical Quarterly; The Opera Quarterly; Political Analysis; Public Opinion Quarterly; Publius: The Journal of Federalism; The Review of Financial Studies; Schizophrenia Bulletin; Social Politics; Toxicological Sciences; The World Bank Economic Review; The World Bank Research Observer*

University of Pennsylvania Press

3905 Spruce Street
Philadelphia, PA 19104-4112

Phone: (215) 898-6261
Fax: (215) 898-0404
E-mail: (user I.D.)@upenn.edu
Web site: www.pennpress.org

Warehouse & Returns:
Maple Press Company
Lebanon Distribution Center
704 Legionaire Drive
Fredericksburg, PA 17026

UK Representative:
University Presses Marketing

Order Department:
PO Box 50370
Baltimore, MD 21211-4370
Phone: (800) 537-5487
Fax: (410) 516-6998
E-mail (inquiries only):
custerv@pobox.upenn.edu

Canadian Representative:
Scholarly Book Services

Staff
Director: Eric Halpern (215/898-1672; e-mail: ehalpern)
 Assistant to the Director and Rights Administrator: Mariellen Smith (215/898-6263; e-mail: mariells)
Acquisitions: Peter Agree, Editor-in-Chief (anthropology, human rights, political science) (215/573-3816; e-mail: agree)
 Senior Editors: Jerome E. Singerman (humanities, Jewish studies) (215/898-1681; e-mail: singerma); Jo Joslyn (art, architecture, ancient studies) (215/898-5754; e-mail: joslyn);

Robert Lockhart (American history, regional books) (215/898-1677; e-mail: rlockhar)
Development Editor: Bill Finan (public policy, international relations) (215/573-7129; e-mail: wfinan)
Acquisitions Assistants: Mariana Martinez (215/898-3252; e-mail: marianaj); Christopher Hu (215/898-6262; e-mail: hucd)

Manuscript Editing and Production: George Lang, Editing & Production Manager (215/898-1675; e-mail: gwlang)
Assistant Production Manager: William Boehm (215/573-4059; e-mail: boehmwj)
Managing Editor: Alison Anderson (215/898-1678; e-mail: anderaa)
Associate Managing Editor: Erica Ginsburg (215/898-1679; e-mail: eginsbur)
Production Editor: Noreen O'Connor (215/898-1709; e-mail: nmoconno)
Editing & Production Coordinator: Susan Day (215/898-7588; e-mail: susanld)
Editorial / Production Assistant: Susan Staggs (215/898-1676; e-mail: sstaggs)
Art Director: John Hubbard (215/573-6118; e-mail: wmj)
Journals Coordinator: Paul Chase (215/573-1295; e-mail: paulbc)

Marketing: Laura Waldron, Marketing Director (215/898-1673; e-mail: lwaldron)
Publicity & Public Relations Manager: Ellen Trachtenberg (215/898-1674; e-mail: ellenpt)
Electronic Promotion Coordinator: Stephanie Brown (215/898-8678; e-mail: browns2)
Direct Mail & Advertising Manager: Christopher Bell (215/898-9184; e-mail: bellcw)
Marketing Assistant: Sandy Haviland (215/898-6264; e-mail: sht)

Business: Joseph Guttman, Business Manager (215/898-1670; e-mail: josephgg)
Financial Coordinator: Kathy Ranalli (215/898-1682; e-mail: ranalli)
Customer Service Representative: Marlene DeBella (215/898-1671; e-mail: custserv@pobox.upenn.edu)

Full Member

Established: 1890

Admitted to AAUP: 1967

Title output 2006: 98

Title output 2007: 108

Titles currently in print: 1,057

Journals published: 8

Editorial Program

Scholarly and semipopular nonfiction, with special interests in American history and culture; ancient, medieval, and Renaissance studies; anthropology; landscape architecture; studio arts; human rights; urban studies, Jewish studies; Pennsylvania regional studies; and political science.

Journals: *Early American Studies*; *Hispanic Review*; *Jewish Quarterly Review*; *Magic, Ritual, and Witchcraft*; *Journal of Medical Toxicology*; *Journal of the Early Republic*; *Journal of the History of Ideas*; and *Revista Hispanica Moderna*

Special series: The Arts and Intellectual Life in Modern America; Contemporary Ethnography; The City in the 21st Century; Divinations: Rereading Late Ancient Religion; Early American Studies; Encounters with Asia; Ethnography of Political Violence; Hagley Perspectives on Business and Culture; Jewish Culture and Contexts; Material Texts; Metropolitan Portraits; Middle Ages Series; Penn Studies in Landscape Architecture; Pennsylvania Studies in Human Rights; Personal Takes; Politics and Culture in Modern America

Copublishing programs: Ceramics Handbooks, The Complete Potter, Textile Handbooks

Imprint: Pine Street Books

Penn State University Press

820 North University Drive
USB1, Suite C
University Park, PA 16802-1003

Orders:
Phone: (800) 326-9180
Fax: (877) 778-2665

Phone: (814) 865-1329
Fax: (814) 863-1408
E-mail: (user I.D.)@psu.edu
Web site: www.psupress.org

UK Representative:
Eurospan

Canadian Distributor:
University of Toronto Press

Staff

Director: Sanford G. Thatcher (e-mail: sgt3)

Acquisitions Editorial: Editor-in-Chief and Associate Director: Patrick Alexander (814/867-2209; e-mail: pha3)

  Art History and Humanities Editor: Eleanor Goodman (814/867-2212; e-mail: ehg11)

  Editorial Assistants: Cali Buckley (814/865-1328; e-mail: ceb214); Kathryn Yahner (814/865-1329; e-mail: kby3)

Manuscript Editorial: Cherene Holland, Managing Editor (814/867-2214; e-mail: cah8)

  Manuscript Editors: Patricia Mitchell (814/867-2216; e-mail: pam18); Laura Reed-Morrisson (814/865-1606; e-mail: lxr168)

Design and Production: Jennifer Norton, Manager (814/863-8061; e-mail: jsn4)

  Chief Designer: Steven Kress (814/867-2215; e-mail: srk5)

  Production and Marketing Assistant: Jon Gotshall (814/867-2213; e-mail: jeg31)

  Production Assistant (Journals): Whittney Trueax (814/863-5992; e-mail: wst110)

Marketing: Tony Sanfilippo, Marketing and Sales Director (814/863-5994; e-mail: ajs23)

  Exhibits and Publicity Manager: Heather Smith (814/863-0524; e-mail: hms7)

  Advertising Manager: Brian Beer (814/867-2210; e-mail: bxb110)

  Marketing Assistant: Kathy Scholz-Jaffe (814/867-2224; e-mail: kxs56)

Business: Clifford Way Jr., Manager (814/863-5993; e-mail: cgw3)

  Group Leader, Shipping Clerk: Kevin Trostle (e-mail: kjt2)

  Accounting Assistant: Kathy Vaughn (814/863-6771; e-mail: kmv1)

Information Systems Manager: Ed Spicer (e-mail: res122)

Full Member

Established: 1956
Title output 2006: 60
Titles currently in print: 1,375

Admitted to AAUP: 1960
Title output 2007: 65
Journals published: 11

Editorial Program

Scholarly books in the humanities and social sciences, with current emphasis on architecture; art history; philosophy; Latin American studies; Russian and East European studies; international relations, political theory, comparative politics, US politics; American and European history; medieval studies; religion; sociology; women's studies; and rural studies. Submissions are not invited in fiction, poetry, or drama.

Journals: (* available online): *Book History**; *Chaucer Review**; *Comparative Literature Studies**; *The Good Society**; *Journal of General Education**; *Journal of Nietzsche Studies**; *Journal of Policy History**; *Journal of Speculative Philosophy**; *Pennsylvania History*; *Philosophy and Rhetoric**; *SHAW: The Annual of Bernard Shaw Studies**

Special series: American and European Philosophy; Buildings, Landscapes, and Societies; Edinburgh Edition of Thomas Reid; Essays on Human Rights; Issues in Policy History; Literature and Philosophy; Magic in History; Max Kade Institute German-American Research Series; Penn State Library of Jewish Literature; Penn State Series in the History of the Book; Pennsylvania German History and Culture; Refiguring Modernism; Re-Reading the Canon; Romance Studies; Rural Studies; Studies of the Greater Philadelphia Philosophy Consortium

Special imprints: Keystone Books

Edizioni PLUS—PISA University Press

Lungarno Pacinotti, 43
56126 Pisa Italy

Phone: +39 050 2212056
Fax: + 39 050 2212945
E-mail: info.plus@adm.unipi.it
Web site: www.edizioniplus.it

Orders:
Phone: +39 050 550042
Fax: +39 050 8311614

UK / North American Representatives:
Libro Co. Italia
Herder Editrice e Libreria

Board of Directors
President: Aldo Pinchera
Honorary President: Luciano Modica
Vice President: Tommaso Fanfani
Chief Executive: Riccardo Grasso
Councillors: Francesco Ciardelli, Alessandro Pizzorusso, Franco Russo, Patrizia Alma Pacini
Staff
Marketing Manager and Acquisitions Editorial: Claudia Napolitano (+39 050 2212056;
    e-mail: c.napolitano@adm.unipi.it, info.plus@adm.unipi.it)
Central Administration/Order Processing: Ambra Seymons (+39 050 550042; e-mail:
    aseymons@edizioniplus.it)

International Member
Established: 2000
Title output 2006: 83
Titles currently in print: 500

Admitted to AAUP: 2005
Title output 2007: 80
Journals published: 14

Editorial Program
Edizioni PLUS—Pisa University Press supports the academic mission of Pisa University by publishing scholarly books and journals for a diverse, worldwide readership. These publications, written by authors representing a broad range of intellectual perspectives, reflect the academic and institutional strengths of the university. Edizioni Plus publishes handbooks and peer-reviewed works of academic distinction, of very good editorial and production quality, in many subjects. These publications primarily service the scholarly community, and many also reach the general reading public.

Journals: *Agogè; Agricoltura Mediterranea; Agrochimica; Archives Italiennes de Biologie; Atti della Società Toscana di Scienze Naturali A and B; Atti e Sipari; Egitto e Vicino Oriente; EuMA: Proceedings of the European Microwave Association; Frustula Entomologica; Laboratorio Universitario Volterrano; Paleontographia Italica; Polittico; Studi Classici e orientali*

Special Series: Clioh's Workshop; Cliohres.net, Conversations at the "Sapienza"; Eco-history Notebooks; History and Sociology of Modernity; Greek, Arabic, Latin: Roads to Knowledge; Methexis Project; Peace Studies; The Phoenix:Studies and Sources for the History of Sculpture; Pisan Linguistics Studies: Russian Literature: Teaching in a University Context

University of Pittsburgh Press

Eureka Building, 5th Floor
3400 Forbes Avenue
Pittsburgh, PA 15260

Phone: (412) 383-2456
Fax: (412) 383-2466
E-mail: (user I.D.)@pitt.edu
Web site: www.upress.pitt.edu

Order Fulfillment:
University of Pittsburgh Press
Chicago Distribution Center
11030 South Langley Avenue
Chicago, IL 60628
Phone: (773) 568-1550; (800) 621-2736
Fax: (773) 660-2235

UK Representative:
Eurospan

Canadian Representative:
Scholarly Book Services

Staff

Director: Cynthia Miller (e-mail: cymiller)
  Assistant to the Director: Kelley Johovic (e-mail: khj4)
  Subsidiary Rights Manager: Margie Bachman (e-mail: mkbachma)
Editorial Director: Peter Kracht (e-mail: pek6)
  Acquisitions Editor: Joshua Shanholtzer (e-mail: uppacq)
  Assistant Acquisitions Editor: Devin Fromm (e-mail: djf4)
Editorial, Production, and Design: F. Ann Walston, Production Director (e-mail: awalston)
  Managing Editor: Deborah Meade (e-mail: dmeade)
  Production Editor: Alex Wolfe (e-mail: apw20)
Marketing: Lowell Britson, Marketing Director (e-mail: lbritson)
  Direct Mail / Advertising Manager: David Bauman (e-mail: ddb13)
  Publicist: Maria Sticco (e-mail: mes5)
Business: Cindy Wessels, Business Manager (e-mail: caw1)

Full Member

Established: 1936
Title output 2006: 57
Titles currently in print: 420

Admitted to AAUP: 1937
Title output 2007: 41

Editorial Program

History; history of architecture, urban studies, international studies; composition and literacy studies; poetry; philosophy of science; Pittsburgh and western Pennsylvania. The Press does not invite submissions in the hard sciences, original fiction (except DHLP), festschriften, memoirs, symposia, or unrevised doctoral dissertations.

The Press distributes and copublishes selected titles with the Carnegie Museum of Art, the Carnegie Museum of Natural History, the Frick Art and Historical Center, the Historical Society of Western Pennsylvania, the Mattress Factory, and the Westmoreland Museum of American Art.

Special series: The Agnes Lynch Starrett Poetry Prize; Cuban Studies; Drue Heinz Literature Prize; Golden Triangle Books; Illuminations: Cultural Formations of the Americas; Milton Studies; Pitt Latin American Series; Pitt Poetry Series; Pitt Series in Russian and East European Studies; Pittsburgh Series in Composition, Literacy, and Culture; Pittsburgh/Konstanz Series in Philosophy and History of Science; The Security Continuum: Global Politics in the Modern Age

Princeton University Press

Executive Offices:
41 William Street
Princeton, NJ 08540-5237

Phone: (609) 258-4900
Fax: (609) 258-6305
E-mail:
(firstname_lastname)@press.princeton.edu
Web site: press.princeton.edu

European Editorial Office:
3 Market Place
Woodstock, Oxfordshire OX20 1SY
United Kingdom
Phone: +44 1993 81 4500
Fax: +44 1993 81 4504
E-mail: (firstinitial)(lastname)@pupress.co.uk

UK / European Sales Representation:
University Presses of California, Columbia, and Princeton, Ltd.
1 Oldlands Way, Bognor Regis
West Sussex PO22 9SA
United Kingdom
Phone: +44 1243 842165
Fax: +44 1243 842167

Order Fulfillment (US and Canada):
California/Princeton Fulfillment Services
1445 Lower Ferry Road
Ewing, NJ 08618
Phone: (800) 777-4726; (609) 883-1759
Fax: (800) 999-1958; (609) 883-7413

UK Distributor:
John Wiley & Sons

Staff

Director: Peter J. Dougherty (609/258-6778)
   Assistant to the Director: Martha Camp (609/258-4953)
   Associate Director and Controller: Patrick Carroll (609/258-2486)
Acquisitions Editorial: Brigitta van Rheinberg, Editor-in-Chief and Group Publisher, Humanities (history) (609/258-4935); Robert Kirk, Executive Editor and Group Publisher, Science (biology, ornithology, natural history) (609/258-4884); Charles Myers, Executive Editor and Group Publisher, Social Sciences (political science) (609/258-4922); Linny Schenck, Editorial Administrator (609/258-0183)

Executive Editors: Vickie Kearn (mathematics) (609/258-2321)
Senior Editors: Fred Appel (anthropology, religion) (609/258-2484); Seth Ditchik (finance, economics) (609/258-9428); Ingrid Gnerlich (physical sciences) (609/258-5775); Anne Savarese (reference) (609/258-4937); Tim Sullivan (economics, sociology) (609/258-4908)
Acquisitions Editors: Alison Kalett (biology, earth science) (609/258-9232); Clara Platter (history) (609/258-2409); Ben Tate (translations) (609/248-5121); Rob Tempio (philosophy, classics, ancient world) (609/258-0843); Hanne Winarsky (art, literature) (609/258-4569)
Manuscript Editorial: Neil Litt, Director of Editing, Design and Production (609/258-5066)
   Managing Editor: Elizabeth Byrd (609/258-2589)
   Electronic Manuscripts Manager: Eileen Reilly (609/258-2719)
   Production Manager: Betsy Litz (609/258-1253)
Marketing: Adam Fortgang, Assistant Press Director and Marketing Director (609/258-4896)
   Advertising Manager: Steffen Mathis (609/258-4924)
   Associate Marketing Director: Leslie Nangle (609/258-5881)
   Exhibits Manager: Melissa Burton (609/258-4915)
   Senior Text Promotion Manager: Julie Haenisch (609/258-6856)
   Sales Director: Eric Rohmann (609/258-4898)
   Subsidiary Rights Manager: Ben Tate (609/258-5121)
   Publicity Director: Andrew DeSio (609/258-5165)
Business: Patrick Carroll, Associate Director and Controller (609/258-2486)
   Assistant to the Controller: Victoria Hansard (609/258-2485)
   Associate Controller: Debbie Greco (609/882-0550)
   Director of Intellectual Property and Documentary Publishing: Daphne Ireland (609/258-5228)
Information Systems: Patrick Carroll, Acting Director of Information Technology (609/258-2846)
   Director of Publishing Technology: Chuck Creesy (609/258-5745)
   Website Administrator: Ann Ambrose (609/258-7749)
European Office:
   Publishing Director, Europe: Richard Baggaley (economics, finance) (+44 1993 81 4501)
   Senior Editor: Ian Malcolm (philosophy, political theory) (+44 1993 81 4502)
   Publicity and Marketing Manager: Caroline Priday (+44 1993 81 4503)

Full Member

Established: 1905   Admitted to AAUP: 1937
Title output 2006: 312   Title output 2007: 327
Titles currently in print: 5,615

Editorial Program

Humanities: American, European, World, Asian, Slavic, and Jewish history; ancient world; classics; art history, philosophy; political theory; literature; religion
Reference: humanities; social science; and science
Science: astrophysics; biology; earth science; mathematics; natural history; ornithology; physics

Social science: anthropology; economics; finance; law; political science; sociology. The Press does not publish drama or fiction

Special imprints: The Bollingen Series, established in 1941 by the Bollingen Foundation, has been published by Princeton University Press since 1967. The Press is not accepting further contributions to the series.

Special monograph series: 20/21; Advances In Financial Engineering; America in the World; A.W. Mellon Lectures in the Fine Arts; Annals of Mathematics Studies; The Bard Music Festival; British Artists; Buddhism; The Cultural Lives of Law; The Econometric Institute Lectures; Encountering Jung; The Ethikon Series in Comparative Ethics; Frontiers of Economic Research; The Gorman Lectures in Economics; Human Rights and Crimes against Humanity; In a Nutshell; In-formation; Index of Christian Art Resources; Investigations in Physics; The Isaac Newton Insitute Lectures; James Madison Library in American Politics; Jews, Christians, and Muslims from the Ancient to the Modern World; Jung Extracts; Jung Seminars; Literature in History Series; London Mathematical Society Monograph Series; Magie Classical Publications; Martin Classical Lectures; Mathematical Notes; Monographs in Behavior and Ecology; Monographs in Population Biology; Mythos; New Forum Books; New French Thought; Papers from the Eranos Yearbooks; Philosophy and Public Affairs Reader; Philosophy Now; Physical Chemistry; Physics Notes; Politics and Society in Twentieth-Century America; Porter Lectures; Portland Press; Princeton Classic Editions; Princeton Computer Science Notes; Princeton Economic History of the Western World; Princeton Environmental Institute Series; Princeton Essays in Literature; Princeton Field Guides; Princeton Illustrated Checklists; Princeton Landmarks in Biology; Princeton Landmarks in Mathematics and Physics; Princeton Lectures in Finance; Princeton Library of Asian Translations; Princeton Mathematical Series; Princeton Modern Greek Studies; Princeton Monographs in Philosophy; Princeton Pocket Guides; Princeton Readings in Religion; Princeton Science Library; Princeton Series in Applied Mathematics; Princeton Series in Astrophysics; Princeton Series in Computer Science; Princeton Series in Evolutionary Biology; Princeton Series in Finance; Princeton Series in Geochemistry; Princeton Series in Geophysics; Princeton Series in International Economics; Princeton Series in Physics; Princeton Series in Theoretical and Computational Biology; Princeton Studies in American Politics; Princeton Studies in Business and Technology; Princeton Studies in Complexity; Princeton Studies in Cultural Sociology; Princeton Studies in Culture/Power/History; Princeton Studies in International History and Politics; Princeton Studies in Muslim Politics; Princeton Studies in Opera; Princeton Studies on the Near East; Proceedings of the Pontifical Academy of Sciences; The Public Square; The Roundtable Series in Behavioral Economics; Science Essentials; Studies in Church and State; Studies in Intellectual History and the History of Philosophy; Studies in Moral, Political, and Legal Philosophy; Studies of the East Asian Institute, Columbia University; Studies of the Harriman Institute, Columbia University; The Toulouse Lectures in Economics; Translation/Transnation; The University Center for Human Values Series; W. H. Auden: Critical Editions; Where to Watch Birds

Poetry series: Facing Pages; The Lockert Library of Poetry in Translation

Original source series: The Collected Papers of Albert Einstein; Collected Works of Spinoza; The Complete Works of W. H. Auden; Kierkegaard's Writings; The Papers of Thomas Jefferson (also Second Series; Retirement Series); The Papers of Woodrow Wilson; The Philosophical, Political and Literary Works of David Hume; Selected Writings of Wilhelm Dilthey; The Writings of Henry D. Thoreau

University of Puerto Rico Press

Street Address:
Edificio Editorial/ Diálogo
Jardín Botánico Área Norte
Carretera No. 1, KM 12.0
Río Piedras, San Juan, PR 00931

Mailing Address:
PO Box 23322
U.P.R. Station
San Juan, PR 00931-3322

Phone: (787) 250-0435
Fax: (787) 753-9116, 751-8785
Web site: www.laeditorialupr.com

Staff
President, Editorial Board: Angel Collado Schwarz
Executive Director: Manuel G. Sandoval (e-mail: msandoval@upr.edu)
Editorial: Marta Aponte, Director of Acquisitions and Editorial (e-mail: maponte@upr.edu)
    Editors: Jesús Tomé; Rosa V. Otero; Salvador O. Rosorio
Sales Director: José A. Burgos (e-mail: jburgos@upr.edu)
    Promotions Manager: Ruth Morales
    Exhibits Manager: Moraima Clavell
Chief Financial Officer and Administrator: Hector D. Stevenson
    (e-mail: hstevenson@upr.edu)
    Accountant: Clara Ortiz
    Accounts Receivable: Anibal Sanabia
Warehouse Manager: Miguel Rodríguez
    Inventory Manager: Amoury de Jesús
Journals: *Revista La Torre,* Director: Juan Nieves
    Journals Marketing: Judith de Ferdinandy

Full Member
Established: 1932
Title output 2006:
Titles currently in print: 900

Admitted to AAUP: 1977
Title output 2007:
Journals published: 1

Editorial Program
Scholarly studies on Puerto Rico, the Caribbean and Latin America; philosophy; history; architecture; law; social sciences; health; women's studies; economics; literary theory and criticism; creative poetry and prose; literary anthologies; nature studies; flora; fauna; ecosystems; children' s books; reference; other general interest publications.
Journal: *Revista La Torre* (the humanities). In distribution: *Revista de Estudios Hispánicos* (Spanish language studies); and *Historia y Sociedad* (Puerto Rican and Caribbean history); *Diálogos* (philosophy)
Special series: literary anthologies; philosophy; creative literature; scholarly nonfiction; nature
Special imprints: Aquí y Ahora (current literature); Colección Puertorriqueña (literary classics); Colección Eugenio María de Hostos (complete works); San Pedrito (children's books); Mujeres de Palabra (women's literature); Colección Sinsonate (poetry)

Purdue University Press

South Campus Courts, Building E
509 Harrison Street
West Lafayette, IN 47907-2025

Phone: (765) 494-2038
Fax: (765) 496-2442
E-mail: pupress@purdue.edu
Indiv: (user I.D.)@purdue.edu
Web site: www.thepress.purdue.edu

Orders:
Purdue University Press
PO Box 388
Ashland, OH 44805
Phone: (800) 247-6553
Fax: (419) 281-6883
E-mail: order@bookmaster.com

US Distributor:
AtlasBooks
2541 Ashland Road
Mansfield, OH 44905

European Distributor:
Eurospan

Canadian Distributor:
Scholarly Book Service

Staff
Director: Thomas Bacher (765/494-2038; e-mail: bacher)
Managing Editor: Margaret Hunt (765/494-6259; e-mail: mchunt)
Design & Production Manager: Bryan Shaffer (765/494-8428; e-mail: bshaffer)
Marketing & Sales: Thomas Bacher
Marketing Assistant / Author Liaison: Becki Corbin (765/494-8144; e-mail: rlcorbin)
Information Associate: Beth Robertson (e-mail: berobert)

Full Member
Established: 1960
Title output 2006: 26
Titles currently in print: 390

Admitted to AAUP: 1993
Title output 2007: 23
Journals published: 7

Editorial Program
Dedicated to the dissemination of scholarly and professional information, the Press provides quality resources in several key subject areas including business, technology, health, veterinary medicine and other selected disciplines in the humanities and sciences.

Journals: *Anthrozoös: A Multidisciplinary Journal of the Interactions of People and Animals*; *Comparative Literature and Culture: A WWWeb Journal*; *Education and Culture: The Journal of the John Dewey Society*; *The Interdisciplinary Journal of Problem Based Learning*; *Journal of Problem Solving*; *Shofar: An Interdisciplinary Journal of Jewish Studies*; *Studies in American Jewish Literature*

Special series: Central European Studies; Comparative Cultural Studies; History of Philosophy; New Directions in the Human-Animal Bond; Philosophy/Communication; Purdue Studies in Romance Literatures; Advances in Homeland Security; International Series on Technology Policy and Innovation; Shofar Supplements in Jewish Studies

Imprints: NotaBell Books—an eclectic reprint collection of non-traditional classics; Ichor Business Books—practical, high-level, how-to titles for today's business and professional challenges; Litera Scripta Manet—a non-traditional reprint series that re-publishes out-of-print scholarly information; PuP Books—reprint series that will bring back to publication out-of-print stories illuminating other times in American history

RAND Corporation

Street Address:
1776 Main Street
Santa Monica, CA 90407

Mailing Address:
PO Box 2138
Santa Monica, CA 90407-2138

Phone: (310) 393-0411
Fax: (310) 451-7026
Web site: www.rand.org/publications

Customer Service:
Phone: (877) 584-8642
Fax: (412) 802-4981
E-mail: order@rand.org

US Distributor:
National Book Network
Phone: (800) 462-6420 or (717) 794-3800
Fax: (800) 338-4550

UK / European Distributor:
NBN International

Staff
Director, Publications: Jane Ryan (ext. 7260; e-mail: ryan@rand.org)
Associate Director, Publications: Paul Murphy (ext. 7806; e-mail: murphy@rand.org)
Business Manager: Claudia McCowan (ext. 6320; e-mail: cmccowan@rand.org)
Managing Editor: Peter Hoffman (ext. 7556; e-mail: peterh@rand.org)
Production Manager: David Bolhuis (ext. 6194; e-mail: bolhuis@rand.org
Marketing Director: John Warren (ext. 6293; e-mail: jwarren@rand.org)
Art Director: Ron Miller (ext. 6384; e-mail: ronkm@rand.org)
Editor, RAND Journal of Economics: Paula Larich (ext. 6617; e-mail: larich@rand.org)
Computing Manager: Edward Finkelstein (ext. 7417; e-mail: edwardf@rand.org)

Associate Member
Established: 1948
Title output 2006: 150
Titles currently in print: 18,000

Admitted to AAUP: 2000
Title output 2007: 160
Journals published: 1

Editorial Program
For more than 50 years, decision-makers in the public and private sectors have turned to the RAND Corporation for objective analysis and effective solutions that address the challenges facing the nation and the world. Publication topics include policy issues such as education; environment and energy; health care; immigration, labor, and population; international affairs; national security; public safety and justice; science and technology; and terrorism and homeland security. Unsolicited manuscripts are not accepted.
Journal: *RAND Journal of Economics*

Resources for the Future / RFF Press

1616 P Street, N.W.
Washington, DC 20036-1400

Phone: (202) 328-5000
Fax: (202) 328-5002
E-mail: rffpress@rff.org
Indiv: (user I.D)@rff.org
Web site: www.rffpress.org

Book Orders and Customer Service:
c/o Hopkins Fulfillment Services
PO Box 50370
Baltimore, MD 21211-4370
Phone: (410) 516-6965; (800) 537-5487
Fax: (410) 516-6998

UK / European Distributor:
John Wiley & Sons

Canadian Distributor:
Renouf Books

Staff
Publisher and Acquisitions: Don Reisman (202/328-5064; e-mail: reisman)
Manuscript Editorial, Production: Grace Hill (202/328-5067; e-mail: hill)
Marketing, Sales, Exhibits, Publicity, Advertising, Business: Tom Harnish (202/328-5086; e-mail: harnish)

Associate Member
Established: 1952
Title output 2006: 11
Titles currently in print: 98

Admitted to AAUP: 1988
Title output 2007: 10

Editorial Program
Scholarly, text, and general interest books in environmental and resource economics; environmental politics, policy, and regulation; risk analysis and management; climate change; land, forest, water, and mineral use; conservation; biodiversity; environmental history; sustainable development at local, national, and global levels; urban planning; land-use policy; technological change; and the use of scientific and expert information in formulating public policy.
Special series: Issues in Water Resource Policy

The Rockefeller University Press

1114 First Avenue, 3rd Floor
New York, NY 10065-8325

Phone: (212) 327-7938
Fax: (212) 327-8587
E-mail: (user I.D.)@mail.rockefeller.edu
Web site: www.rockefeller.edu/rupress

Staff
Executive Director: Mike Rossner (212/327-8881; e-mail: rossner)
   Assistant to the Executive Director: JoAnn Greene (212/327-8025; e-mail: greenej)

Manuscript Editorial: Emma Hill, Executive Editor, *The Journal of Cell Biology* (212/327-8011; e-mail: ehill); Heather L. Van Epps, Executive Editor, *The Journal of Experimental Medicine* (212/327-7031); David Greene, Managing Editor, *The Journal of General Physiology* (212/327-8615; e-mail: jgp)
Advertising: Lorna Petersen, Sales Director (212/327-8880; e-mail: petersl)
Journals: Robert O'Donnell, Electronic Publishing and Production Director (212/327-8545; e-mail: odonner)
Business: Raymond T. Fastiggi, Finance Director (212/327-8567; e-mail: fastigg)
Business Development Director: Gregory Malar (212/327-7948; e-mail: malarg)

Full Member

Established: 1958	Admitted to AAUP: 1982
Title output 2006: 1	Title output 2007: 0
Titles currently in print: 39	Journals published: 3

Editorial Program

Scholarly works on scientific subjects, primarily in the biomedical sciences. The Press is interested in related subjects, such as historical, philosophical, or biographical studies that illuminate the goals of our scientific frontiers, along with problems and opportunities that this research poses. Manuscripts from nonscientific fields are unlikely to be considered. Occasionally a book is published under a joint imprint and/or copublishing arrangement.
Journals: *The Journal of Cell Biology*; *The Journal of Experimental Medicine*; *The Journal of General Physiology*

Russell Sage Foundation

112 East 64th Street
New York, NY 10065

Phone: (212) 750-6000
Fax: (212) 371-4761
E-mail: pubs@rsage.org
Indiv: (firstname)@rsage.org
Web site: www.russellsage.org

Orders:
Russell Sage Foundation
CUP Services
750 Cascadilla St.
PO Box 6525
Ithaca, NY 14851
Phone: (800) 666-2211; (607) 277-2211
Fax: (800) 688-2877; (607) 277-6292

UK / European Representative:
University Presses Marketing

Staff

Director of Publications: Suzanne Nichols (212/750-6026)
Publications Assistant: Dana Adams (212/750-6038)
Production Manager: Matthew Callan (212/750-6034)
Director of Public Relations: David A. Haproff (212/750-6037)
Public Relations Assistant: Angela Gloria (212/750-6021)
Exhibits / Permissions: Dana Adams (212/750-6038)
Foundation President: Eric Wanner

Associate Member

Established: 1907
Title output 2006: 39
Titles currently in print: 450

Admitted to AAUP: 1989
Title output 2007: 40

Editorial Program
Scholarly books on current research and policy issues in the social sciences. Recent research programs sponsored by the Russell Sage Foundation include the future of work, sustainable employment, current US immigration, the analysis of the 1990 and 2000 US Census, the social psychology of cultural contact, the role of trust in shaping social relations, the social dimensions of inequality, and behavioral economics.

Copublishing programs: joint publications with Harvard University Press and Princeton University Press

Rutgers University Press

Livingston Campus
100 Joyce Kilmer Avenue
Piscataway, NJ 08854-8099

Phone: (732) 445-7762
Fax: (732) 445-7039
E-mail: (user I.D.)@rutgers.edu
Web site: rutgerspress.rutgers.edu

Warehouse, Fulfillment, & Cust. Service:
c/o Longleaf Services, Inc.
PO Box 8895
Chapel Hill, NC 27515-8895
Phone: (800) 848-6224
Fax: (800) 272-6817
E-mail: longleaf@unc.edu

UK / European Representative:
Eurospan

Canadian Representative:
Scholarly Book Services

Staff
Director: Marlie Wasserman (ext. 624; e-mail: marlie)
  Assistant to the Director / Permissions and Subsidiary Rights Manager / E-book Coordinator: Christina Brianik (ext. 623; e-mail: cbrianik)
  Acquisitions Editorial: Leslie Mitchner, Associate Director and Editor-in-Chief (humanities, literature, visual culture, Latino studies, and film) (ext. 601; e-mail: lmitch)
  Editors: Adi Hovav (social sciences, Latin American studies, and anthropology) (ext. 604; e-mail: adih); Kendra Boileau (history, Asian studies, and Asian American studies) (ext. 602; e-mail: kboileau); Doreen Valentine (science, health, and medicine) (ext. 605; e-mail: dvalen)
  Associate Editor: Beth Kressel (Jewish studies) (ext. 603; e-mail: bkres)
  Editorial Assistant: Rachel Friedman (ext. 630; e-mail: rachfr)
Manuscript Editorial and Production: Marilyn Campbell, PrePress Director (ext. 606; e-mail: marilync)
  Production Manager: Anne Hegeman (ext. 608; e-mail: hegeman)
  Production Coordinator: Alison Hack (ext. 605; e-mail: ahack)
  Production Editor: Alicia Nadkarni (ext. 636; e-mail: anadkarn)
  Imports and Reprints Manager: Suzanne Kellam (ext. 607; e-mail: skellam)
Marketing: Elizabeth Scarpelli, Sales and Marketing Director (ext. 627; e-mail: escarpel)
  Advertising and Direct Marketing Manager: Donna Liese (ext. 628; e-mail: dliese)
  Webmaster and E-Marketing Manager: Michael Tomolonis (ext. 625; e-mail: mtomolon)

Publicity Director: Jeremy Wang-Iverson (ext. 626; e-mail: jwi)
Marketing Assistant / Exhibits Coordinator: TBA (ext. 622)
Business: Molly Venezia, Director of Finance and Administration / Assistant Director
(ext. 610; e-mail: mvenezia)
Accountant: Winnie Westcott (ext. 614; e-mail: wwestcot)
Customer Service Liason: Penny Burke (ext. 613; e-mail: pborden)

Full Member

Established: 1936   Admitted to AAUP: 1937
Title output 2006: 95   Title output 2007: 98
Titles currently in print: 1,850

Editorial Program

American studies; anthropology; Asian studies; Asian American studies; African American
studies and literature; environmental studies; film and media; history; history of science/
technology; Jewish studies; life and health sciences; public policy; regional studies; religion;
sociology; women's studies; Latin American studies; Latino Studies.

Special series: Rutgers Series in Childhood Studies; Critical Issues in Crime and Society;
Critical Issues in Health and Medicine; Depth of Field; Key Words in Jewish Studies; MELA
(Multi-Ethnic Literatures of the Americas); The Public Life of the Arts; Screen Decades:
American Culture/American Cinema; Studies in Medical Anthropology; New Directions in
International Studies; Star Decades: American Culture/American Cinema; La Raza: Latino
Culture, Politics, and Society; Signifying (on) Scriptures; Jewish Cultures of the World;
Thought and Culture in the United States since 1945
Imprints: Rivergate Books
Joint Imprint: The Jane Voorhees Zimmerli Art Museum

Society of Biblical Literature

The Luce Center   Orders:
825 Houston Mill Road, Suite 350   Phone: (877) 725-3334
Atlanta, GA 30329   Fax: (802) 864-7626

Phone: (404) 727-3100   Journal Subscriptions and Membership:
Fax: (404) 727-3101   Phone: (866) 727-9955
E-mail: sblexec@sbl-site.org   Fax: (404) 727-2419
Indiv: (firstname.lastname)@sbl-site.org
Web site: www.sbl-site.org

Staff

Executive Director: Kent Richards (404/727-3038)
Editorial Director: Bob Buller (970/669-9900)
Managing Editor: Leigh Andersen (404/727-2327)
Acquisitions Editor: Billie Jean Collins (404/727-0807)
Marketing Manager: Kathie Klein (404/727-2325)
Director of Accounting: Susan Madara (404/727-3103)
Director of Administrative and Technology Services: Missy Colee (404/727-3124)

Technology Manager: Lauren Hightower
Web Site Manager: Sharon Johnson (404/727-3102)
Manager of Development & Customer Services: Sandra Stewart-Kruger (404/727-9484)
Director of Congresses and Professions: Matthew Collins (404/727-3095)
Manager of Congresses: Trista Krock (404/727-3137)
Software Developer: Chris O'Connor (404/727-2187)
Customer Services Coordinator: Deon King (404/727-9498)

Associate Member

Established: 1880	Admitted to AAUP: 2003
Title output 2006: 36	Title output 2007: 30
Titles currently in print: 502	Journals published: 2

Editorial Program

The SBL publishes works in biblical and religious studies. Monographic publications include major reference works; commentaries; text editions and translations; collections of essays; doctoral dissertations; and tools for teaching and research fields; archaeological, sociological, and historical studies; volumes that use archaeological and historical data to illuminate Israelite religion or the culture of biblical peoples; scholarly works on the history, culture, and literature of early Judaism; scholarly works on various aspects of the Masorah; scholarly congress proceedings; critical texts of the Greek Fathers including evaluations of data; philological tools; studies employing the methods and perspectives of linguistics, folklore studies, literary criticism, structuralism, social anthropology, and postmodern studies; studies of the Septuagint including textual criticism, manuscript witnesses and other versions, as well as its literature, historical milieu, and thought; studies related to the Jewish apocrypha and pseudepigrapha of the Hellenistic period, and the subsequent development of this literature in Judaism and early Christianity; studies in biblical literature and/or its cultural environment; text-critical works related to Hebrew Bible/Old Testament and New Testament including investigations of methodology, studies of individual manuscripts, critical texts of a selected book or passage, or examination of more general textual themes; translations of ancient Near Eastern texts; translations of ancient texts from the Greco-Roman world.

SBL is the exclusive North American distributor for Sheffield Phoenix Press (UK), and the sole producer and distributor of volumes in the Brown Judaic Studies series (Brown University).

Journals: *Journal of Biblical Literature, Review of Biblical Literature*

Special series: Academia Biblica; Archaeology and Biblical Studies; Biblical Encyclopedia Translations; Commentary on the Septuagint; Early Judaism and Its Literature; Global Perspectives on Biblical Scholarship; History of Biblical Studies; Masoretic Studies; The New Testament in the Greek Fathers; Resources for Biblical Study; Semeia Studies; Septuagint and Cognate Studies; Studia Philonica Annual and Monographs; Studies in Biblical Literature; Symposium Series; Text-Critical Studies; Writings from the Ancient World; Writings from the Greco-Roman World

Joint imprints and copublishing programs: SBL Handbook of Style for Ancient Near Eastern, Biblical, and Early Christian Studies with Hendrickson Publishers; HarperCollins Study Bible (NRSV), HarperCollins Bible Dictionary, Revised Edition, HarperCollins Bible Commentary, Revised Edition, and Harper's Bible Pronunciation Guide with HarperCollins; Hardback editions with Brill Academic Publishers of Leiden, The Netherlands

The University of South Carolina Press

1600 Hampton Street
5th Floor
Columbia, SC 29208

Phone: (803) 777-5243
Fax: (803) 777-0160
E-mail: (user I.D.)@sc.edu
Web site: www.sc.edu/uscpress

Business Office and Warehouse:
718 Devine Street
Columbia, SC 29208
Phone: (800) 768-2500
Fax: (800) 868-0740
E-mail: (user I.D.)@sc.edu

UK / European Distributor:
Eurospan

Canadian Distributor:
Scholarly Book Services

Staff

Director: Curtis L. Clark (803/777-5245; e-mail: cclark)
  Assistant Director for Operations: Linda Fogle (803/777-4848; e-mail: lfogle)
  Assistant Director for Sales and Marketing: Jonathan Haupt (803/777-2021; e-mail: jhaupt)
  Assistant to the Director: Karen Riddle (803/777-5245; e-mail: riddlek)
Acquisitions Editors: Linda Fogle (regional, trade) (803/777-4848; e-mail: lfogle); Alexander Moore (African American studies, history, Southern studies) (803/777-8070; e-mail: alexm); Jim Denton (literature, religious studies, rhetoric/communication, social work) (803/777-4859; e-mail: dentoja)
Manuscript Editorial: Bill Adams, Managing Editor (803/777-5075; e-mail: adamswb)
  Editor: Karen Rood (803/777-5877; e-mail: roodk)
  Editorial Assistant: Karen Beidel (803/777-9055; e-mail: kcbeidel)
Design and Production: Pat Callahan, Design and Production Manager (803/777-2449; e-mail: mpcallah)
  Book Designer: Brandi Lariscy-Avant (803/777-9056; e-mail: lariscyb)
  Design and Production Assistant: Ashley Mathias (803/777-2238; e-mail: samathi)
Marketing: Jonathan Haupt, Manager (803/777-2021; e-mail: jhaupt)
  Sales Assistant: Carolyn Dibble (803/777-5029; e-mail: cdibble)
  Advertising and Direct Mail Manager: Lynne Parker (803/777-5231; e-mail: parkerll)
Business/Warehouse: Dianne Smith, Business Manager and Permissions (803/777-1773; e-mail: dismith)
  Assistant Business Manager: Vicki Sewell (803/777-7754; e-mail: sewellv)
  Customer Service Representative: Libby Mack (803/777-1774; e-mail: lmack)
  Warehouse Assistant: Eddie Hill (803/777-0184; e-mail: jehill)

Full Member

Established: 1944
Title output 2006: 42
Titles currently in print: 750

Admitted to AAUP: 1948
Title output 2007: 52

Editorial Program

Scholarly works, mainly in the humanities and social sciences, and general interest titles, particularly those of importance to the state and region. Subjects include African-American studies; history, especially American history, military history, maritime history, and Southern history; literature and literary studies; religious studies, including comparative religion; Southern studies; rhetoric/communication; and social work.

Special series, joint imprints, and/or copublishing programs: The Belle W. Baruch Library in Marine Science; Chief Justiceships of the United States Supreme Court; The Papers of Henry Laurens; Historians in Conversation: Recent Themes in Understanding the Past; The Papers of John C. Calhoun; Social Problems and Social Issues; South Carolina Poetry Initiative Book Prize; Southern Classics; Studies in Comparative Religion; Studies in Maritime History; Studies in Rhetoric/Communication; Studies on Personalities of the New Testament; Studies on Personalities of the Old Testament; Understanding Contemporary American Literature; Understanding Contemporary British Literature; Understanding Modern European and Latin American Literature; Women's Diaries and Letters of the South

Southern Illinois University Press

1915 University Press Drive
SIUC Mail Code 6806
Carbondale, IL 62901-6806

Phone: (618) 453-2281
Fax: (618) 453-1221
E-mail: (user I.D.)@siu.edu
Web site: www.siu.edu/~siupress

Orders:
Southern Illinois University Press
c/o Chicago Distribution Center
11030 South Langley Avenue
Chicago, IL 60628-3830
Phone: (800) 621-2736
Fax: (800) 621-8476
Phone: (618) 453-6619; (800) 346-2680
Fax: (618) 453-3787; (800) 346-2681
E-mail: custserv@press.uchicago.edu
EDI; PUBNET at 202-5280

UK / European Distributor:
Eurospan

Canadian Representative:
Scholarly Book Services

Staff

Director: A.M. (Lain) Adkins (618/453-6615; e-mail: ladkins)
　Rights and Permissions (618/453-6619; e-mail: rights)
Acquisitions Editorial: Karl Kageff, Editor-in-Chief (American literature, film, regional studies, rhetoric and composition) (618/453-6629; e-mail: kageff)
　Executive Editor: Sylvia Frank Rodrigue (Civil War, Reconstruction) (508/297-2162; e-mail: sylvia@sylverlining.com)
　Acquisitions Editor: Kristine Priddy (composition, theater) (618/453-6631; e-mail: mkpriddy)
　Assistant Acquisitions Editor: Bridget Brown (communication, poetry) (618/453-2178; e-mail: bcbrown)
Editorial, Design, and Production: Barbara Martin, EDP Manager (618/453-6614; e-mail: bbmartin)
　Project Editors: Wayne Larsen (618/453-6628; e-mail: wlarsen); Kathleen Kageff (618/453-6613; e-mail: kbkageff)

Book Designer: Mary Rohrer (618/453-6612; e-mail: mrohrer)
Compositor: Kyle Lake (618/453-6635; e-mail: kylelake)
Marketing and Sales: Larry Townsend, Director of Marketing and Sales (618/453-6623;
e-mail: townsend)
Exhibits and Promotions Manager: Jennifer Fandel (618/453-6624; e-mail: jfandel)
Publicity Manager: Robert Carroll (618/453-6633; e-mail: rcarroll)
Internet Sales Manager: J.D. Tremblay (618/453-6634; e-mail: shipper2)
Business: Lisa Falaster, Manager (618/453-6610; e-mail: lisafala)
Database Manager: Angela Moore-Swafford (618/453-6619; e-mail: angmoore)
Accounting Specialist: Dawn Vagner (618/453-3786; e-mail: dvagner)

Full Member

Established: 1956
Title output 2006: 50
Titles currently in print: 1,200

Admitted to AAUP: 1980
Title output 2007: 47

Editorial Program
Scholarly books, primarily in the humanities and social sciences. Particular strengths are film
studies; theatre and stagecraft; regional and Civil War history; communication, rhetoric, and
composition studies; American literature; criminology; philosophy; aviation; contemporary
poetry. Submissions in fiction and festschriften are not invited.
Special series: Aviation Management; Civil War Campaigns in the Heartland; The Crab Or-
chard Series in Poetry; The Holmes-Johnson Series in Criminology; The Illustrated Flora of
Illinois; Landmarks in Rhetoric and Public Address; The North & South Series; The Papers
of Ulysses S. Grant; Shawnee Classics; Shawnee Books; Studies in Rhetorics and Feminisms;
Studies in Writing and Rhetoric; Theater in the Americas; The Collected Works of John
Dewey

Southern Methodist University Press

Street Address:
314 Fondren Library West
6404 Hilltop Lane
Dallas, TX 75275

Mailing Address:
PO Box 750415
Dallas, TX 75275-0415

Phone: (214) 768-1432
Fax: (214) 768-1428
E-mail: (user I.D.)@smu.edu
Web site: www.tamu.edu/upress/smu/smugen.html

Orders:
Phone: (800) 826-8911

Staff
Director: Keith Gregory (214/768-1432; e-mail: keithg)
Acquisitions Editor: Kathryn M. Lang (214/768-1433; e-mail: klang)
Marketing and Production Manager: George Ann Ratchford (214/768-1434;
e-mail: ggoodwin)

Full Member

Established: 1937
Title output 2006: 7
Titles currently in print: 212

Admitted to AAUP: 1946
Title output 2007: 7

Editorial Program

Creative nonfiction; ethics and human values; fiction; medical humanities; performing arts; Southwestern studies; and sport.
Special series: Medical Humanities; Sport in American Life

Stanford University Press

1450 Page Mill Road
Palo Alto, CA 94304-1124

Phone: (650) 723-9434
Fax: (650) 725-3457
E-mail: (user I.D.)@stanford.edu
Web site: www.sup.org

Orders:
Stanford University Press
Chicago Distribution Center
11030 South Langley Avenue
Chicago, IL 60628
Phone: (800) 621-2736; (773) 702-7000
Fax: (800) 621-8471; (773) 702-7212

European Representative:
Eurospan

Canadian Representative:
Lexa Publishers' Representatives

Staff

Director: Geoffrey Burn (650/736-1942; e-mail: grhburn) (business and security studies)
Associate Director & Editor-in-Chief: Alan Harvey (650/723-6375; e-mail: aharvey) (finance and IT)
Rights, Permissions, and Contracts: Ariane de Pree-Kajfez, Rights Manager (650/725-0815; e-mail: arianep)
Director of Scholarly Publishing: Norris Pope (650/725-0827; e-mail: npope) (humanities)
    Acquiring Editors: Kate Wahl (sociology, law, Middle East studies) (650/723-9598; e-mail: kwahl); Margo Beth Crouppen (economics, social and organizational studies) (650/724-7079; e-mail: mbcrouppen); TBA (anthropology and education); TBA (Asian studies, political science)
    Associate Editor: Emily-Jane Cohen (650/725-7717; e-mail: beatrice)
    Editorial Assistants: Joa Suorez (650/724-7080; e-mail: jsuorez); Jessica Walsh (650/736-0924; e-mail: jwalsh)
Editorial, Design, and Production: Patricia Myers, EDP Director (650/724-5365; e-mail: pmyers)
    Senior Production Editor: Judith Hibbard (650/736-0719; e-mail: jhibbard)
    Production Editors: Mariana Raykov (650/725-0835; e-mail: mraykov); John Feneron (650/725-0828; e-mail: johnf); Emily Smith (650/736-0686; e-mail emilys); Carolyn Brown (650/724-9990; e-mail: carolynb)
    Art & Design Manager: Rob Ehle (650/723-1132; e-mail: ehle)
    Designer: Bruce Lundquist (650/723-6808; e-mail: brucel)
    Production Manager: Harold Moorehead (650/725-0836; e-mail: hmoorehead)
    Production Coordinator Mike Sagara (650/725-0839; e-mail: msagara)
Marketing: David Jackson, Marketing Director (650/736-1782; e-mail: david.jackson)
    Marketing and Publicity Manager: Puja Sangar (650/724-4211; e-mail: psangar)

Advertising and Direct Mail Coordinator: Elizabeth Miles (650/725-0823;
e-mail: elizabeth.miles)
Exhibits Manager: Christie Cochrell (650/725-0820; e-mail: cochrell)
Marketing Assistants: Sylvie Kim (650/736-1781; e-mail: sylviek); Sarah Crane Newman
(650/725-0822; e-mail: sarahcn)
Business: John Zotz, Chief Operating Officer (650/723-3230; e-mail: jnzotz)
Business Manager: Jean Kim (650/725-0838; e-mail: jean.h.kim)
Systems Manager: Chris Cosner (650/724-7276; e-mail: ccosner)

Full Member

Established: 1925   Admitted to AAUP: 1937
Title output 2006: 140   Title output 2007: 145
Titles currently in print: 1,800

Editorial Program
Scholarly titles and textbooks in philosophy, history, literature, religion, sociology, anthropology, and political science; and on Asia, Latin America, and the Western United States.
Scholarly titles, textbooks, and professional titles in business, economics, security studies,
law, policy, and education.
Special series: The Amherst Series in Law, Jurisprudence, and Social Thought; Asian
America; Asian Religions and Cultures; Asian Security; Cold War International History Project; Comparative Studies in History, Institutions, and Public Policy; The Complete Works
of Friedrich Nietzsche; Contemporary Issues in Asia and the Pacific; Critical Perspectives on
Crime and Law; The Cultural Lives of Law; Cultural Memory in the Present; Cultural Sit-
ings; Figurae: Reading Medieval Culture; Innovation and Technology in the World Econo-
my; Jurists: Profiles in Legal Theory; Latin American Development Forum; Law, Society, and
Culture in China; The Making of Modern Freedom; Meridian: Crossing Aesthetics; Social
Science History; Stanford Business Classics; Stanford Nuclear Age Series; Stanford Studies in
International Economics and Development; Stanford Studies in Jewish History and Culture;
Studies in Kant and German Idealism; Studies in Social Inequality; Studies of the East Asian
Institute
Special imprints: Stanford Business Books; Stanford Law and Politics; Stanford Social Sci-
ences; Stanford Economics and Finance; Stanford Security Studies; Stanford General Books
Copublishing arrangements: United Nations, the World Bank, and the Woodrow Wilson
Center

State University of New York Press

194 Washington Avenue, Suite 305
Albany, NY 12210-2384

Phone: (518) 472-5000
Fax: (518) 472-5038
E-mail: info@sunypress.edu
Indiv: (firstname.lastname)@sunypress.edu
Web site: www.sunypress.edu

Customer Service:
c/o CUP Services
PO Box 6525
Ithaca, NY 14851
Phone: (607) 277-2211;
(800) 666-2211 (US only)
Fax: (607) 277-6292;
(800) 688-2877 (US only)
E-mail: orderbook@cupserv.org

UK Representative:
Andrew Gilman
University Presses Marketing

UK / European Distributor:
NBN International

Canadian Representative:
Lexa Publishers' Representatives

Staff

Director: Gary Dunham
  Associate Director: James Peltz (518/472-5031) (film studies, literary criticism, literature)
  Assistant to the Director: Janice Vunk (518/472-5025)
  Rights & Permissions: Jennie Doling (518/472-5024)
  Receptionist: Diana Altobello (518/472-5000)
Acquisitions Editorial:
  Editor-in-Chief: Jane Bunker (518/472-5003) (philosophy, psychology, education)
  Senior Acquisitions Editors: Nancy Ellegate (518/472-5004) (Asian studies, criminology, religion, sociology); Michael Rinella (518/472-5030) (political science, African American studies, regional)
  Acquisitions Editors: Larin McLaughlin (518/472-5035) (women's studies, cultural studies, American studies, Latin American studies, communication)
  Editorial Assistants: Amanda Lanne (518/472-5037); Allison Lee (518/472-5018); Andrew Kenyon (518/472-5007)
Production:
  Director of Production: Marilyn Semerad (518/472-5019)
  Senior Production Editors: Diane Ganeles (518/472-5014); Laurie Searl (518/472-5033); Kelli Williams (518/472-5041)
  Production Editors: Eileen Meehan (518/472-5015); Ryan Morris (518/472-5002)
  Assistant Production Editor: Robert Puchalik (518/472-5042)
Marketing:
  Director of Marketing and Publicity: Fran Keneston (518/472-5023)
  Executive Promotions Manager: Anne Valentine (518/472-5032)
  Senior Promotions Manager: Michael Campochiaro (518/472-5043)
  Publicist: Susan Petrie (518/472-5008)
  Exhibits Coordinator: Michelle Alamillo (518/472-5039)
  Review Clerk: Meghan Morris (518/472-5006)

Marketing and Publicity Assistant: TBA (518/472-5044)
Sales:
  Director of Sales and Business Development: Dan Flynn (518/472-5036)
  Administrator of Electronic Marketing and Publishing Services: Greg Smith
  (518/472-5028)
  Sales Assistant: Renee Jones (518/472-5046)
Business:
  Director of Financial Operations: Frank Mahar (518/472-5022)
  Accounts Payable: Judy Trenchard (518/472-5010)
  General Ledger Accountant: Linda Hallak (518/472-5027)
  Royalties Accountant: Sharla Clute (518/472-5016)
Information Systems:
  LAN Administrator: Bob Sajeski (518/472-5021)

Full Member

Established: 1966   Admitted to AAUP: 1970
Title output 2006: 178   Title output 2007: 167
Titles currently in print: 4,037

Editorial Program

Scholarly titles and serious works of general interest in most areas of the humanities and the social sciences, with special interest in African American studies; American studies; Asian studies; communication; cultural studies; education; environmental studies; film studies; Holocaust studies; Jewish studies; literature and literary theory and criticism; Middle Eastern studies; philosophy; political science; psychology; religious studies; rhetoric and composition; sociology; sports studies; and women's studies.

  SUNY Press is the exclusive distributor of books from the Rockefeller Institute Press.

Syracuse University Press

Street Address: Warehouse Address:
621 Skytop Road, Suite 110   1600 Jamesville Avenue
Syracuse, NY 13244-5290   Syracuse, NY 13244-5160

Phone: (315) 443-5534   Orders:
Fax: (315) 443-5545   Phone: (315) 443-2597; (800) 365-8929
E-mail: (user I.D.)@syr.edu   Fax: (866) 536-4771
Web site: syracuseuniversitypress.syr.edu

                                         UK Distributor:
                                         Eurospan

Staff

Director: Alice R. Pfeiffer (315/443-5535; e-mail: arpfeiff)
  Assistant to the Director: Ellen S. Goodman (315/443-5541; e-mail: esgoodma)
Acquisitions Editorial: Mary Selden Evans, Executive Editor (315/443-5543; e-mail:
  msevans)

Acquisitions Editor: Glenn Wright (315/443-5647; e-mail: glwright)
Acquisitions Assistant: Marcia Hough (315/443-2150; e-mail: mshough)
Manuscript Editorial: John Fruehwirth, Managing Editor (315/443-5544; e-mail: jjfruehw)
Copy Editor: Marian Buda (315/443-5542; e-mail: mebuda)
Electronic Manuscripts Manager: Kay Steinmetz (315/443-9155; e-mail: kasteinm)
Design and Production: Mary Peterson Moore, Manager (315/443-5540; e-mail: mpmoore)
Senior Designers: Victoria Lane (315/443-5540; e-mail: vmlane); Fred Wellner (315/443-5540; e-mail: fawellne)
Marketing: Mona Hamlin, Marketing Analyst (315/443-5547; e-mail: mhamlin)
Design Specialist: Lynn Hoppel (315/443-1975; e-mail: lphoppel)
Marketing Coordinator: Lisa Kuerbis (315/443-5546; e-mail: lkuerbis)
Business: Karen Lockwood, Senior Business Manager (315/443-5536; e-mail: kflockwo)
Credit Manager: Karen Boland (315/443-5539; e-mail: kcboland)
Warehouse Coordinator: Anthony Carbone (315/443-5537)
Distribution Assistant: John Vacchiano (315/443-5537)
Order Supervisor: Lori Lazipone (315/443-5538; e-mail: ljlazipo)
Accounting Clerk: Tamra delCostello-Emmi (315/443-3621; e-mail: tdelcost)
Office Assistant: Karen Thompson (315/443-1451; e-mail: kethom02)

Full Member

Established: 1943   Admitted to AAUP: 1946
Title output 2006: 48   Title output 2007: 54
Titles currently in print: 1,250

Editorial Program

Scholarly books and works of general interest in the areas of Jewish, Middle East, Irish, New York State, women's, Native American, and Medieval studies; Arab-American writing; religion; television; sports history; journalism; biography; human and urban geography; politics; peace and conflict resolution. Selected fiction, poetry, and memoirs.

The Press distributes books bearing the imprints of Adirondack Museum; American University of Beirut; Moshe Dayan Center for Middle Eastern and African Studies (Tel-Aviv University); American University in Cairo Press; New Netherlands Project; Jusoor; National Library of Ireland; Arlen House, Dedalus Press, Munson-Williams-Proctor Institute; Corning Museum of Glass, and the Pucker Gallery, Boston.

Special series, joint imprints, and/or copublishing programs: The Adirondack Museum; The Albert Schweitzer Library; Arab-American Writing; Contemporary Issues in the Middle East; Gender, Culture, and Politics in the Middle East; Gender and Globalization; Irish Studies; Iroquois and Their Neighbors; Judaic Traditions in Literature, Music, and Art; Library of Modern Jewish Literature; The Martin Buber Library; Medieval Studies; Middle East Literature in Translation; Modern Intellectual and Political History of the Middle East; Modern Jewish History; Mohamad El-Hindi Books on Arab Culture and Islamic Civilization; New York State Studies; Religion and Politics; Religion, Theology and the Holocaust; Space, Place, and Society; Sports and Entertainment; Syracuse Studies in Peace and Conflict Resolution; The Television Series; Women in Religion

Teachers College Press

1234 Amsterdam Avenue
New York, NY 10027-6696

Phone: (212) 678-3929
Fax: (212) 678-4149
E-mail: (user I.D.)@columbia.edu
(unless otherwise indicated)
Web site: www.tcpress.com

Warehouse:
Teachers College Press
PO Box 20
Williston, VT 05495-0020
Phone: (800) 864-7626

Returns:
12 Winter Sport Lane
Williston, VT 05495

European Representative:
Eurospan

Canadian Representative:
Guidance Centre

Staff

Director: Carole Pogrebin Saltz (212/678-3927; e-mail: saltz@tc.edu)
   Assistant to the Director: Golnar Nikpour (212/678-3965; e-mail:
   nikpour@tc.columbia.edu)
   Rights and Permissions Manager/Special Sales Coordinator: Leah Wonski (212/678-3827;
   e-mail: wonski@tc.edu)
Acquisitions Editorial: Brian Ellerbeck, Executive Acquisitions Editor (administration, school
   change, leadership, policy, special and gifted education, curriculum studies, cultural studies) (212/678-3908; e-mail: bhe3)
   Senior Acquisitions Editor: Marie Ellen Larcada (early childhood education, sociology,
   educational research, teacher education/foundations, higher education, women's studies)
   (212/678-3928; e-mail: larcada@tc.columbia.edu)
   Acquisitions Editor: Meg Lemke (language and literacy, teacher research, counseling/psy-
   chology, infancy/child development) (212/678-3909; e-mail: lemke@tc.edu)
   Assistant Acquisitions Editor: Adee Braun (212/678-3905; e-mail:
   braun@tc.columbia.edu)
Production: Peter Sieger, Production Manager (212/678-3926; e-mail: prs7)
   Senior Production Editor: Karl Nyberg (212/678-3806; e-mail: kan10)
   Production Editors: Lyn Grossman (212/678-3902; e-mail: lg124); Aureliano Vazquez
   (212/678-3945; e-mail: av314); Lori Tate (212/678-3907; e-mail: lat18)
   Production Assistants: Debra Jackson-Whyte (212/678-3926; e-mail: daj61); Shannon
   Waite (212/678-3914; e-mail: stw2005)
Marketing: Leyli Shayegan, Director, Sales and Marketing and Assistant Director
   (212/678-3475; e-mail: ls175)
   Marketing Manager: Nancy Power (212/678-3915; e-mail: nep5)
   Graphic Arts Manager: David Strauss (212/678-3982; e-mail: dms38)
   Publicity Coordinator: Tamar Elster (212/678-3963; e-mail: elster@tc.edu)
   Outreach Coordinator: Michael McGann (212/678-3919; e-mail: mim11)
Business: Mary Lynch, Senior Financial Manager (212/678-3913; e-mail: mal48)
   Business Assistant: Lisa Forsythe (212/678-3917; e-mail: laf2002)
   Secretary / Receptionist: Marcia Ruiz (212/678-3929; e-mail: myr3)

Full Member

Established: 1904

Title output 2006: 58

Titles currently in print: 700

Admitted to AAUP: 1971

Title output 2007: 63

Editorial Program

Scholarly, professional, text, and trade books on education, education-related areas, and feminist studies. Multimedia instructional materials, tests, and evaluation materials for classroom use at all levels of education.

Specific areas of interest in education are: curriculum; early childhood; school administration and educational policy; counseling and guidance; mathematics; philosophy; psychology; language and literacy; science; sociology; special education; social studies; teacher education; cultural studies; women and higher education.

Special series: Advances in Contemporary Educational Thought; Athene Series in Women's Studies; Between Teacher & Text; Counseling and Development; Critical Issues in Curriculum; Critical Issues in Educational Leadership; Early Childhood Education; Education and Psychology of the Gifted; John Dewey Lecture; Language and Literacy; Multicultural Education; Politics of Identity and Education; Practitioner Inquiry; Professional Ethics in Education; Reflective History; The Series on School Reform; Sociology of Education; Teaching for Social Justice; Ways of Knowing in Science and Mathematics

Temple University Press

1601 N. Broad Street, USB Room 306
Philadelphia, PA 19122-6099

Phone: (215) 204-8787; (800) 447-1656
Fax: (215) 204-4719
E-mail: (firstname.lastname)@temple.edu
Web site: www.temple.edu/tempress

UK Distributor:
Combined Academic Publishers

Orders:
Temple University Press
Chicago Distribution Center
11030 South Langley Avenue
Chicago, IL 60628
Phone: (800) 621-2736
Fax: (800) 621-8471

Canadian Distributor:
Lexa Publishers' Representatives

Staff

Director: Alex Holzman (215/204-3436)
Development Director: David Pausch (215/204-0996)
Rights and Permissions Manager: Matthew Kull (215/204-5707)
Acquisitions: Janet M. Francendese, Assistant Director and Editor-in-Chief (215/204-3437)
   Senior Editors: Micah Kleit (215/204-3439); Mick Gusinde-Duffy (215/204-3754)
Production: Charles H. E. Ault, Assistant Director and Director of Production and
   Electronic Publishing (215/204-3389)
   Senior Production Editor: Elena Coler (215/204-3388)
   Production Coordinator: David Wilson (215/204-7296)
Marketing: Ann-Marie Anderson, Assistant Director and Director of Marketing
   (215/204-1108)
   Advertising and Promotion Manager: Irene Imperio (215/204-1099)
   Publicity Manager: Gary Kramer (215/204-3440)

Business: Barry Adams, Assistant Director and Financial Manager (215/204-3444)
  Customer Service/Operations Manager: Karen Baker (215/204-8606)

Full Member

Established: 1969   Admitted to AAUP: 1972
Title output 2006: 46   Title output 2007: 42
Titles currently in print: 1,140

Editorial Program

African American studies; American studies; anthropology; Asian studies; Asian American studies; cinema and media studies; communication; criminology; disability studies; education; ethnicity and race; gay and lesbian studies; gender studies; geography; health; labor studies; Latin American studies; law and society; Philadelphia regional studies; political science and public policy; religion; sociology; sports; urban studies; US and European history; women's studies.

  Temple University Press distributes books for the Asian American Writers' Workshop.
Special series: America in Transition: Radical Perspectives; American Subjects; Animals, Culture, and Society; Asian American History and Culture; Critical Perspectives on the Past; Emerging Media; Gender, Family, and the Law; Labor in Crisis; Mapping Racisms; The New Academy; Place, Culture, and Politics; Politics, History, and Social Change; Queer Politics, Queer Theories; Rhetoric, Culture, and Public Address; Sound Matters; Studies in Latin American and Caribbean Music; Teaching/Learning Social Justice; Voices of Latin American Life; Wide Angle Books

University of Tennessee Press

Mailing Address: Shipping Address:
110 Conference Center   600 Henley Street
Knoxville, TN 37996-4108   Suite 110 Conference Center
                                                   Knoxville, TN 37902-2911

Phone: (865) 974-3321   Orders:
Fax: (865) 974-3724   Univ. of Tennessee Press
E-mail: custserv@utpress.org   Chicago Distribution Center
Indiv: (user I.D.)@utk.edu   11030 South Langley Avenue
(unless otherwise indicated)   Chicago, IL 60628
Web site: utpress.org   Phone: (800) 621-2736
                                                   Fax: (773) 660-2235

Staff

Director: Jennifer M. Siler (e-mail: jsiler)
Acquisitions Editorial: Scot Danforth, Acquisitions Editor (e-mail: danforth)
Manuscript Editorial: Stanley Ivester, Managing Editor (e-mail: ivester)
  Manuscript Editor: Gene Adair (e-mail: gadair)
  Editorial Assistant: Thomas Wells (e-mail: twells)
Design and Production: Barbara Karwhite, Manager (e-mail: bkarwhit)
  Book Designer: Kelly Gray (e-mail: kgray14)

Production Coordinator: Stephanie Thompson (e-mail: sthomp20)
Marketing: Cheryl Carson, Manager (e-mail: ccarson3)
  Exhibits/Publicity Manager: Tom Post (e-mail: tpost)
Business: Tammy Berry, Manager (e-mail: tberry)
  Receptionist/Bookkeeper: Lisa Davis (e-mail: ldavis49)
IT Manager: Maryann Stopha Reissig (e-mail: mstopha)

Full Member

Established: 1940	Admitted to AAUP: 1964
Title output 2006: 40	Title output 2007: 38
Titles currently in print: 730	

Editorial Program
American studies; Appalachian studies; African American studies; history; religion; folklore; vernacular architecture; historical archaeology; material culture; literature; and literary fiction. Submissions in poetry, textbooks, and translations are not invited.
Special series, joint imprints, and/or copublishing programs: Appalachian Echoes; Correspondence of James K. Polk; Legacies of War, Outdoor Tennessee; The Papers of Andrew Jackson; Sport and Popular Culture; Tennesseana Editions; Tennessee Studies in Literature; Vernacular Architecture Studies; and Voices of the Civil War

University of Texas Press

Street Address:	Mailing Address:
2100 Comal Street	PO Box 7819
Austin, TX 78722	Austin, TX 78713-7819

Phone: (512) 471-7233	Orders:
Fax: (512) 232-7178	Phone: (800) 252-3206
E-mail: utpress@uts.cc.utexas.edu	Fax: (800) 687-6046
Indiv: (user I.D.)@utpress.ppb.utexas.edu	
Web site: www.utexaspress.com	

Staff
Director: Joanna Hitchcock (512/232-7604; e-mail: joanna)
  Assistant to the Director: Dreya Johannsen (512/232-7603; e-mail: dreya)
  Development Officer: Celeste Mendoza (512/232-7605; e-mail: celeste)
Rights and Permissions Manager: Laura Young Bost (512/232-7625; e-mail: laura)
  Rights and Permissions Assistant: Peggy Gough (512/232-7624; e-mail: peggy)
Assistant Director and Editor-in-Chief: Theresa May (social sciences, Latin American studies) (512/232 7612; e-mail: theresa)
  Acquisitions Editors: William Bishel (natural sciences, Texas and the Southwest) (512/232-7609; e-mail: wbishel); Jim Burr (humanities) (512/232-7610; e-mail: jim); Allison Faust (art, music, geography, Texas art and culture) (512/232-7615; e-mail: allison)
  Assistant Editor: Casey Kittrell (512/232-7608; e-mail: casey)
Managing Editor: Leslie Tingle (512/232-7614; e-mail: leslie)
  Manuscript Editors: Lynne Chapman (512/232-7607; e-mail: lynne); Victoria Davis (512/232-7613; e-mail: victoria)
  Copyediting Assistant: Megan Giller (512/232-7616; e-mail: megan)

Editorial Fellows: Samantha Allison (512/232-7613, e-mail: samantha); Katherine Jones (512/232-7611; e-mail: katie)
Design & Production Manager: Ellen McKie (512/232-7640; e-mail: ellen)
Designers: Derek George (512/232-7641; e-mail: derek); Lisa Tremaine (512/232-7642; e-mail: lisa)
Production Editor: Regina Fuentes (512/232-7639; e-mail: regina)
Production Coordinator: David Ramonda (512/232-7637; e-mail: dramonda)
Production Assistant: Kaila Wyllis (512/232-7638; e-mail: kaila)
Assistant Director and Sales/Marketing Manager: David Hamrick (512/232-7627; e-mail: dave)
Texas Sales Manager: Darrell Windham (512/471-4032; e-mail: darrell)
Texas Sales Representative: Steve Griffis (979/255-9175; e-mail: steve)
Assistant Marketing Manager: Nancy Bryan (512/232-7628; e-mail: nancy)
Direct Mail and Website Manager: Sharon Casteel (512/232-7631; e-mail: sharon)
Publicist: Stephanie Nelson (512/232-7634; e-mail: stephanie)
Advertising and Exhibits Manager: Lauren Zachry-Reynolds (512/232-7630; e-mail: lauren)
Marketing Assistant: Colleen Devine (512/232-7633; e-mail: colleen)
Journals Manager: Sue Hausmann (512/232-7620; e-mail: sue)
Journals Production Coordinator: Karen Broyles (512/232-7622; e-mail: kbroyles)
Journals Production Coordinator: Stacey Salling (512/232-7619; e-mail: stacey)
Journals Promotion Manager: Leah Dixon (512/232-7618; e-mail: leah)
Journals Circulation and Rights and Permissions Manager: Rebecca Frazier (512/232-7621; e-mail: rebecca)
Journals Circulation Assistant: James McKaskle (512/232-7621; e-mail: james)
Assistant Director and Financial Officer: Joyce Lewandowski (512/232-7646; e-mail: joyce)
Accounts Receivable: Sharon Greensage (512/232-7648; e-mail: sgreensage)
Accounts Payable: Linda Ramirez (512/232-7649; e-mail: linda)
Business Assistant: Nancy Monroe (512/232-7647; e-mail: nmonroe)
Customer Service Supervisor: Brenda Jo Hoggatt (512/232-7650; e-mail: brenda_jo)
Customer Service Assistant: Dawn Bishop (512/232-7652; e-mail: dawn)
Warehouse (512/471-3634)
Warehouse Manager: Donald Martinez (512/232-7654; e-mail: donald)
Warehouse Supervisor: George Mill (512/232-7656; e-mail: george)
Warehouse Staff: Michael Murillo (512/232-7655); Rogelio Rocha Jr. (512/232-7657); Rey Renteria (512/232-7658; e-mail: rey)
Senior LAN Administrator: William Braddock (512/232-7644; e-mail: william)

Full Member

Established: 1950	Admitted to AAUP: 1954
Title output 2006: 106	Title output 2007: 109
Titles currently in print: 1,045	Journals published: 13

Editorial Program

Scholarly books in the humanities, natural sciences, and social sciences; regional books; and serious nonfiction of general interest; humanities (art of the ancient world, classics and the ancient world, Egyptology, film and media studies, literary modernism, Middle Eastern studies and translations of Middle Eastern literature, Old World archaeology, Texas architecture); natural sciences (botany, conservation, cookbooks and gardening, environmental studies, geography, natural history, ornithology); social sciences (American studies, anthropology, applied language, Chicano/a studies, Latin American and pre-Columbian studies, translations of Latin American literature, Mexican American studies, Native American studies, New World archaeology, Texas and the Southwest, women's studies). Original fiction, poetry, and children's books are not invited.

The Press distributes publications for the Austin Museum of Art; Bat Conservation International; Jack S. Blanton Museum of Art; Center for Middle Eastern Studies; Center for Mexican American Studies; McNay Art Museum; Museum of Fine Arts Houston; and Teresa Lozano Long Institute of Latin American Studies.

Journals (*available electronically): *Archaeoastronomy*; Art Lies, Asian Music*; Cinema Journal*; Flow*, The Journal of Individual Psychology*; The Journal of the History of Sexuality*; Latin American Music Review*; Latin American Research Review*; Libraries and the Cultural Record*; Southwestern Historical Quarterly*; Texas Studies in Literature and Language*; The Velvet Light Trap*; Journal of Latin American Geography for the Conference of Latin Americanist Geographers**

Special series, joint imprints, and/or copublishing programs: Center for Mexican American Studies, History, Culture, and Society Series; Chicana Matters Series; Constructs Series; Focus on American History Series; Handbook of Latin American Studies; Harry Ransom Humanities Research Imprint Series; Inter-America Series; Legendary Past Series; Literary Modernism Series; Middle East Monograph Series; Modern Middle East Literature in Translation Series; Modern Middle East Series; New Interpretations of Latin America Series; Oratory of Classical Greece Series; Southwest Writers Series; Surrealist Revolution Series; Texas Archaeology and Ethnohistory Series; Texas Field Guides; Texas Pan American and Literature in Translation Series; Wittliff Gallery Series of Southwestern and Mexican Photography

Endowed book series: Bridwell Texas History Series; Clifton and Shirley Caldwell Texas Heritage Series; Jamal and Rania Daniel Series; M. Georgia Hegarty Dunkerley Contemporary Art Series; Peter T. Flawn Series in Natural Resource Management and Conservation; Roger Fullington Series in Architecture; Jess and Betty Jo Hay Endowment; The Corrie Herring Hooks Series; Jewish History, Life, and Culture Series; Joe R. and Teresa Lozano Long Series in Latin American and Latino Art and Culture; Brad and Michele Moore Roots Music Series; William and Bettye Nowlin Series in Art, History, and Culture of the Western Hemisphere; Linda Schele Series in Maya and Pre-Columbian Studies; Jack and Doris Smothers Series in Texas History, Life, and Culture; Louann Atkins Temple Women and Culture Series; Mildred Wyatt-Wold Series in Ornithology; Bill and Alice Wright Photography Series

Texas A&M University Press

Street Address:
John H. Lindsey Building, Lewis Street
College Station, TX 77843

Mailing Address:
4354 TAMU
College Station, TX 77843-4354

Phone: (979) 845-1436
Fax: (979) 847-8752
E-mail: upress@tampress.tamu.edu
Indiv: (user I.D.)@tampress.tamu.edu
Web site: www.tamu.edu/upress

Orders:
Phone: (800) 826-8911
Fax: (888) 617-2421

European Representative:
Eurospan

Staff

Director: Charles Backus (979/458-3980; e-mail: backus)
  Assistant to the Director/Rights & Permissions: Linda Lou Salitros (979/845-1438; e-mail: lls)
Acquisitions Editorial: Mary Lenn Dixon, Editor-in-Chief (Texas and Western history, borderland studies, presidential studies, anthropology) (979/845-0759; e-mail: mld)
  Louise Lindsey Merrick Editor for the Natural Environment: Shannon Davies (512/327-3183; e-mail: shannondavies@austin.rr.com)
  Acquisitions Assistant: Diana Vance (979/458-3975; e-mail: dlv)
  Intern: Michael Beilfuss (979/458-3977; e-mail: acquistions)
Manuscript Editorial: Thom Lemmons, Managing Editor (979/845-0758; e-mail: tl)
  Assistant Editor: Jennifer Ann Hobson (979/458-3979; e-mail: jah)
  Editorial Assistant: Janet Mathewson (979/458-3978; e-mail: jmm)
Production: Susan Pettey, Production Manager (979/845-0760; e-mail: sap)
Design: Mary Ann Jacob, Design Manager (979/845-3694; e-mail: maj)
  Pre-press and Electronic Publishing Manager: Kevin Grossman (979/458-3995; e-mail: klg)
Marketing: Gayla Christiansen, Marketing Manager (979/845-0148; e-mail: gec)
  Publicity and Advertising Manager: Teresa Laffin (979/458-3982; e-mail: tdl)
  Graphics / Web Manager: Kyle Littlefield (979/458-3983; e-mail: k-littlefield)
  Exhibits and Special Promotions Manager: Jennifer Gardner (979/458-3984; e-mail: jg)
  Sales Manager: David Neel (979/458-3981; e-mail: dn)
Financial: Dianna Sells, Financial Manager (979/845-0146; e-mail: dsh)
  Finance Assistant: Johnny Ruiz (979/458-3974; e-mail: jar)
Business Operations Manager: Sharon Pavlas-Mills (979/458-3994; e-mail: sym)
  Accounts Receivable Manager: Wynona Davis (979/458-3989; e-mail: wsd)
  Order Fulfillment Supervisor: Vicky Ramos (979/458-3990; e-mail: vrr)
  Assistant Business Operations Manager: Brandy Petereit (979/458-3991; e-mail: bjp)
Warehouse Manager: Mike Martin (979/458-3986; e-mail: mam)
  Assistant Warehouse Manager: Chris O'Connell (979/458-3987; e-mail: coc)

Full Member

Established: 1974
Title output 2006: 54
Titles currently in print: 938

Admitted to AAUP: 1977
Title output 2007: 63

Editorial Program

Texas and the Southwest; American and Western history; natural history; the environment; nautical archaeology; women's studies; military history; economics; business; architecture; art; veterinary medicine; presidential studies; borderland studies. Submissions are not invited in poetry.

Special series: C. A. Brannen Series in Military Studies; Canseco-Keck History; Carolyn and Ernest Fay Series in Analytical Psychology; Centennial of Flight Series; Centennial Series of the Association of Former Students; Charles and Elizabeth Prothro Texas Photography; Clayton Wheat Williams Texas Life; Ed Rachal Foundation Series in Nautical Archaeology; Elma Dill Russell Spencer Foundation; Environmental History; Fronteras; Gulf Coast Studies; The Hughes Presidency and Leadership Studies; Joe and Betty Moore Texas Art; Kenneth E. Montague Business and Oil History; Landmark Speeches on American Politics; Louise Lindsey Merrick Texas Environment; Presidential Rhetoric; Rio Grande/Rio Bravo; River Books; Sam Rayburn Rural Life; Sara and John H. Lindsey Series in the Arts and Humanities; Studies in Architecture and Culture; Tarleton State University Southwestern Studies in the Humanities; Texas A&M Economics; Texas A&M Foreign Relations and the Presidency; Texas A&M Military History; Texas A&M Southwestern Studies; Texas A&M University Anthropology; University of Houston Mexican American Studies; W. L. Moody Jr. Natural History; Wardlaw Books; West Texas A&M University

TCU Press

Mailing Address:
Box 298300
Fort Worth, TX 76129

Street Address:
3000 Sandage
Fort Worth, TX 76109

Phone: (817) 257-7822
Fax: (817) 257-5075
Web site: www.prs.tcu.edu

Orders:
Phone: (800) 826-8911

Staff

Director: Judy Alter (e-mail: j.alter@tcu.edu)
Editor: Susan Petty (e-mail: s.petty@tcu.edu)
Production Director: Melinda Esco (e-mail: m.esco@tcu.edu)

Full Member

Established: 1966
Title output 2006: 10
Titles currently in print: 266

Admitted to AAUP: 1982
Title output 2007: 16

Editorial Program

Humanities and social sciences, with special emphasis on Texas and Southwestern history and literature; American studies; fiction; and women's studies.

Special series: Chaparral Books for Young Readers; The Chisholm Trail Series; The Texas Tradition Series; Texas Biography; TCU Texas Poets Laureate

Texas Tech University Press

<u>Street Address:</u>
Administrative Support Center
2903 Fourth Street, Suite 201
Lubbock, TX 79409-1037

<u>Mailing Address:</u>
Box 41037
Lubbock, TX 79409-1037

Phone: (806) 742-2982
Fax: (806) 742-2979
E-mail: (firstname.lastname)@ttu.edu
Web site: www.ttup.ttu.edu

<u>Orders:</u>
Phone: (806) 742-2982; (800) 832-4042

Staff

Director: Noel R. Parsons
Acquisitions: Judith Keeling, Editor-in-Chief (humanities)
    Editor: Noel R. Parsons (sciences)
Managing Editor: Karen Medlin
Design and Production Manager: Barbara Werden
    Design and Production Assistant: Lindsay Starr
Marketing Manager: Barbara Brannon
    Exhibits and Publicity Manager: John Brock
Journals Editor: Lori Vermaas
Business Manager: Joel Nichols
Office Manager: Isabel Williams
    Customer Service: Sandra Fielding; Isabel Williams, Michelle Yost
    Warehouse & Shipping Manager: Ramon Luna

Full Member

Established: 1971
Title output 2006: 25
Titles currently in print: 349

Admitted to AAUP: 1987
Title output 2007: 22
Journals published: 5

Editorial Program

Natural sciences and natural history; environmental studies and literature of place; regional history and culture; Western Americana; Vietnam War and Southeast Asian studies; eighteenth-century studies; Joseph Conrad studies; costume and textile history and conservation; poetry (by invitation only); regional fiction.

Journals: *Conradiana*; *The Eighteenth Century*; *Helios*; *Intertexts*; *The William Carlos Williams Review*

Special series: Costume Society of America; Discourses in Native America; Double Mountain Books: Classic Reissues of the American West; Fashioning the Eighteenth Century; Grover E. Murray Studies in the American Southwest; Modern Southeast Asia; Plains Histories; and Walt McDonald First-Book Series in Poetry

Texas Western Press

University of Texas at El Paso
500 West University Avenue
El Paso, TX 79968-0633

Orders:
Phone: (800) 488-3789; (915) 747-5688

Phone: (915) 747-5688
Fax: (915) 747-7515
E-mail: twpress@utep.edu
Web site: www.utep.edu/twp

Staff
Director: Robert L. Stakes (915/747-5688; e-mail: rlstakes@utep.edu)
Accounts Supervisor and Secretary: Carmen Tavarez (915/747-5688; e-mail: ctavarez)

Full Member
Established: 1952
Title output 2006: 2
Titles currently in print: 54

Admitted to AAUP: 1986
Title output 2007: 2

Editorial Program
Scholarly books and serious nonfiction with special interests in the history and cultures of the
Southwest; selected art and photography; US-Mexico border studies; environmental studies;
and the following series: Southwestern Studies and The Borderlands/La Frontera.

University of Tokyo Press

7-3-1 Hongo, Bunkyo-ku
Tokyo 113-8654, Japan

Phone: +81-3-3811-0964, +81-3-3811-8814
Fax: +81-3-3814-9458, +81-3-3812-6958
E-mail: info@utp.or.jp

US Representative:
Columbia University Press

Staff
President: Hiroshi Komiyama
Chairman of the Board: Kazuo Okamoto
Managing Director: Masami Yamaguchi (e-mail: ajup@utp.or.jp)
Associate Director & Editor-in-Chief: Hidetoshi Takenaka
Marketing Director: Tomohiko Takahashi
Production Director: Masayuki Nagasaka
Executive Assistant, International Publications: Mitsuo Takayanagi

International Member
Established: 1951
Title output 2006: 114
Titles currently in print: 3,950

Admitted to AAUP: 1970
Title output 2007: 124

Editorial Program

Titles published in Japanese reflect the research carried out at the university in the humanities, social sciences, and natural sciences. Continuing series are published in biology, earth sciences, sociology, economics, philosophy, and Japanese art and historical studies. Special projects include publication of textbooks and reprinting of historical source materials.

English-language publishing began in 1960; special strengths include Japanese and Asian studies (including art, history, economics, law, and sociology). English-language publications also include translations of historical and important literary works and diaries.

University of Toronto Press, Inc.

Scholarly Publishing Division:
10 St. Mary Street, Suite 700
Toronto, ON M4Y 2W8
Canada

Phone: (416) 978-2239
Fax: (416) 978-4738
E-mail: publishing@utpress.utoronto.ca
Indiv: (user I.D.)@utpress.utoronto.ca
Web site: www.utppublishing.com

European Representative:
Wolfgang Wingerter

Journals Division/Orders/Customer Service:
5201 Dufferin Street
North York, ON M3H 5T8
Canada
Phone: (416) 667-7810
Fax: (416) 667-7881; (800) 221-9985
E-mail: journals@utpress.utoronto.ca
Web site: www.utpjournals.com

US Warehouse:
2250 Military Road
Tonawanda, NY 14150
Phone: (716) 693-2768

UK Representative:
Yale University Press

Staff

President, Publisher and CEO: John Yates (ext. 222; e-mail: jyates)
  Senior Vice President, Administration: Kathryn Bennett (ext. 224; e-mail: kbennett)
  Vice President, Scholarly Publishing: Lynn Fisher (ext. 243; e-mail: lfisher)
  Vice President, Order Fulfillment and Management Information Services: Hamish
  Cameron (ext. 252; e-mail: hcameron)
  Vice President, Journals: Anne Marie Corrigan (416/667-7838; e-mail: acorrigan)
Executive Editor: Virgil Duff (social sciences) (ext. 240; e-mail: vduff)
  Senior Humanities Editor and Foreign Rights: Suzanne Rancourt (medieval and Renaissance studies) (ext. 239; e-mail: srancourt)
  Editors: Len Husband (history, philosophy) (ext. 238; e-mail: lhusband); Siobhan McMenemy (Canadian film, literature, cultural studies, book history, communications, gender studies) (ext. 231; e-mail: smcmenemy); Ron Schoeffel (Erasmus, Italian studies) (ext. 241; e-mail: rschoeffel); Jill McConkey (humanities) (ext. 233; e-mail: jmcconkey); Stephen Kotowych (Social Sciences) (ext. 229; e-mail: skotowych)
  Permissions: Walter Brooker (ext. 226; e-mail: wbrooker)
  Reference Division Manager: Elizabeth Lumley (ext. 245; e-mail: elumley)

Managing Editor: Anne Laughlin (ext. 236; e-mail: alaughlin)
Production: Ani Deyirmenjian, Manager (ext. 227; e-mail: adeyirmenjian)
Sales and Marketing Manager: Douglas Hildebrand, (ext. 251; e-mail: dhildebrand)
  Publicity Coordinator: Andrea-Jo Wilson (ext 248; e-mail: awilson)
  Advertising, Journal Review & Reference Marketing Coordinator: Deepshikha Dutta (ext. 247; e-mail: ddutta)
  Sales Coordinator: Amanda O'Boyle (ext. 250; e-mail: aoboyle)
  Catalogue & Copy Coordinator: Daniel Quinlan (ext 254; e-mail: dquinlan)
  Exhibits & Examination Copies Coordinator: Ryan Van Huijstee (ext. 257; e-mail: rvanhuijstee)
  Data & Web Coordinator: Bob Currer (ext. 249; e-mail bcurrer)
Journals: (5201 Dufferin St.)
  Vice-President, Journals: Anne Marie Corrigan (416/667-7838; e-mail: acorrigan)
  Supervisor, Editorial Services: Sylvia Hunter (416/667-7806; e-mail: shunter)
  Journals Advertising and Marketing Coordinator: Audrey Greenwood (416/667-7766; e-mail: agreenwood)

Full Member

Established: 1901	Admitted to AAUP: 1937
Title output 2006: 155	Title output 2007: 154
Titles currently in print: 1,650	Journals published: 32

Editorial Program

Classical studies; medieval studies; Renaissance studies; Slavic studies; environmental studies; Erasmian studies; Victorian studies; English literature; Canadian studies; Canadian literature; literary theory and criticism; modern languages and literatures; philosophy; political science; law and criminology; religion and theology; education; music; art history; geography; Canadian and international history; sociology; anthropology; Native studies; social work; and women's studies. Submissions are not invited in poetry or fiction.

Journals: *Bookbird*; *Canadian Historical Review*; *Canadian Journal of Information and Library Sciences*; *Canadian Journal of Linguistics*; *Canadian Journal of Mathematics*; *Canadian Journal of Women and the Law*; *Canadian Journal on Aging*; *Canadian Mathematical Bulletin*; *Canadian Modern Language Review*; *Canadian Public Policy*; *Canadian Review of American Studies*; *Canadian Theatre Review*; *Cartographica*; *Diaspora: A Journal of Transnational Studies*; *Eighteenth Century Fiction*; *Histoire Sociale*; *INFOR*; *Journal of Canadian Studies*; *Journal of Scholarly Publishing*; *Journal of Veterinary Medical Education*; *Modern Drama*; *Seminar*; *Simile: Studies in Media and Information Literacy Education*; *The Tocqueville Review*; *Ultimate Reality and Meaning*; *University of Toronto Law Journal*; *University of Toronto Quarterly*; *Victorian Periodicals Review*

Special series, joint imprints and/or copublishing programs: Anthropological Horizons; Benjamin Disraeli Letters; Canadian Cinema; Chaucer Bibliographies; Collected Works of A.M. Klein; Collected Works of Bernard Lonergan; Collected Works of E.J. Pratt; Collected Works of Erasmus; Collected Works of George Grant; Collected Works of John Stuart Mill; Collected Works of Northrop Frye; Cultural Spaces; Dictionary of Canadian Biography; Digital Futures; Erasmus Studies; Historical Atlas of Canada; Hong Kong Bank of Canada Papers on Asia; Italian Linguistics and Language Pedagogy; Lonergan Studies; McMaster Old English Studies and Texts; Medieval Academy Reprints for Teaching; Mental and Cultural World of Tudor and Stuart England; Ontario Historical Studies Series; Phoenix Supplementary Volumes; Publications of the Osgoode Society; Records of Early English Drama;

Renaissance Society of America Reprint Texts; Reprints in Canadian History; Robson Classical Lectures; Royal Inscriptions of Mesopotamia; State and Economic Life Series; Studies in Gender and History; Studies in Social History; Themes in Canadian Social History; Toronto Italian Studies; Toronto Medieval Bibliographies; Toronto Medieval Texts and Translations; Toronto Old English Series; Toronto Studies in Philosophy; Studies in Early English Drama; Toronto Studies in Semiotics; University of Toronto Romance Series; University of Toronto Ukrainian Studies

United Nations University Press

53-70, Jingumae 5-chome
Shibuya-ku, Tokyo 150-8925
Japan

Orders:
Fax: +81-3-3406-7345
E-mail (orders): sales@hq.unu.edu

Phone: +81-3-3499-2811
Fax: +81-3-3406-7345
E-mail: press@hq.unu.edu
Indiv: (user I.D.)@hq.unu.edu
Web site: www.unu.edu/unupress

US Distributor:
Brookings Institution Press

UK Distributor:
UPM (through Brookings)

Staff
Officer-in-Charge: Max Bond (+81 3 5467-1219; e-mail: bond)
Editor: Robert Davis (+81 3 5467-1315; e-mail: davis)
Design and Production: Yoko Kojima, Manager (+81 3 5467-1316; e-mail: kojima)
Marketing and Sales: Marc Benger, Manager (+ 81 3 5467-1310; e-mail: benger)
    Sales Assistant: Mikako Torii (+81 3 5467-1313; e-mail: torii)

International Member
Established: 1990
Title output 2006: 16
Titles currently in print: 190

Admitted to AAUP: 1997
Title output 2007: 16

Editorial Program
United Nations University Press is the publishing arm of the United Nations University, which was established as a subsidiary organ of the United Nations by General Assembly resolution 2951 (XXVII) in 1972. UNU Press publishes scholarly and policy-oriented books and periodicals on the issues facing the United Nations and its peoples and member states, with particular emphasis on international, regional and trans-boundary policies.

United States Institute of Peace Press

1200 17th Street, N.W., Suite 200
Washington, DC 20036-3011

Phone: (202) 457-1700
Fax: (202) 429-6063
E-mail: (user I.D)@usip.org
Web site and online catalog: www.usip.org

Customer Service:
PO Box 605
Herndon, VA 20172
Phone: (800) 868-8064 ;(703) 661-1590
Fax: (703) 661-1501

UK / European Representative:
University Presses Marketing

Canadian Representative:
Renouf Books

Staff
Director of Publications: Valerie Norville (202/429-4147; e-mail: vnorville)
Managing Editor: Michelle Slavin (202/429-3821; e-mail: mslavin)
Production Manager: Marie Marr (202/429-3815; e-mail: mmarr)
Sales and Marketing Manager: Kay Hechler (202/429-3816; e-mail: khechler)

Associate Member
Established: 1991
Title output 2006: 9
Titles currently in print: 80

Admitted to AAUP: 1993
Title output 2007: 17

Editorial Program
The Press publishes books that are based on work supported by the Institute. The Institute is an independent, nonpartisan federal institution mandated by Congress to promote research, education, and training on the peaceful resolution of international conflicts. The Institute's publications range across the entire spectrum of international relations, including: conflict management and resolution, diplomacy and negotiation, human rights, mediation and facilitation, foreign policy, ethnopolitics, political science, and religion and ethics. The Institute also publishes reports and a newsletter, *Peace Watch*.

W. E. Upjohn Institute for Employment Research

300 Westnedge Avenue
Kalamazoo, MI 49007-4686
Phone: (269) 343-4330
Fax: (269) 343-7310
E-mail: publications@upjohninstitute.org
Indiv: (lastname)@upjohninstitute.org
Web site: www.upjohninstitute.org

Orders:
(888) 227-8569

Staff
Director of Publications: Kevin Hollenbeck (269/343-5541)
  Assistant to the Director: Claire Black (269/343-5541)
Manager of Publications and Marketing: Richard Wyrwa (269/343-5541)
Assistant Editor: Ben Jones (269/343-5541)
Production Coordinator: Erika Jackson (269/343-5541)

Associate Member

Established: 1945
Title output 2006: 7
Titles currently in print: 200

Admitted to AAUP: 1997
Title output 2007:

Editorial Program

Scholarly works on employment-related issues; labor economics; current issues in the social sciences, with an emphasis on public policy. Books are authored mainly by researchers awarded grants through the Institute's annual Competitive Grant Program; also by resident research staff and other scholars in the academic and professional communities. The Institute also publishes working papers and technical reports authored by the resident research staff; a quarterly journal on the West Michigan economy, Business Outlook for West Michigan, and a quarterly newsletter, Employment Research.

The Urban Institute Press

2100 M Street, NW
Washington, DC 20037

Orders:
Phone: (877) 847-7377

Phone: (202) 261-5687
Fax: (202) 467-5775
E-mail: pubs@ui.urban.org
Indiv: (user I.D.)@ui.urban.org (unless otherwise indicated)
Web site: www.uipress.org

Staff

Director and Acquisitions: Kathleen Courrier (202/261-5730; e-mail: kcourrie)
Permissions: Grenda Townsend-Hudson (202/261-5724; e-mail: ghudson)
Editorial / Production / Marketing Manager: Scott Forrey (202/261-5647; e-mail: sforrey)
Editors: Fiona Blackshaw, Devlan O'Connor, Will Bradbury
Customer Service: Dawn Inscoe (202/261-5885; e-mail: dinscoe)

Associate Member

Established: 1968
Title output 2006: 9
Titles currently in print: 180

Admitted to AAUP: 2006
Title output 2007:13

Editorial Program

The Urban Institute Press publishes data-driven, rigorously analytical books on domestic social issues and policy. Books in these and related fields are eligible for publication: public budgets and finance, childcare, child and family well-being, community development, crime and criminal justice, domestic demographic trends, education, family violence, federalism, income, employment and job training, homelessness, health care, housing, immigration, marriage, performance measurement and public management, philanthropy and nonprofits, public benefits and programs, racial and ethnic disparities, retirement, social service delivery, taxes, and welfare.

University of Utah Press

1795 E. South Campus Drive, #101
Salt Lake City, UT 84112-9402

Phone: (801) 581-6771
Fax: (801) 581-3365
Indiv: (user I.D.)@utah.edu
Web site: www.uofupress.com

Orders:
The University of Utah Press
c/o Chicago Distribution Center
11030 S. Langley Ave.
Chicago IL 60628
Phone: (800) 621-2736
Fax: (800) 621-8476

Canadian Representative:
Scholarly Book Services

Staff
Director: John Herbert (e-mail: john.herbert)
Acquisitions Editor: Peter DeLafosse (e-mail: peter.delafosse)
Managing Editor: Glenda Cotter (e-mail: glenda.cotter)
Production Manager: Virginia Fontana (e-mail: jinni.fontana)
Marketing Manager: TBA
Marketing and Sales Assistant: Maritza Herrera-Diaz (e-mail: m.herrera)
Business Manager: Sharon Day (e-mail: sharon.day)

Full Member
Established: 1949
Title output 2006: 24
Titles currently in print: 310

Admitted to AAUP: 1979
Title output 2007: 30

Editorial Program
Anthropology and archaeology, linguistics, Mesoamerica, Native America, Utah and Western history, Mormon studies, Middle East studies, natural history, Utah and regional guidebooks, and general titles of regional interest.
Special series: Agha Shahid Ali Prize in Poetry; Anthropology of Pacific North America; Foundations of Archaeological Inquiry; Publications in the American West; Publications in Mormon Studies; Tanner Lectures on Human Values; Utah Series in Turkish and Islamic Studies; University of Utah Anthropological Papers

Utah State University Press

Utah State University
7800 Old Main Hill
Logan, UT 84322-7800

Phone: (435) 797-1362
Fax: (435) 797-0313
E-mail: (firstname.lastname)@usu.edu
Web site: www.usu.edu/usupress

Orders:
Utah State University Press
Chicago Distribution Center
Phone: (800) 621-2736
Fax: (800) 621-8476

Staff
Director: Michael Spooner
Executive Editor: John R. Alley Jr.
Marketing Manager: Kathleen Kingsbury
Office Assistant: Sandra Reed
Production Assistant: Dan Miller

Full Member
Established: 1972
Title output 2006: 18
Titles currently in print: 236

Admitted to AAUP: 1984
Title output 2007: 18

Editorial Program
Scholarly books with special emphasis on Western American history; regional (Mountain West) studies; composition studies; folklore studies; regional natural history; Native American studies; Western women's history; and Mormon history. Submission by invitation only in fiction and poetry.
Special series: Kingdom in the West; Life Writings of Frontier Women; May Swenson Poetry Award; Leonard J. Arrington Lecture Series

Vanderbilt University Press

Street Address:
2014 Broadway
Suite 320
Nashville, TN 37203

Mailing Address:
VU Station B 351813
Nashville, TN 37235

Phone: (615) 322-3585
Fax: (615) 343-8823
E-mail: vupress@vanderbilt.edu
Indiv: (firstname.lastname)@vanderbilt.edu
Web site: www.vanderbiltuniversitypress.com

Customer Service/Order Fulfillment:
OU Press Book Distribution Center
2800 Venture Drive
Norman, OK 73069
Phone: (800) 627-7377
Fax: (800) 735-0476

UK / European Distributor:
Eurospan

Canadian Distributor:
Scholarly Book Services

Staff
Director: Michael Ames
Marketing and New Media Associate: Betsy Phillips
Editing and Production Manager: Dariel Mayer
Marketing Manager: Sue Havlish
Business Manager: Donna Gruverman

Full Member
Established: 1940
Title output 2006: 22
Titles currently in print: 180

Admitted to AAUP: 1993
Title output 2007: 18

Editorial Program
Scholarly books and serious nonfiction in most areas of the humanities, the social sciences, health care, and higher education. Special interests include Hispanic and Latin American studies, health care and social issues, English and American literature, gender studies, human rights, and regional books.
Copublishing program: Country Music Foundation

The University of Virginia Press

Street Address:
Bemiss House
210 Sprigg Lane
Charlottesville, VA 22903-0608

Mailing Address:
PO Box 400318
Charlottesville, VA 22904-4318

Phone: (434) 924-3468
Fax: (434) 982-2655
E-mail: vapress@virginia.edu
Indiv: (user I.D.)@virginia.edu
Web site: www.upress.virginia.edu

Warehouse Address:
500 Edgemont Road
Charlottesville, VA 22903-0608
Phone: (434) 924-6305
Fax: (434) 982-2655

UK/European Representative:
Eurospan

Canadian Representative:
Scholarly Book Services

Staff

Director: Penelope Kaiserlian (434/924-3131; e-mail: pkaiserlian)
  Assistant to the Director and Rights & Permissions Manager: Mary E. MacNeil (434/924-3361; e-mail: mmm5w)
  Acquisitions Editorial: Cathie Brettschneider (humanities) (434/982-3033; e-mail: cib8b); Richard K. Holway (history and social sciences) (434/924-7301; e-mail: rkh2a); Boyd Zenner (architecture, environmental studies, ecocriticism, and regional) (434/924-1373; e-mail: bz2v)
  Editorial Assistant: Angie Hogan (434/924-4725; e-mail: arh2h)
Electronic Imprint: Mark H. Saunders, Manager (434/924-6064; e-mail: mhs5u)
  Editorial and Technical Manager: David Sewell (434/924-9973; e-mail: dsewell)
  Project Editors: Mary Ann Lugo (434/982-2310; e-mail: ml2z); John Carlson (e-mail: jic7r)
Systems Engineer/Programmer: Oludotun Akinola (434/924-4423; e-mail: oa2m)
  Programmer/Analysts and XML Designers: Shannon Shiflett (434/924-4544; e-mail: shiflett)
Manuscript Editorial: Ellen Satrom, Managing Editor (434/924-6065; e-mail: egs6s)
  Project Editors: Mark Mones (434/924-6066; e-mail: emm4t); Ruth Steinberg (434/924-6067; e-mail: rs9er)
Design and Production: Martha Farlow, Production Manager (434/924-3585; e-mail: mfarlow)
  Assistant Design/Production Manager: Chris Harrison (434/924-6069; e-mail: crh4w)
  Design/Production Assistant: Brooke Kelley (434/982-2704; e-mail: bwk4u)
Marketing: Mark H. Saunders, Assistant Director, Marketing and Sales (434/924-6064; e-mail: mhs5u)
  Marketing Manager: Nancy Mills (434/924-6070; e-mail: njm8j)
  Publicist: Loren Biggs (434/982-2932; e-mail: lrb6c)
Electronic Marketing and Exhibits Manager: Jason Coleman (434/924-4150; e-mail: jgc3h)
Accountant: F. Duncan Pickett (434/924-6068; e-mail: fdp7e)
  Customer Service Manager: Brenda Fitzgerald (434/924-3469; e-mail: bwf)

Business Assistant: Leslie Fitzgerald (434/924-3468; e-mail: lbs6h)
Warehouse Manager: Johnny Tyler (434/924-6305; e-mail: jrt3u)

Full Member

Established: 1963
Title output 2006: 69
Titles currently in print: 1,026

Admitted to AAUP: 1964
Title output 2007: 62

Editorial Program

Scholarly publications in humanities and social sciences, with concentrations in American history; African American studies; Southern studies; political science; literary and cultural studies, with particular strengths in African and Caribbean studies; Victorian studies; religious studies; architecture and landscape studies; regional trade; Virginiana.

The Press also publishes digital publications, primarily critical and documentary editions, through its electronic imprint, Rotunda. Documentary editions (ongoing): The Dolly Madison Digital Edition; The Papers of George Washington; The Papers of James Madison; The Papers of Abraham Lincoln.

Special series: The American South; CARAF BOOKS (Caribbean and African Literature translated from French); The Carter G. Woodson Institute Series in Black Studies; Cultural Frames, Framing Cultures; History of Early Modern Germany; Jeffersonian America; A Nation Divided: New Studies in Civil War History; Race and Ethnicity in Urban Politics; Reconsiderations in Southern African History; Studies in Religion; Under the Sign of Nature; Victorian Literature and Culture; The Virginia Bookshelf

University of Washington Press

Street Address:
1326 Fifth Avenue, Suite 555
Seattle, WA 98101-2604

Mailing Address:
PO Box 50096
Seattle, WA 98145-5096

Phone: (206) 543-4050
Fax: (206) 543-3932
E-mail: (user I.D.)@u.washington.edu
Web site: www.washington.edu/uwpress/

Orders:
Hopkins Fulfillment Services
Phone: (410) 516-6956
Fax: (410) 516-6998

UK Representative:
Combined Academic Publishers

Canadian Sales Group:
University of British Columbia Press

Staff

Director: Pat Soden (206/543-8271; e-mail: patsoden)
  Assistant to Director and Subsidiary Rights Manager: Denise Clark (206/543-4057; e-mail: ddclark)
  Associate Director and General Manager: Mary Anderson (206/221-5892; e-mail: maryande)
  Development Director: Nina McGuinness (206/543-4053; e-mail: ninamg)
  Development Assistant: Hady De Jong (206/221-4991; e-mail: hadydej)
Acquisitions Editorial: Michael Duckworth, Executive Editor (206/221-4940; e-mail: michaeld)
  Senior Editor: Lorri Hagman (206/221-4989; e-mail: lhagman)
  Acquisitions Editors: Jacqueline Ettinger (206/221-4984; e-mail: jetting);

Marianne Keddington-Lang (206/450-5383; e-mail: mkedlang)
  Assistant Acquisitions Editor: Beth Fuget (206/616-0818; e-mail: bfuget)
Manuscript Editorial: Marilyn Trueblood, Managing Editor (206/221-4987;
  e-mail: marilynt)
  Assistant Managing Editor: Mary Ribesky (206/685-9165; e-mail: ribesky)
  Copyeditor: Kerrie Maynes (206/221-5889; e-mail: maynesk)
  Assistant Editor and Web Site Manager: Kathleen Pike Jones (206/221-4986;
  e-mail: kpike)
Design and Production: John Stevenson, Production Manager (206/221-5893;
  e-mail: jasbooks)
  Production Coordinator: Diane Murphy (206/221-4992; e-mail: kdm)
  Designer and Assistant Production Manager: Pamela Canell (206/221-4993;
  e-mail: pcanell)
  Senior Designer: Ashley Saleeba (206/221-7004; e-mail: asaleeba)
Marketing Manager: Alice Herbig (206/221-4994; e-mail: aherbig)
  Sales Manager: Lori Barsness (206/221-4996; e-mail: lorijo)
Publicist: Rachael Mann (206/221-4995; e-mail: remann)
  Director Marketing Manager: Beth DeWeese (206/221-5890; e-mail: edeweese)
  Exhibits Coordinator: Gerlinde van Lagen (206/221-4997; e-mail: gvlagen)
Business Manager: Shelley Rial (206/543-2857; e-mail: srial)
  Assistant Business Manager: Patricia Kain (206/685-3286; e-mail: pkain)

Full Member

Established: 1909   Admitted to AAUP: 1937
Title output 2006: 75   Title output 2007: 71
Titles currently in print: 1,400

Editorial Program

African American Studies; Anthropology; Architecture; Asian American studies; Asian stud-
ies; art; environmental studies; regional history and culture of the Northwest; Native American studies; Slavic studies; Middle Eastern studies; international studies; Western American
history; Jewish studies.

Special series, joint imprints, and/or copublishing programs: American Ethnic and Cultural Studies; Asian Law Series; China Program Books; Classics of Chinese Thought; Classics
of Tlingit Oral Literature; Critical Dialogues in Southeast Asian Studies; Culture, Place,
and Nature: Studies in Anthropology and Environment; Donald R. Ellegood International
Publications; Earl and Edna Stice Lecture-Book Series in Social Science; Emil and Kathleen
Sick Lecture-Book Series in Western History and Biography; Gandharan Buddhist Texts; A
History of East Central Europe; In Vivo: The Cultural Mediations of Biomedical Science;
Jacob Lawrence Series on American Artists; Korean Studies of the Henry M. Jackson School
of International Studies; Literary Conjugations; New Directions in Scandinavian Studies; Pa-
cific Northwest Poetry Series; Pastora Goldner Series in Post-Holocaust Studies; Publications
on the Near East; Robert B. Heilman Books; Samuel and Althea Stroum Lectures in Jewish
Studies; Samuel and Althea Stroum Books; Scott and Lauri Oki Series in Asian American
Studies; Studies on Ethnic Groups in China; Studies in Modernity and National Identity;
Sustainable Design Solutions from the Pacific Northwest; V Ethel Willis White Books; Wey-
erhaeuser Environmental Books

Washington State University Press

Cooper Publications Building
Grimes Way
PO Box 645910
Pullman, WA 99164-5910

Orders:
Phone: (800) 354-7360; (509) 335-7880

Phone: (509) 335-3518
Fax: (509) 335-8568
E-mail: wsupress@wsu.edu
Indiv: (user I.D.)@wsu.edu
Web site: wsupress.wsu.edu

Canadian Representative:
University of British Columbia Press

Staff
Director: Mary Read (509/335-3518; e-mail: read)
Permissions: Marc Lindsey (509/335-3518; e-mail: lindseym)
Editor-in-Chief: Glen Lindeman (509/335-3518; e-mail: lindeman)
Production Coordinator: Jean Taylor (509/335-3518; e-mail: taylorj)
Production Editor, Journals: Nancy Grunewald (509/335-3518; e-mail: grunewan)
Marketing Coordinator: Caryn Lawton (509/335-3518; e-mail: lawton)
Order Fulfillment Coordinator: Jennifer Lynn (509/335-7880; e-mail: jslynn)

Full Member
Established: 1927
Title output 2006: 5
Titles currently in print: 164

Admitted to AAUP: 1987
Title output 2007: 5
Journals published: 1

Editorial Program
Pacific Northwest; natural history; history, politics, and culture relating to the region; Western American history; ethnic studies; Native American studies; women's studies; and environmental issues. The Press distributes publications for the Hutton Settlement, Oregon Writers Colony, Pacific Institute, Tornado Creek Publications, Wenatchee Valley Museum and Cultural Center, WSU Center to Bridge the Digital Divide, WSU Museum of Art, and WSU Thomas S. Foley Institute.
Journal: *Northwest Science*

Wayne State University Press

4809 Woodward Avenue
Detroit, MI 48201-1309

Orders:
Phone: (800) WSU-READ (978-7323)

Phone: (313) 577-6120
Fax: (313) 577-6131
E-mail: (user I.D.)@wayne.edu
Web site: wsupress.wayne.edu

Canadian Distributor:
Scholarly Book Services

UK / European Distributor:
Eurospan

Staff

Director: Jane Hoehner (313/577-4606; e-mail: jane.hoehner)
Acquisitions Editorial: Kathryn Wildfong, Acquisitions Manager (313/577-6070; e-mail:
k.wildfong) (Great Lakes, Africana, Judaica, German literary criticism)
   Editor: Annie Martin (313/577-8335; e-mail: annie.martin) (film and television, fairy tale
   studies, childhood studies)
   Assistant Editor: TBA
Editorial and Production: Kristin Harpster Lawrence, Managing Editor (313/577-4604;
   e-mail: khlawrence)
   Production Editors: Carrie Downes Teefey (313/577-6123; e-mail: carrie.downes)
   Production Coordinator: Maya Rhodes (313/577-4600; e-mail: m.rhodes)
Marketing: TBA, Marketing / Sales Manager
   Promotion and Direct Mail Manager: Sarah Murphy (313/577-6077; e-mail: murphysa)
   Marketing and Sales Assistant: Emily Nowak (313/577-6128; e-mail: aj3076)
Journals: Betty Pilon, Journals Coordinator (313/ 577-6127; e-mail: betty.pilon)
Business: Theresa Mahoney, Business Manager (313/577-3671; e-mail: ab7620)
   Fulfillment Manager: Theresa Martinelli (313/577-6126; e-mail: theresa.martinelli)
   Customer Service: Colleen Stone (313/577-6120; e-mail: colleen.stone)
   Warehouse Manager: Todd Richards (313/577-4619; e-mail: aa5624)
   Shipping: John Twomey (313/577-4609; e-mail: ai7331)
Systems Administrator: James Lee (313/577-2109; e-mail: jameslee)

Full Member

Established: 1941
Title output 2006: 31
Titles currently in print: 785

Admitted to AAUP: 1956
Title output 2007: 30
Journals published: 6

Editorial Program

Scholarly books and serious nonfiction, with special interests in regional and local history
and literature; Africana; Judaica; film and television studies; childhood studies; fairy tales and
folklore; speech and language pathology; labor studies; urban studies; and gender and ethnic
studies.

Journals: *Criticism; Discourse; Framework; Human Biology; Marvels and Tales; Merrill-Palmer
Quarterly*

Special series: African American Life; Classical Studies: Pedagogy; Contemporary Approaches to Film and Television; Fairy Tale Studies; Great Lakes Books; Kritik: German Literary Theory and Culture; Landscapes of Childhood; Made in Michigan Writers Series; Painted Turtle Books; Raphael Patai Series in Jewish Folklore and Anthropology; TV Milestones; William Beaumont Hospital Series in Speech and Language Pathology
Joint imprints, copublishing, and distribution programs: Grand Rapids Historical Commission; Hebrew Union College Press; Cranbrook Institute of Science; Detroit Institute of Arts; Marick Press; and Saugatuck-Douglas Historical Society

Wesleyan University Press

Editorial Offices:
215 Long Lane
Middletown, CT 06459

Phone: (860) 685-7711
Fax: (860) 685-7712
E-mail: (user I.D.)@wesleyan.edu
Web site: www.wesleyan.edu/wespress/

Book Distribution Center:
Wesleyan University Press
c/o University Press of New England
1 Court Street, Suite 250
Lebanon, NH 03766-1358
Phone: (800) 421-1561
Fax: (603) 643-1540

UK / European Representative:
Eurospan

Canadian Representative:
University of British Columbia Press

Staff
Director / Editor-in-Chief: Suzanna Tamminen (860/685-7727; e-mail: stamminen)
Acquisitions Editor: Parker Smathers (860/685-7730; e-mail: psmathers)
Marketing: Leslie Starr, Assistant Director / Marketing Manager (860/685-7725;
    e-mail: lstarr)
Publicist: Stephanie Elliot (860/685-7723; e-mail: selliott)

Full Member
Established: 1957

Title output 2006: 24
Titles currently in print: 445

Admitted to AAUP: 2001
(Former membership: 1966-1991)
Title output 2007: 24

Editorial Program
The current editorial program focuses on poetry, music, dance, science fiction studies, film/TV/media studies, regional studies, and American studies.
Special series: Early Classics of Science Fiction; Music / Culture; Wesleyan Poetry; Wesleyan Film; Garnet Books

University of the West Indies Press

7A Gibraltar Hall Road
Kingston 7
Jamaica West Indies
Phone: (876) 977-2659
Fax: (876) 977-2660
Web site: www.uwipress.com

US and Caribbean Orders:
Longleaf Services
P.O. Box 8895
Phone: (800) 848-6224

UK / European Distributor:
Eurospan

Canadian Distributor:
Scholarly Book Services

Staff

Director: Linda Speth (e-mail: lspeth@cwjamaica.com)
Editorial and Production Manager: Shivaun Hearne (e-mail: shivearne@gmail.com)
Marketing and Sales Manager: Donna Muirhead
   (e-mail: uwipress_marketing@cwjamaica.com)
Finance Manager: Nadine Buckland (e-mail: nbuckland@cwjamaica.com)

International Member

Established: 1992
Title output 2006: 25
Titles currently in print: 236

Admitted to AAUP: 2005
Title output 2007: 26
Journals published: 3

Editorial Program

Scholarly books in the humanities and social sciences with lists emphasizing a Caribbean context in the fields of cultural studies, gender studies, history, literature, economics, education, environmental studies, sociology, and political science.
Journals: *Journal of Caribbean History; Journal of Caribbean Geography; Journal of Caribbean Literature*

The West Virginia University Press

Street Address:
G3 White Hall
Morgantown, WV 26506

Mailing Address:
PO Box 6295
Morgantown, WV 26506

Phone: (304) 293-8400
Fax: (304) 293-6585
Web site: www.wvupress.com

Staff

Director/Editor: Patrick Conner (ext. 4505; e-mail: pconner@wvu.edu)
Office Manager: Floann Downey (ext. 4500; e-mail: fdowney2@wvu.edu)
Marketing Director: Sara Pritchard (ext. 4504; e-mail: sara.pritchard@mail.wvu.edu)
Production Manager/Designer: Than Saffel (ext. 4503; e-mail: than.saffel@mail.wvu.edu)
Journals Manager: Hilary Attfield (ext. 4502; e-mail: hattfiel@wvu.edu)
Business Manager: Michelle Marshall (304/293-3107 ext. 33407; e-mail: michele.marshall@mail.wvu.edu)

Full Member

Established: 1963	Admitted to AAUP: 2003
Title output 2006: 16	Title output 2007: 18
Titles currently in print: 54	Journals published: 5

Editorial Program

Serious works of nonfiction in American history, with an emphasis on West Virginia and Appalachia; art history, economic history; ethnic studies; West Virginia and Appalachian fiction; medieval studies, especially Anglo-Saxon studies; regional studies in Appalachia; American studies; natural history. A second imprint, Vandalia Press, publishes fiction and non-fiction of interest to the general reader concerning Appalachia and, more specifically, West Virginia.
Journals: *Essays in Medieval Studies*; *Tolkien Studies*; *Education and Treatment of Children*; *West Virginia History*; *Victorian Poetry*
Special series: Medieval European Studies; Sound Archive Series; West Virginia and Appalachia, Mountain Studies

Wilfrid Laurier University Press

75 University Avenue West
Waterloo, ON N2L 3C5
Canada

Phone: (519) 884-0710 ext. 6124
Fax: (519) 725-1399
E-mail: press@wlu.ca
Indiv: (user I.D.)@press.wlu.ca
Web site: www.wlupress.wlu.ca

US Distributor:	UK Representative:
UTP Distribution Service	Gazelle Book Services, Ltd.

Staff

Director: Brian Henderson (ext. 6123; e-mail: brian)
Acquisitions Editorial: Lisa Quinn, Acquisitions Editor (ext. 2843; e-mail: quinn)
Manuscript Editorial: Rob Kohlmeier, Managing Editor (ext. 6119; e-mail: rob)
Design and Production: Heather Blain-Yanke, Production and Editorial Projects Manager
    (ext. 6122; e-mail: heather)
Marketing: Penny Grows, Marketing Manager (ext. 6605; e-mail: pgrows)
    Web Page and Marketing Coordinator: Leslie Macredie (ext. 6281; e-mail: leslie)
    Publicist: Clare Ferguson (ext. 2665; e-mail: clare)
Journals: Cheryl Beaupré, Coordinator, Distribution & Journals (ext. 6124, e-mail: cheryl)
Business: Cathy Hebbourn, Financial Administrator (ext. 6030; e-mail: cathy)
Information Systems: Steve Izma, Computing Systems Administrator (ext. 6125;
    e-mail: steve)

Full Member

Established: 1974	Admitted to AAUP: 1986
Title output 2006: 25	Title output 2007: 28
Titles currently in print: 222	Journals published: 10

Editorial Program
Canadian literature; cultural studies; history; literary criticism; poetry; literature in translation; philosophy; life writing; sociology/anthropology; native studies; film studies; art and art history; religious studies; social work; women's studies.

Journals (*available electronically): *Anthropologica**; *Canadian Bulletin of Medical History*; *Canadian Journal of Community Mental Health**; *Canadian Social Work Review*; *Dialogue: Canadian Philosophical Review*; *Indigenous Law Journal*; *Leisure/Loisir*; *Studies in Religion**; *Topia: A Canadian Journal of Cultural Studies*; *Toronto Journal of Theology*

Special series and joint imprints: Aboriginal Studies; Canadian Corporation for Studies in Religion; Comparative Ethics; Editions SR; Environmental Humanities; Studies in Christianity and Judaism; Studies in Women and Religion; Collected Works of Florence Nightingale; Cultural Studies; Film and Media Studies; Laurier Poetry; Life Writing; New Political Philosophy; Studies in Childhood and Family in Canada

The University of Wisconsin Press

1930 Monroe Street, 3rd Floor
Madison, WI 53711-2059

Phone: (608) 263-1110
Fax: (608) 263-1120
E-mail: uwiscpress@uwpress.wisc.edu
Indiv: (user I.D)@wisc.edu
Web site: www.wisc.edu/wisconsinpress

Orders:
The University of Wisconsin Press
Chicago Distribution Center
11030 South Langley Avenue
Chicago, IL 60628-3892
Phone: (800) 621-2736; (773) 702-7000
Fax: (800) 621-8476; (773) 702-7212

UK Distributor:
Eurospan

Staff
Interim Director: Sheila Leary (608/263-1101; e-mail: smleary)
Subsidiary Rights & Permissions Manager: Margaret Walsh (608/263-1131; e-mail: mawalsh1)
Acquisitions Editorial: Raphael Kadushin, Senior Acquisitions Editor (608/263-1062; e-mail: kadushin)
  Acquisitions Editor: Gwen Walker (608/263-1123; e-mail: gcwalker)
Manuscript Editorial: Adam Mehring, Managing Editor (608/263-0856; e-mail: amehring)
  Editor: Sheila Moermond (608/263-1133; e-mail: samoermond)
Design and Production: Terry Emmrich, Production Manager (608/263-0731; e-mail: temmrich)
  Assistant Production Manager: Carla Aspelmeier (608/263-0732; e-mail: cjaspelmeier)
  Senior Editor / In-House Compositor: Scott Lenz (608/263-0794; e-mail: sjlenz)
Marketing: Andrea Christofferson, Marketing & Sales Manager (608/263-0814; e-mail: aschrist)
  Advertising and Web Manager: Kirt Murray (608/263-0733; e-mail: kdmurray)
  Publicity Manager: Christopher Caldwell (608/263-0734; e-mail: publicity@uwpress.wisc.edu or ccaldwell)

Exhibits and Direct Mail Manager: Kara Zavada (608/263-1136; e-mail: kazavada)
Sales Manager: Fred Lauing (608/263-0795; e-mail: flauing)
Journals: Pam Wilson, Manager (608/263-0667; e-mail: pjwilson2)
  Assistant Manager: Susan Kau (608/263-0669; e-mail: szkau)
  Advertising: Adrienne Omen (608/263-0534; e-mail: amomen)
  Marketing: Toni Gunnison (608/263-0753; e-mail: gunnison)
  Subscription Information/Renewal: Rita Emmert (608/263-0668; e-mail: rmemmert);
  Judith Choles (608/263-0654; e-mail: jmcholes); Beth Johnson (608/263-1135; e-mail:
  bajohnso)
Business: Russell Schwalbe, Business Manager (608/263-0263; rschwalbe)
  Accounts Payable: Anne Herger (608/263-1137; e-mail: abherger)
  Business Assistant: Jim Hahn (608/263-1128, e-mail: jhahn3)
  Business office fax: (608/263-1120)
Information Systems: James Leaver, Network and Data Administrator (608/263-1121;
  e-mail: jleaver)

Full Member

Established: 1937	Admitted to AAUP: 1945
Title output 2006: 68	Title output 2007: 55
Titles currently in print: 1,745	Journals published: 11

Editorial Program

Scholarly and general interest works in African studies; American cultural and intellectual history; Classical studies; film / dance / performance; gay and lesbian studies and memoirs; human rights; Latin American and Latino studies and memoirs; modern European & Irish history; Russian and East European studies; Southeast Asian studies; and Wisconsin and the Upper Midwest (all aspects, including politics, folklore, natural history, Native studies, travel, sports, ethnic heritage, etc.). For the Brittingham & Felix Pollak Poetry Prize, contest guidelines are available online at www.wisc.edu/wisconsinpress/poetryguide.html

Journals: *American Orthoptic Journal; Arctic Anthropology; Contemporary Literature; Ecological Restoration; Journal of Human Resources; Land Economics; Landscape Journal; Luso-Brazilian Review; Monatshefte; Ecquid Novi (African Journalism Studies); SubStance*

Special series: Africa and the Diaspora: History, Politics, Culture; Brittingham Prize in Poetry; Felix Pollak Prize in Poetry; George L. Mosse Series in Modern European Cultural and Intellectual History; History of Anthropology; History of Ireland and the Irish Diaspora; Living Out: Gay and Lesbian Autobiographies; New Perspectives in Southeast Asian Studies; Print Culture History in Modern America; Publications of the Wisconsin Center for Pushkin Studies; Sources in Modern Jewish History; Studies in American Thought and Culture; Studies in Dance History; Wisconsin Film Studies; Wisconsin Land and Life; Wisconsin Studies in Autobiography; Wisconsin Studies in Classics; Women in Africa and the Diaspora; Writing in Latinidad

The Woodrow Wilson Center Press

Woodrow Wilson International Center for Scholars
One Woodrow Wilson Plaza
1300 Pennsylvania Avenue, N.W.
Washington, DC 20004-3027

Phone: (202) 691-4041
Fax: (202) 691-4001
E-mail: press@wilsoncenter.org
Indiv: (firstname.lastname)@wilsoncenter.org
Web site: www.wilsoncenter.org/press

Staff
Director: Joseph Brinley (202/691-4042; e-mail: joe.brinley)
Editor: Yamile Kahn (202/691-4041; e-mail: yamile.kahn)
Editorial Assistant: Erin Mosely (202/691-4266; e-mail: erin.mosely)
Administrative Assistant: TBA

Associate Member
Established: 1987   Admitted to AAUP: 1992
Title output 2006: 8   Title output 2007: 11
Titles currently in print: 180

Editorial Program
Woodrow Wilson Center Press publishes work written at or for the Woodrow Wilson
International Center for Scholars, the official memorial of the United States to its twenty-
eighth president. The Center was created by law in 1968 as a living memorial "symbolizing
and strengthening the fruitful relation between the world of learning and the world of public
affairs." The Press's books come from both the work of the Center's scholars in residence and
from some of the six hundred meetings held at the Center each year.

The Center's interests range widely in areas associated with questions of public policy. The
Press has published in American studies; history; international relations; political science;
economics and finance; religious studies; urban studies; women's studies; and the study of
Africa, Asia, Europe, Latin America, and the Middle East.

All the Press's books are copublished. Partners include Johns Hopkins University Press,
Stanford University Press, University of California Press, University of Pennsylvania Press,
and Columbia University Press. The Cold War International History Project Series is copublished with Stanford.

Yale University Press

Street Address:
302 Temple Street
New Haven, CT 06511

Mailing Address:
PO Box 209040
New Haven, CT 06520-9040

Phone: (203) 432-0960
Faxes: (203) 432-0948 (Main)
(203) 432-1064/2394 (Editorial)
(203) 432-4061 (Production)
(800) 406-9145 (Customer Service)
(203) 432-8485 (Marketing)
(203) 432-5455 (Promotion)
(203) 432-6862 (Computer room)
(203) 432-6862 (Accounting)
E-mail: (firstname.lastname)@yale.edu
Web site and online catalog: www.yale.edu/yup/

London Office:
47 Bedford Square
London WCIB 3DP
United Kingdom
Phone: +44-207-079-4900
Fax: +44-207-079-4901
E-mail:(firstname.lastname)@yaleup.co.uk

Staff

Director: John E. Donatich (203/432-0933)
  Deputy Director for Finance and Operations: John D. Rollins (203/432-0938)
  Associate Director and Publishing Director: Tina C. Weiner (203/432-0962)
  Associate Director and Editorial Director: Jonathan Brent (203/432-0905)
  Development Associate: Janyce P. Siress (203/432-0934)
Acquisitions Editorial: Jean E. Thomson Black (science and medicine) (203/432-7534);
  Jonathan Brent (literature, literary studies, theater, Slavic studies) (203/432-0905); Keith
  Condon (political science, psychology) (203/432-0924); Patricia Fidler (art and archi-
  tectural history) (203/432-0927); TBA (literature, philosophy, and political science)
  (203/432-6807); Christopher Rogers (history, intellectual history, American studies, biog-
  raphy, and women's studies) (203/432-0935); Mary Jane Peluso (language and reference)
  (203/432-8013); Michael O'Malley (business, economics, law) (203/432-0904); Ileene
  Smith (general interest, history, Jewish studies, current affairs) (212/396-4317)
Manuscript Editorial: Jenya Weinreb, Managing Editor (203/432-0913)
  Assistant Managing Editor: Mary Pasti (203/432-0911)
  Editors: Laura Jones Dooley (203/432-0915); Dan Heaton (203/432-1017); Jessie
  Hunnicutt (203/432-4823); Ann-Marie Imbornoni (203/432-0903); Lawrence Kenney
  (203/432-0908); Phillip King (203/432-1015); Susan Laity (203/432-0922); Margaret
  Otzel (203/432-0918); Jeffrey Schier (203/432-4001)
Design and Production: Christina Coffin, Director of Production (203/432-4062)
  Assistant Production Manager: Maureen Noonan (203/432-4064)
  Production Controllers: Orna Johnston (203/432-4060); Mary Mayer (203/432-0925)
  Art Director: Nancy Ovedovitz (203/432-4067)
  Designers: Rebecca Gibb (203/432-4065); James L. Johnson (203/432-4068); Sonia Scan-
  lon (203/432-4066); Mary Valencia (203/432-8092)
Marketing & Sales: Jay Cosgrove, Sales Director (203/432-0968)
  Promotion Director: Sarah F. Clark (203/432-0965)
  Advertising Manager: Peter Sims (203/432-0974)
  Electronic Marketing Manager: Daniel Lee (203/432-3819)

Publicity Manager: Heather D'Auria (203/432-0971)
Assistant Publicity Manager: Brenda King (203/432-0917)
Publicists: Jessica Holahan (203/432-0971); Paige Jokl (203/432-0964); Robert Pranzatelli (203/432-0972)
Promotion Designer: Amy Andersen (203/432-7086)
Direct Mail Manager: Debra Bozzi (203/432-0959)
Electronic Promotion Manager, Language Books Promotion: Timothy Shea (203/436-1321)
Business: John D. Rollins, Deputy Director for Finance and Operations (203/432-0938)
Accounting: Susan Kelly (203/436-1924)
Operations Manager: Jim Stritch (203/432-0939)
Computer Services Manager: Milton Kahl (203/432-0937)
Permissions and Ancillary Rights Manager: Donna Anstey (203/432-0932)
Intellectual Property and Contracts Director: Linda B. Klein (203/432-0936)
London Office:
Managing Director: Robert Baldock
Acquisitions Editors: Gillian Malpass, Heather McCallum, Sally Salvesen
Head of Marketing: Kate Pocock
Foreign Rights Manager: Anne Bihan

Full Member

Established: 1908
Title output 2006: 281
Titles currently in print: 4,485

Admitted to AAUP: 1937
Title output 2007:

Editorial Program

Humanities, social and behavioral sciences, natural sciences, medicine. Poetry is not accepted except for submissions to the Yale Series of Younger Poets contest, held annually. Festschriften and collections of previously published articles are not invited and very rarely accepted.
Special series, joint imprints and/or copublishing programs: Agrarian Studies; American Icons; Annals of Communism; The Annotated Shakespeare; Babylonian Collection; Bard Graduate Center; Broadway Masters; Carnegie Endowment for International Peace; The Castle Lectures in Ethics, Politics, and Economics; A Century Foundation Book; Complete Prose Works of John Milton; Complete Works of St. Thomas More; Composers of the Twentieth Century; Council on Foreign Relations; Cowles Foundation; Culture and Civilization of China; Current Perspectives in Psychology; Current Thinking in the Behavioral Sciences; Darden Innovation and Entrepreneurship; David Brion Davis Lectures; Democracy in America; The Diary of Joseph Farington; Dodge Lectures; Dura-Europos; Economic Census Studies; Economic Growth Center; Elizabethan Club; English Monarchs; The Fetished Object; George Elliot Letters; The Henry McBride Series in Modernism and Modernity; History of the Soviet Gulag System; Horace Walpole Correspondence; Institute for Social and Policy Studies; Institute of Far Eastern Languages; Institution of Human Relations; Intellectual History of the West; Italian Literature and Culture; James Boswell; Library of Medieval Philosophy; Music Theory Translation Series; Musical Instrument Series; Neighborhoods of New York City; The New Republic; New Yiddish Library; Oak Spring Garden Library; Okun; Open University; Page Lectures; The Papers of Benjamin Franklin; The Papers of Benjamin

Latrobe; Papers of Frederick Douglass; Papers on Soviet & East European, Economic & Political Science; Paul Mellon Centre for Studies in British Art; Pelikan History of Art; Percy Letters; Petroleum Monographs; Pevsner Series: Buildings of England, Scotland, and Ireland; Phillips Andover Archaeology; Philosophy and Theory and Art; Poems of Alexander Pope; Posen Library of Jewish Culture and Civilization; Psychoanalytic Study of the Child; The Relations of Canada and the United States; Rethinking the Western Tradition; Russian Classics; Science in Progress; The Selected Papers of Charles Willson Peale and His Family; Silliman Lectures; Society and the Sexes; Stalin Archives; Storrs Lectures; Studies in Comparative Economics; Studies in Hermeneutics; Studies in Modern European Literature and Thought; Terry Lectures; Theoretical Perspectives in Archaeological History; Wall Street Journal; Western Intellectual Trail Series; Why X Matters; Writings on American History; The Works of Jonathan Edwards; The Works of Samuel Johnson; Yale Classical Monographs; Yale Classical Studies; Yale Contemporary Law Series; Yale Drama Series; Yale Edition of the Unpublished Works of Gloria Stein; Yale French Studies; Yale Guide to English Literature; Yale Health and Wellness; Yale Historical Publications; Yale Judaica; Yale Law Library Publications; Yale Law School Studies; Yale Library of Military History; Yale Liebniz; Yale Linguistics; Yale New Classics; Yale Publications in Religion; Yale Romantic Studies; Yale Series of Younger Poets; Yale Studies in Economics; Yales Studies in English; Yale Studies in History & Theory of Religious Education; Yale Studies in Political Science

Sales Agents and Distributors: Canada, UK, Europe

Aldington Books
Unit 3(b) Frith Business Centre
Frith Road
Aldington, Ashford
Kent TN25 7HJ
United Kingdom
Phone: +44 1233 720123
Fax: + 44 1233 721272
E-mail: sales@aldingtonbooks.co.uk
Web site: www.aldingtonbooks.co.uk

Baker & Taylor International
1120 Route 22 East
Bridgewater, NJ 08807
Phone: (800) 775-1500; (908) 541-7000
E-mail: btinfo@btol.com
Web site: www.btol.com

Bill Bailey Publishers' Representatives
16 Devon Square
Newton Abbot
Devon TQ12 2HR
United Kingdom
Phone: +44 1626 331079
Fax: +44 1626 331080

Book Representation and Distribution, Ltd.
Hadleigh Hall
London Road, Hadleigh
Essex SS7 2DE
United Kingdom
Phone: +44 1702 552912
Fax: +44 01702 556095
E-mail: info@bookreps.com
Web site: www.bookreps.com

Broadview Press
280 Perry St., Unit 5
P.O. Box 1243
Peterborough, ON K95 7H5 Canada
Phone: (705) 743-8990
Fax: (705) 743-8353
E-mail: customerservice@
  broadviewpress.com
Web site: www.broadviewpress.com

Canadian Manda Group
165 Dufferin Street
Toronto, ON M6K 3H6 Canada
Phone: (416) 516-0911
Fax: (416) 516-0917
E-mail: general@mandagroup.com
Web site: www.mandagroup.com

Cariad, Ltd.
180 Bloor St. West
Suite 801
Toronto, ON M5S 2V6 Canada
Phone: (416) 929-2774
Fax: (416) 929-1926

Combined Academic Publishers, Ltd.
15a Lewin's Yard
East Street
Chesham, Buckinghamshire, HP5 1HQ
United Kingdom
Phone: +44 1494 581601
Fax: +44 1494 581602
E-mail: nickesson@combinedacademic.
  demon.co.uk
Web site: www.combinedacademic.co.uk

The Crowood Press
The Stable Block
Crowood Lane
Ramsbury
Wiltshire SN8 2HR
United Kingdom
Phone: +44 1672 520320
Fax: +44 1672 520280
E-mail: admin@crowood.com
Web site: www.crowoodpress.co.uk

Eurospan University Press Group
3 Henrietta Street, Covent Garden
London WC2E 8LU
United Kingdom
Phone: +44 2072 400856
Fax: +44 2073 790609
E-mail: info@eurospan.co.uk
Web site: www.eurospan.co.uk

Fitzhenry & Whiteside
195 Allstate Parkway
Markham, ON L3R 4T8 Canada
Phone: (800) 387-9776
Fax: (800)-260-9777
E-mail: godwit@fitzhenry.ca
Web site: www.fitzhenry.ca

Forest Book Services
The New Building
Ellwood Road
Milkwall Coleford
Gloucestershire GL16 7LE
United Kingdom
Phone: +44 1594 833858
Fax: +44 1594 833446
Web site: www.forestbooks.com

Gazelle Book Services, Ltd./
Gazelle Drake Academic
White Cross Mills
High Town
Lancaster LA1 4XS
United Kingdom
Phone: +44 1524-68765
Fax: +44 1524-63232
E-mail: sales@gazellebooks.co.uk
Web site: www.gazellebooks.co.uk

Georgetown Publications, Inc.
579 Richmond Street West, Suite 100
Toronto, ON M5V 1Y6 Canada
Phone: (416) 364-8741
Fax: (416) 367-4242

Gracewing Publishing
2 Southern Avenue
Leominster, Herefordshire HR6 0QF
United Kingdom
Phone: +44 1568 616835
Fax: +44 1568 613289
E-mail: gracewingx@aol.com (orders)
Web site: www.gracewing.co.uk

Guidance Centre Suppliers
5201 Dufferin St.
Toronto, ON M3H 5T8 Canada
Phone: (416) 667-7791
Fax: (416) 667-7832
E-mail: utp@utpress.utoronto.ca
Web site: www.utpress.utoronto.ca/
    GCentre/index.html

Hargreaves, Fuller & Paton
4335 W. 10th Ave, Suite # 13
Vancouver, BC V6R 2H6 Canada
Phone: (604) 222-2955
Fax: (604) 222-2965
E-mail: harful@telus.net

Herder Editrice e Libreria
Piazza Montecitorio 120 - 00186
Rome Italy
Phone: + 39 (06) 679 46 28 / 679 53 04
Fax: +39 (06) 678 47 51
E-mail: distr@herder.it
Web site: www.herder.it

Jacqueline Gross and Associates Inc.
165 Dufferin Street
Toronto, ON M6K 3H6   Canada
Phone: (416) 531- 6737
Fax: (416) 531- 4259
E-mail: gayle@jaquelinegross.com
Web site: www.jaquelinegross.com

John Wiley & Sons, Ltd.
The Atrium
Southern Gate, Chichester
West Sussex, PO19 8SQ
United Kingdom
Phone: +44 1243 779777
Fax: + 44 1243 775878
E-mail: customer@wiley.co.uk
Web site: www.wiley.com

Kellington & Associates
338 Riverdale Drive
Toronto, ON M4J 1A2 Canada
Phone: (416) 461-7472
Fax: (416) 461-9173
E-mail: r.kellingtonl@sympatico.ca

Lavis Marketing
73 Lime Walk
Headington, Oxford
Oxfordshire OX3 7AD
United Kingdom
Phone: +44 1865 767575
Fax: +44 1865 750079

Lexa Publishers' Representatives
215 Ashworth Avenue
Toronto, ON M6G 2A6 Canada
Phone: (416) 535-6494
Fax: (416) 535-6599
E-mail: lynnmcclory@sympatico.ca

Libro Co. Italia s.r.l.
Via Borromeo, 48
50026 San Casciano V.P.
Florence
Italy
E-mail: libroco@libroco.it
Web site: www.libroco.it/

Login Brothers Canada
324 Saulteaux Crescent
Winnipeg, MB R3J 3T2 Canada
Phone: (800) 665-1148; (204) 837-2987
Fax: (800) 665-0103; (204) 837-3116
E-mail: sales@lb.ca
Web site: www.lb.ca

Marston Book Services, Ltd.
PO Box 269
Abingdon Oxfordshire OX14 4YN
United Kingdom
Phone: +44 1235 465540
Fax: +44 1235 465555
E-mail: direct.enq@marston.co.uk
Web site: www.marston.co.uk

Premier Book Marketing, Ltd.
Clarendon House
52, Cornmarket St.
Oxford OX1 3HJ
United Kingdom
Phone: +44 1865-304059
Fax: +44 1865-304035
E-mail: mail@premierbookmarketing.com
Web site: www.premierbookmarketing.com

NBN International
Plymbridge House,
Estover Road,
Plymouth, Devon PL6 7PY
United Kingdom
Phone: +44 1752 202300
Fax: +44 1752 202330
E-mail: enquiries@nbninternational.com
Web site: www.nbninternational.com

Publishers Group UK
8 The Arena
Mollison Ave.
Enfield, Middlesex EN3 7NL
United Kingdom
Phone: +44 2088 040400
Fax: +44 2088 040044
E-mail: info@pubilshersgroupuk.co.uk
Web site: www.pguk.co.uk

Renouf Publishing Co. Ltd.
1-5369 Canotek Road
Ottawa, ON K1J 9J3 Canada
Phone: (888) 551-7470, (613) 745-2665
Fax: (613) 745-7660
E-mail: order.dept@renoufbooks.com
Web site: www.renoufbooks.com

Roundhouse Publishing, Ltd.
Millstone, Limers Lane
Northam, North Devon EX39 2RG
United Kingdom
Phone: +44 1237 474 474
Fax: +44 1237 474 774
E-mail: roundhouse.group@ukgateway.net
Web site: www.roundhouse.net

Scholarly Book Services, Inc.
127 Portland Street
3rd Floor
Toronto, ON M5V 2N4 Canada
Phone: (800) 847-9736, (416) 504-6545
Fax: (800) 220-9895, (416) 504-0641
E-mail: customerservice@sbookscan.com
Web site: www.sbookscan.com

Taylor and Francis
2 Park Square
Milton Park, Abingdon
Oxfordshire OX14 4RN
United Kingdom
Phone: +44 207017 6000
Fax: +44 207017 6699
E-mail: tf.enquiries@tfinforma.com
Web site: www.taylorandfrancisgroup.com

Turnaround Publishers Services
Unit 3 Olympia Trading Estate
Coburg Rd.
Wood Green, London N22 6TZ
United Kingdom
Phone: +44 20 8829 3000
Fax: +44 20 8881 5088
E-mail: enquires@turnaround-uk.com
Web site: www.turnaround-psl.com

The University Press Group
164 Hillsdale Avenue East
Toronto, ON M4S 1T5 Canada
Phone: (416) 484-8296
Fax: (416) 484-0602
E-mail: dcstimpson@yahoo.com

University Presses Marketing
The Tobacco Factory
Raleigh Road,
Southville, Bristol BS3 1TF
United Kingdom
Phone: +44 117 9020275
Fax: +44 117 9020294
E-mail: upm01bristol@compuserve.com
Web site: www.universitypressesmarketing.
 co.uk

Vanwell Publishing Ltd.
1 Northrup Crescent
PO Box 2131
St. Catharines, ON L2R 7S2 Canada
Phone: (905) 937-3100 / (800) 661-6136
Fax: (905) 937-1760
E-mail: sales@vanwell.com
Web site: www.vanwell.com/

William Gills & Associates
7 Yew Lane
Ardargie Forgandenny
Perthshire PH2 9QX
United Kingdom
Phone: +44 1738 812619
Fax: +44 1738 812480
E-mail: bill@booksfromamerica.co.uk
Web site: www.booksfromamerica.co.uk

Windsor Books International
Roundhouse Group
Millstone
Limers Lane
Northam, N Devon EX39 2RG
United Kingdom
Phone: +44 1237 474474
Fax: +44 1237 474774
E-mail: geoffcowen@windsorbooks.co.uk
Web site: www.windsorbooks.co.uk

Yale Representation, Ltd.
47 Bedford Square
London WC1B 3DP
United Kingdom
Phone: +44 20 7079 4900
Fax: +44 20 7079 4901

THE ASSOCIATION

The Association of American University Presses (AAUP) was established by a small group of university presses in 1937. In the subsequent years, the association has grown steadily. Today AAUP consists of 126 member presses, ranging in size from those publishing a handful of titles each year to those publishing more than a thousand.

AAUP is a nonprofit organization. Its sources of financing are limited to membership dues and to revenues derived from such activities as organizing national conferences and seminars, producing publishing-related books and catalogs, and operating cooperative marketing programs. In addition, grants provided by foundations and government bodies help to finance special projects.

AAUP's member presses provide much of the personnel that guide the association and carry out its work. A thirteen-member board of directors sets policy for the organization. Many individuals serve on committees and task forces. Their activities reflect the diverse concerns of the membership, including keeping up with emerging electronic publishing technologies, production and analysis of industry statistics, maintaining copyright protections, professional development, marketing, and scholarly journals publishing.

The AAUP Central Office, located in New York City, consists of an executive director and a small professional staff. The office manages member programs and coordinates the work of the board and committees.

AAUP members currently fall into three categories—full, international, and associate. A fourth category of introductory membership was created in June 2007. For a complete description of membership requirements, consult the "Guidelines on Admission to Membership and Maintenance of Membership," reproduced on page 201.

AAUP Central Office

Association of American University Presses
71 W. 23rd St., Suite 901
New York, NY 10010

Phone: (212) 989-1010
Fax: (212) 989-0275/0176
E-mail: info@aaupnet.org
Web site: www.aaupnet.org

Staff

Executive Director: Peter J. Givler (e-mail: pgivler@aaupnet.org)
Assistant Director and Controller: Timothy Muench (e-mail: tmuench@aaupnet.org)
Administrative Manager: Linda McCall (e-mail: lmccall@aaupnet.org)
Marketing Manager: Rachel Weiss-Feldman (e-mail: rweiss@aaupnet.org)
Electronic and Strategic Initiatives Director: Brenna McLaughlin (518/436-3586; e-mail:
    bmclaughlin@aaupnet.org)
Membership Manager: Susan Patton (e-mail: spatton@aaupnet.org)
Marketing and Membership Coordinator: Kim Miller (e-mail: kmiller@aaupnet.org)
Communications Coordinator: Shaun Manning (e-mail: smanning@aaupnet.org)

2007-2008 AAUP Board of Directors

Sanford Thatcher, Penn State University Press, President (2007-08)
Alex Holzman, Temple University Press, President-elect (2007-08)
Penelope Kaiserlian, University of Virginia Press, Past President (2007-2008)
John Zotz, Stanford University Press, Treasurer (2007-2008)
Rebecca Schrader, MIT Press, Treasurer-elect (2007-2008)
Richard Brown, Georgetown University Press (2007-2010)
MaryKatherine Callaway, Louisiana State University Press (2006-2009)
Philip Cercone, McGill-Queen's University Press (2005-08)
Sylvia Hecimovich, University of Chicago Press (2005-08)
Kathleen Keane, John Hopkins University Press (2007-10)
Joanne O'Hare, University of Nevada Press (2007-10)
Rebecca Simon, University of California Press (2007-10)
Peter J. Givler, AAUP Central Office, ex officio

2007-2008 AAUP Committees and Task Forces

Admissions and Standards
Stephen A. Cohn, Duke, Chair
Gail Grella, Georgetown
Eric Halpern, Pennsylvania
Elaine Maisner, North Carolina
David Nicholls, MLA
Darrin Pratt, Colorado

Annual Meeting Program
Philip Cercone, McGill-Queen's, Chair
Chris Cosner, Stanford
Anthony Crouch, California
Dennis Lloyd, Florida
Joanne O'Hare, Nevada
Jennifer Reichlin, Georgia
Alan Thomas, Chicago
Laura Westlund, Minnesota
Mark Zandrozny, Cambridge

Business Handbook
Mike Bieker, Arkansas, Chair
Barry Adams, Temple
Conrad Roberts, Kansas

Business Systems
Roger Hubbs, Cornell, Chair
Linda Frech, Missouri
William Lindsay, Harvard
John Rollins, Yale
Molly Venezia, Rutgers
Anna Weidman, California

Copyright
Vicky Wells, North Carolina, Chair
Laura Bost, Texas
Christina Brianik, Rutgers
Rick Huard, Ohio
Daphne Ireland, Princeton
Marc Lindsey, Washington State
Sandy Thatcher, Penn State

Design and Production
Will Powers, Minnesota Historical Society, Chair
Liz Cosgrove, Oxford
David Graham, Florida
Todd Lape, Mississippi
Betsy Litz, Princeton
Maya Rhodes, Wayne State
Laurie Searl, SUNY
Linda Secondari, Columbia
   Eco Subcommittee
   Julie, Fauci, Northwestern, Chari
   Anthony Crouch, California
   Holly Keller, British Columbia
   Karen Schmidt, Getty
   Annette Tanner, Michigan State

Electronic
Alan Harvey, Stanford, Chair
Tom Bacher, Purdue
Dean Blobaum, Chicago
Michael Jensen, National Academies
Daniel Lee, Yale
Paul Murphy, RAND
Tony Sanfilippo, Penn State
Linda Secondari, Columbia
Mark Simpson-Vos, North Carolina
Wendy Queen, Johns Hopkins

Marketing
Mahinder Kingra, Cornell, Chair
Colleen Lanick, MIT
James McCoy, Iowa
Jessica Pellien, Princeton
Amanda Sutton, New Mexico
Erich van Rijn, California
Alison Vandenberg, Minnesota Historical Society

Nominating
Holly Carver, Iowa, Chair
Meredith Morris Babb, Florida
Carol Kasper, Chicago
Will Underwood, Kent State
Molly Venezia, Rutgers

Professional Development
Jane Bunker, SUNY, Chair
Lisa Bayer, Illinois
Greg Britton, Minnesota Historical Society
Jennifer Crewe, Columbia
Cope Cumpston, Illinois
Kristin Harpster Lawrence, Wayne State
Maria Lindenfeldar, Princeton
Nicole Mitchell, Georgia
Molly Venezia, Rutgers

Scholarly Journals
Clydette Wantland, Illinois, Chair
Bill Breichner, Johns Hopkins
Sue Hausmann, Texas
Nick Lindsay, California
Pam Wilson, Wisconsin

By-Laws (As revised June 14, 2007)

ARTICLE I Preamble
ARTICLE II Purposes
ARTICLE III Membership
Section 1. Definition of Full Membership
Section 2. Definition of a University Press
Section 3. Eligibility for Full Membership
Section 4. Associate Membership
Section 5. International Membership
Section 6. Introductory Membership
Section 7. Voting and Other Privileges
Section 8. Cancellation of Membership and Resignation
ARTICLE IV Membership Meetings
Section 1. The Annual Meeting
Section 2. Special Meetings
Section 3. Notice of Meetings
Section 4. Representation by Proxy
Section 5. Quorum
Section 6. Voting
ARTICLE V Directors and Officers
Section 1. The Board of Directors
Section 2. Election Procedure and Term of Office
Section 3. Officers
Section 4. Duties of Officers
Section 5. Removal from Office and Replacement
Section 6. Board Meetings
Section 7. Board Quorum
Section 8. Board Voting
ARTICLE VI Executive Committee
ARTICLE VII Standing Committees
ARTICLE VIII Other Committees and Task Forces
ARTICLE IX The Executive Director
ARTICLE X Regional Organizations
ARTICLE XI Dues
ARTICLE XII Books and Records
ARTICLE XIII Changes in By-Laws and Guidelines

ARTICLE I: PREAMBLE

This Corporation, existing under the Not-for-Profit Corporation Law of the State of New York, shall be known as the Association of American University Presses, Inc. (hereinafter referred to as the "Association"). The Association expects members to recruit, employ, train, compensate, and promote their employees without regard to race, ethnic background, national origin, status as a veteran or handicapped individual, age, religion, gender, marital status, or sexual preference.

ARTICLE II: PURPOSES

The purposes of the Association shall be:

a) To encourage dissemination of the fruits of research and to support university presses in their endeavor to make widely available the best of scholarly knowledge and the most important results of scholarly research;
b) To provide an organization through which the exchange of ideas relating to university presses and their functions may be facilitated;
c) To afford technical advice and assistance to learned bodies, scholarly associations, and institutions of higher learning; and
d) To do all things incidental to and in furtherance of the foregoing purposes without extending the same.

ARTICLE III: MEMBERSHIP

The Association admits members in four categories: (1) full membership, (2) associate membership, (3) international membership, and (4) introductory membership.

Section 1: Definition of Full Membership.

The full membership of the Association shall consist of those members who were in good standing at the time of the incorporation of the Association in 1964, except those who have since resigned or whose membership has been otherwise terminated, and all other members who have since been admitted in accordance with the procedures set forth in Section 3 of this Article. Presses with affiliate status as of June 2007 will be instated as full members upon approval of the membership.

Section 2: Definition of a University Press.

A university press eligible for full membership is hereby defined as the nonprofit scholarly publishing arm of a university or college, or of a group of such institutions within a state or geographic region, located within the Americas and publishing primarily in English. A university press as here defined must be an integral part of one or more such colleges and universities, and should be so recognized in the manual of organization, catalogue, website, or other official publication of at least one such parent institution. The organization and functions of the university press must lie within the prescription of its parent institution or institutions.

Section 3: Eligibility for Full Membership.

Any university press satisfying the requirements set forth in the "Guidelines on Admission to Membership and Maintenance of Membership" (hereinafter, the "Guidelines") that are in force at the time of application shall be eligible for election to full membership in the Association. A university press shall be elected to membership by a majority vote of the membership on the recommendation of the Board of Directors at the Annual or a Special Meeting of the membership. Such action shall be taken by the Board only on the prior recommendation of the Committee on Admissions and Standards, which shall be responsible for determining that the applying university press satisfies the minimum requirements for membership. Annual dues for full members shall be set from time to time by the Board of Directors.

Section 4: Associate Membership.

The associate membership of the Association shall consist of those associate members who have been admitted since the time of the incorporation of the Association in 1964, in accordance with the procedures in force at the time of application.

Presses of non-degree-granting scholarly institutions and associations may apply for associate membership, provided that those institutions are incorporated as not-for-profit and that the presses satisfy the requirements for full membership, except that the auspices and structures of the parent organizations of such presses will in all instances be those of non-degree-granting institutions or scholarly associations rather than those of universities. Associate members should be located within the Americas and publishing primarily in English. In the absence of an editorial committee or board, an applicant for associate membership shall observe commonly accepted standards of editorial review.

Admission to associate membership shall be by a majority vote of the membership at an Annual or Special Meeting, a quorum being present, on the prior recommendation of the Committee on Admissions and Standards and the Board of Directors. Associate members shall enjoy such rights and privileges as determined by the Board of Directors, including the right to serve on the Board of Directors or on the Standing Committees of the Association and the right to vote on any business conducted by the Association. Associate members shall not be eligible to participate in the Association's statistical programs for full members. Annual dues for associate members shall be set from time to time by the Board of Directors. The number of associate members shall not exceed thirty-five percent of the number of full members of the Association and no more than one associate member representative may serve on the Board at any one time.

Section 5: International Membership.

The international membership of the Association shall consist of those international members who have been admitted since the time of the incorporation of the Association in 1964, in accordance with the procedures in force at the time of application.

International membership may be applied for by (a) university-affiliated scholarly publishers and presses of non-degree-granting scholarly institutions and associations in parts of the world not embraced by the Americas and (b) such presses within the Americas that publish primarily in languages other than English. To qualify for international membership in the Association, a publisher in either class must submit the same application as applicants for full and associate member status but will not be expected to meet precisely the staffing and organizational requirements for those members. Admission to international membership shall be by a majority vote of the membership at an Annual or Special Meeting, a quorum being present, on the prior recommendation of the Committee on Admissions and Standards and the Board of Directors.

International members shall enjoy all rights and privileges of membership except the right to vote in any business being conducted by the Association, the Board of Directors, or the membership. Any reference elsewhere in these By-Laws to a voting right, therefore, shall be read so as to exclude international members. Annual dues for international members shall be set from time to time by the Board.

Section 6: Introductory Membership.

Eligible for introductory membership are nonprofit scholarly publishers that intend to apply for AAUP membership in one of the other categories either during their introductory term or at the end of that term. Presses may not stay in the introductory category for more than three years.

Candidates for introductory membership will be expected to provide evidence concerning the scholarly character of their publishing programs and information about present staffing, reporting relationships, review processes, and also any changes or developments proposed in these areas, but they will not be expected to meet the publication rate, staffing, or organizational requirements of full membership. Admission to introductory membership shall be made at the discretion of the Executive Director of the Association in consultation with the Board upon receipt by the Membership Manager of a letter of application that includes the requested information.

At any time during the introductory period introductory members may apply for regular membership in the appropriate category. After three years, the introductory membership is automatically terminated.

Introductory members shall enjoy such rights and privileges as determined by the Board of Directors, but in no event shall their rights and privileges extend to service on the Board of Directors or on the Standing Committees of the Association or voting in any business conducted by it. Any reference elsewhere in the By-Laws to a voting right, therefore, shall be so read as to exclude introductory members. Annual dues for introductory members shall be set from time to time by the Board.

Section 7: Voting and Other Privileges.

Each full member and each associate member of the Association shall be entitled to one vote in such business as may come before the Association. Only members in good standing shall be entitled to vote or otherwise enjoy the privileges of membership in the Association.

Section 8: Cancellation of Membership and Resignation.

A university press, by its very nature, must be devoted to scholarly and educational ends; the failure of a university press to pursue such ends as its fundamental business shall constitute grounds for canceling its membership in the Association. Any accusation of such a failure will be brought to the Committee on Admissions and Standards for a recommendation to the Board.

A membership may also be canceled for continued nonpayment of dues or for continued failure, after admission to membership, to meet the minimum requirements set forth in the Guidelines.

Cancellation of full, associate, or international membership shall be effected, on recommendation of the Board of Directors, by a two-thirds vote of the members present and voting at the Annual Meeting or a Special Meeting, a quorum being present.

Any member may resign at any time if its current annual dues are paid, provided its resignation is confirmed in a written communication to the Executive Director and President of the Association from a responsible officer or group of officers of the parent institution or institutions.

Should a member in any class of membership resign after the due date of the annual dues payment and before the next annual dues payment date, the member is responsible for the payment of such dues at the time of resignation.

ARTICLE IV: MEMBERSHIP MEETINGS

Section 1: The Annual Meeting.

The Annual Meeting of members shall be held at such time and place within or without the State of New York as may be designated by the Board of Directors after giving due weight to preferences expressed by members. Such meetings shall be held for the purpose of electing the Board of Directors, approving the annual budget, and transacting such other business as may be properly brought before the meeting. At each Annual Meeting of members, the Board of Directors shall cause to be presented to the membership a report verified by the President and the Treasurer, or by a majority of the Board, in accordance with the requirements of Section 519 of the New York Not-for-Profit Corporation Law.

Section 2: Special Meetings.

Special Meetings of the members shall be held at such time and place within or without the State of New York as may be designated by the Board of Directors. Such meetings may be called by (a) the Board of Directors; or (b) the Executive Committee; or (c) the President, the President-elect, or the Executive Director acting on a request received in writing that states the purpose or purposes of the meeting and is signed by 30 percent or more of the members of the Association.

Section 3: Notice of Meetings.

Notice of the purpose or purposes and of the time and place of every meeting of members of the Association shall be in writing and signed by the President, President-elect, or the Executive Director, and a copy thereof shall be delivered personally or by the U.S. Postal Service not less than ten or more than fifty days before the meeting, to each member entitled to vote at such meeting.

Section 4: Representation by Proxy.

A member may authorize a person or persons to act by proxy on all matters in which a member is entitled to participate. No proxy shall be valid after the expiration of eleven months from the date thereof unless otherwise provided in the proxy. Every proxy shall be revocable at the pleasure of the member executing it.

Section 5: Quorum.

Except for a special election of Directors pursuant to Section 604 of the New York Not-for-Profit Corporation Law, the presence at a meeting in person or by proxy of a majority of the members entitled to vote thereat shall constitute a quorum for the transaction of any business, except that the members present may adjourn the meeting even if there is no quorum.

Section 6: Voting.

In the election of members of the Board of Directors and the election of Officers, a plurality of the votes cast at an Annual Meeting shall elect. Any other action requires a majority of votes cast except as otherwise specifically provided in these By-Laws. A vote may be taken without a meeting if a majority of the members in good standing submit written votes in response to a request to this effect from the President, the President-elect, or the Executive Director.

ARTICLE V: DIRECTORS AND OFFICERS

Section 1: The Board of Directors.

The Association shall be managed by its Board of Directors, and, in this connection, the Board of Directors shall establish the policies of the Association while considering the wishes of the membership and the constituency of the Association (which constituency consists of the employees of the member presses), and shall evaluate the performance of the Executive Director. The Board of Directors shall meet at least three times each year, once in the fall and once in the winter and in conjunction with the Annual Meeting of the membership of the Association. The Board of Directors shall consist of not fewer than nine or more than thirteen Directors, all of whom shall be at least nineteen years of age, at least two-thirds of whom shall be citizens of the United States, four of whom shall be the elected Officers of the Association. Directors other than Officers (Directors-at-Large), like Officers, must be on the staff of a member press, except that the Executive Director is an ex officio (nonvoting) member of the Board of Directors and the Executive Committee.

Section 2: Election Procedure and Term of Office.

Directors shall be elected by a plurality vote of the members present at the Annual Meeting. Candidates may be nominated by the Nominating Committee appointed by the Executive Committee, or from the floor. Officers shall be elected for a one-year term, except that the President shall remain on the Board of Directors for an additional year as Past-President; Directors-at-Large shall be elected for a three-year term. Directors shall not succeed themselves except that (a) Directors who are elected Officers shall continue as Directors as long as they remain Officers, and (b) the Treasurer shall remain on the Board for an additional year as a Director-at-large. Each newly elected Director and Officer shall assume office at the close of the Annual Meeting at which the election is held. Any Director or Officer may resign by notifying the President, the President-elect, or the Executive Director. The resignation shall take effect at the time therein specified. Except as provided for in Article IX ("The Executive Director"), Directors shall not receive any compensation for serving as Directors. However, nothing herein shall be construed to prevent a Director from serving the Association in another capacity for which compensation may be received.

Section 3: Officers.

The elected Officers of the Association, each of whom must be on the staff of a member press, shall be a President, a President-elect, a Treasurer, and a Treasurer-elect, each to be elected for a one-year term by a plurality vote of the members present at the Annual Meeting. Between Annual Meetings of members, a Special Meeting of members may elect, by a plurality vote of the members present, an Officer to complete the term of an Officer who has resigned or otherwise ceased to act as an Officer.

Section 4: Duties of Officers.

The President shall serve as presiding officer at all meetings of the membership and all meetings of the Board of Directors and the Executive Committee. The President, with the Executive Director, serves as spokesperson for the Association. At the Annual Meeting of members, the President and the President-elect shall provide a forum for the Association membership and constituency to discuss and assess the Association's program. The President-elect shall discharge the duties of the President in the President's absence, and shall succeed to the office of President in the event of a vacancy in that office, filling out the unexpired term as well as the term to which he or she is elected President.

The Treasurer shall be custodian of the Association's funds, shall be responsible for the preparation of its financial records as the basis for an annual audit, and shall report at the Annual Meeting of members on the Association's financial condition. The Treasurer-elect shall discharge the duties of the Treasurer in the Treasurer's absence, and shall succeed to the office of Treasurer in the event of a vacancy in that office, filling out the unexpired term as well as the term to which he or she is elected Treasurer.

Section 5: Removal from Office and Replacement.

Any Director or elected Officer may be removed from office at any time, for cause or without cause, by a majority vote of the membership or may be removed for cause by a majority vote of the Board acting at a meeting duly assembled, a quorum being present. If one or more vacancies should occur on the Board for any reason, the remaining members of the Board, although less than a quorum, may by majority vote elect a successor or successors for the unexpired term.

Section 6: Board Meetings.

Meetings of the Board of Directors shall be held at such place within or without the State of New York as may from time to time be fixed by resolution of the Board, or as may be specified in the notice of the meeting. Notice of any meeting of the Board need not be given to any Director who submits a signed waiver of such notice. Special Meetings of the Board may be held at any time upon the call of the Executive Committee, the Executive Director, the President, or the President-elect.

Section 7: Board Quorum.

A majority of the members of the Board of Directors then acting, but in no event less than one-half of the entire board of Directors, acting at a meeting duly assembled, shall constitute a quorum for the transaction of business. If at any meeting of the Board there shall be less than a quorum present, a majority of those present may adjourn the meeting without further notice from time to time until a quorum shall have been obtained. The "entire Board of Directors" shall mean the total number of Directors that the Association would have if there were no vacancies.

Section 8: Board Voting.

Except as otherwise specified in these By-Laws, all decisions of the Board shall be by majority vote of the Directors in attendance, a quorum being present. Any Board action may be taken without a meeting if all members of the Board or committee thereof consent in writing to the adoption of a resolution authorizing the action. The resolution and the written consents thereto shall be filed with the minutes of the proceedings of the Board. Any member of the Board or of any committee thereof may participate in a meeting of such Board or committee thereof by means of a telephone or similar communications equipment allowing all persons participating in the meeting to hear each other at the same time. Participation by such means shall constitute presence in person at a meeting.

ARTICLE VI: EXECUTIVE COMMITTEE

The Executive Committee of the Board of Directors shall consist of the Past-President and President of the Association and the President-elect, Treasurer, Treasurer-elect, and the Executive Director (ex officio, nonvoting). The Executive Committee shall advise and confer with the Executive Director, call Special Meetings of the Board of Directors as necessary, appoint committee members not otherwise appointed pursuant to these By-Laws, and serve as the investment committee for the Association. The Executive Committee shall, if necessary, act for the full Board of Directors between meetings of the Board, but only in those matters not establishing policy or not requiring a vote of more than a majority of Directors in attendance.

ARTICLE VII: STANDING COMMITTEES

The Standing Committees of the Association (in addition to the Executive Committee) shall be the Committee on Admissions and Standards, the Committee on the Annual Meeting Program, and the Nominating Committee. The Committee on Admissions and Standards shall be constituted as provided in the Guidelines. Appointments to the Committee on the Annual Meeting Program and the Nominating Committee shall be made in accordance with Article VIII of these By-Laws.

ARTICLE VIII: OTHER COMMITTEES AND TASK FORCES

Other committees and task forces may be established by agreement of the Executive Director and the Board. The President-elect shall appoint chairs of said committees (and the Standing Committees) and such of their members as the Executive Committee may care to designate. The President-elect shall charge the said committees with such duties, including reporting duties, as he or she may deem appropriate. Task forces shall be established for a limited time to accomplish a specific goal. The President shall appoint chairs of task forces and provide their charges. Reports of standing and all other committees and task forces shall be made to the Board of Directors, in writing or orally, as requested by the Executive Director.

ARTICLE IX: THE EXECUTIVE DIRECTOR

The Board of Directors may appoint at such times, and for such terms as it may prescribe, an Executive Director of the Association who shall report to the Board of Directors and who is responsible for implementing policy through fiscally sound programs; monitoring the work of committees and task forces; and managing the Central Office (such Central Office consisting of salaried employees hired by the Executive Director in order to carry out the business of the Association). The Executive Director shall prepare an operating plan and budget and shall participate in meetings of the Board of Directors and Executive Committee in an ex officio nonvoting capacity as appropriate. Under the authority of the Board of Directors, the Executive Director shall have responsibility for the execution of Association policy, for the furtherance of the Association's interests, and for the day-to-day operation of the Association's business and programs. The Executive Director shall act as secretary at all Board meetings, Executive Committee meetings, and Annual and Special Meetings of the Association, and shall prepare and distribute minutes of the same. The Executive Director shall serve as Corporate Secretary. The Executive Director's salary shall be fixed annually by the Board.

ARTICLE X: REGIONAL ORGANIZATIONS

The Board of Directors may recognize geographical regions within which members of the Association and others may organize themselves for regional meetings to further the aims of the Association.

ARTICLE XI: DUES

The amount of the annual dues payment by members shall be voted each year at the Annual Meeting on recommendation of the Board of Directors. The fiscal year of the Association shall be April 1 to March 31. Dues shall be payable by September 30, at which time any member press that has not paid its dues shall be subject to suspension at the Board's discretion. When a member is suspended for nonpayment of dues, the President of the Association shall so notify the director of the said member and the responsible officer or officers of its parent institution or group of institutions, and shall further advise them that if such member has not paid its dues by the end of the Association's fiscal year its membership shall be subject to cancellation.

ARTICLE XII: BOOKS AND RECORDS

The Association shall keep at its office within the State of New York correct and complete books and records of account; minutes of meetings of the members, of the Board of Directors, and of the Executive Committee; and an up-to-date list of the names and addresses of all members. These books and records may be in written form or in any other form capable of being converted to written form within a reasonable time.

ARTICLE XIII: CHANGES IN BY-LAWS AND GUIDELINES

The members may amend or repeal these By-Laws by two-thirds of the votes cast at any Annual or Special Meeting called for that purpose at which a quorum is present. The members may revise, amend, or repeal the Guidelines by a majority of votes cast at any Annual or Special Meeting of members called for that purpose at which a quorum is present. Whenever there is a conflict between these By-Laws and the Guidelines, any Statement of Governance, or a resolution of the membership, Board of Directors, or Executive Committee, or any other document published by the Association, these By-Laws shall prevail.

Guidelines on Admission to Membership and Maintenance of Membership

As revised June 14, 2007

A. Preamble

The purposes of the Association are to encourage dissemination of the fruits of research and to support university presses in their endeavor to make widely available scholarly knowledge and the most important results of scholarly research; to provide an organization through which the exchange of ideas relating to university presses and their functions may be facilitated; to afford technical advice and assistance to learned bodies, scholarly associations, and institutions of higher learning; and to do all things incidental to and in furtherance of the foregoing purposes without extending the same.

B. Types of Membership

The Association admits members in four categories: (1) full membership, (2) associate membership, (3) international membership, and (4) introductory membership.

1. Full Membership

Eligible for full membership are nonprofit university presses, defined as the scholarly publishing arm of a university or college or a group of such institutions within a state or geographic region, located within the Americas and publishing primarily in English, that satisfy the following criteria:

(a) Eligible presses must be an integral part of one or more such colleges and universities, and should be so recognized in the manual of organization, catalogue, website, or other official publication of at least one such parent institution. The organization and functions of the university press must lie within the prescription of its parent institution or institutions.

(b) A committee or board of the faculty of the parent institution or institutions shall be charged with certifying the scholarly quality of the publications that bear the institutional imprint.

(c) Publication of ten or more scholarly titles in the twenty-four months preceding the date of application shall be required for admission to full membership. Scholarly books, journals, and digital projects that include original scholarly content will all be counted to satisfy this requirement. The word "scholarly" is used here in the sense of original research of a character usually associated with the scholarly interests of a university or college. (Textbooks, manuals of a synthetic character or intended for class use, and publications for which the press serves primarily as a printer and/or distributor for other departments or divisions of the university or college are not to be included in the aforementioned minimum scholarly publishing requirement.)

(d) An acceptable scholarly publishing program shall have the benefit of the service of not fewer than three full-time equivalent employees, of whom one shall have the rank and functions of director. This official shall report, organizationally, to the President of the university or college, or to an officer at the vice-presidential or decanal level (i.e., an officer reporting either to the President or to the chief academic officer) having both academic and fiscal authority, or to the designated representative of a group of such institutions who shall have both kinds of authority.

Any press satisfying these requirements shall be eligible in principle for election to full membership in the Association. Annual dues for full members shall be set from time to time by the Board.

2. Associate Membership

Presses of non-degree-granting scholarly institutions and associations may apply for associate membership, providing those institutions are incorporated as not-for-profit and that the presses satisfy the requirements for membership, except that the auspices and structures of the parent organizations of such presses will in all instances be those of non-degree-granting institutions or scholarly associations rather than those of universities. Applicants for associate membership should be in a state or geographic region located within the Americas and publishing primarily in English. In the absence of an editorial committee or board, an applicant for associate membership shall observe commonly accepted standards of editorial review.

Associate members shall enjoy such rights and privileges as determined by the Board of Directors, including the right to serve on the Board of Directors and on the Standing Committees of the Association and the right to vote on any business conducted by it. Associate members shall not be eligible to participate in the Association's statistical programs for full members. The number of associate members shall not exceed thirty-five percent of the number of full members of the Association and no more than one associate member representative may serve on the Board at any one time. Annual dues for associate members shall be set from time to time by the Board.

3. International Membership

International membership may be applied for by (a) university-affiliated scholarly publishers and presses of non-degree-granting scholarly institutions and associations in parts of the world not embraced by the Americas and (b) such presses within the Americas that publish primarily in languages other than English.

Candidates for international membership will be expected to provide evidence concerning the size and scholarly character of their publishing programs but will not be expected to meet the staffing or organizational requirements of full membership.

International members shall enjoy all rights and privileges of full membership except the right to vote in any business conducted by the Association. Any reference elsewhere in the By-Laws to a voting right, therefore, shall be so read as to exclude international members. International members shall not be eligible to participate in the Association's statistical programs. Annual dues for international members shall be set from time to time by the Board.

4. Introductory Membership

Eligible for introductory membership are nonprofit scholarly publishers that intend to apply for AAUP membership in one of the other categories either during their introductory term or at the end of that term.

Candidates for introductory membership will be expected to provide evidence concerning the scholarly character of their publishing programs and information about present staffing, reporting relationships, review processes, and also any changes or developments proposed in these areas, but they will not be expected to meet the publication rate, staffing, or organizational requirements of full membership. Presses may not stay in the introductory category for more than three years.

At any time during the introductory period introductory members may apply for regular membership in the appropriate category. If a press does not wish to continue as an introductory member for three years, it may resign from the Association after payment of its current annual dues. After three years, the introductory membership is automatically terminated.

Introductory members shall enjoy such rights and privileges as determined by the Board of Directors, but in no event shall their rights and privileges extend to service on the Board of Directors or on the Standing Committees of the Association or voting in any business conducted by it. Any reference elsewhere in the By-Laws to a voting right, therefore, shall be so read as to exclude introductory members. Annual dues for introductory members shall be set from time to time by the Board.

C. Application, Admission, and Cancellation

1. Application

All inquiries from prospective applicants for membership in the Association are to be directed to the Membership Manager of AAUP. The Membership Manager shall advise the candidate of the substance of these Guidelines on Admission to Membership and Maintenance of Membership, and shall require as evidence of satisfactory compliance with them for all membership categories, except the Introductory Membership, the following materials for submission to the Committee on Admissions and Standards:

(a) One copy of each of 10 or more different scholarly titles published by the applicant and certified by its faculty editorial board or committee in the twenty-four months preceding the date on which the application for membership is filed, and full runs of the issues of any journals for the year or years in which a journal serves as one of the titles. If original digital publications are submitted, the applicant will provide access to committee members.

(b) A list of the peer reviewers (names and affiliations) for each of the books or original digital publications submitted as part of the application. Published reviews of the titles and information about scholarly awards received may be submitted as part of the application.

(c) Copies of the applicant press's catalogs for the past two years for each member of the Committee on Admissions and Standards.

(d) A complete list, by name and title, of the staff of the applicant press, to be prepared in that form in which such information is given for active members in the most recent edition of the Directory of the Association of American University Presses. For part-time staff the list should indicate the percentage of time each person devotes to the press.

(e) A statement from a senior administrative officer of the parent institution, or the designated representative of a group of institutions, outlining the immediate and long-term intentions and financial expectations of the institution or group of institutions for its press, and reflecting a realistic appreciation of the cost of supporting a serious program of scholarly publication.

(f) Copies of its financial operating statements for the two most recently completed fiscal years.

With respect to the scholarship of published works, the Association will in general accept the certification of the press's own faculty board or committee and will not pass judgment on the scholarship of any individual work. However, the Committee on Admissions and Standards will take into account the observance by the press of commonly accepted standards of editorial review, ordinarily including at least one positive evaluation by a qualified scholar not affiliated with the author's own institution.

2. Admission

Following the filing of a formal application for full, associate, or international membership and notification by the Membership Manager of AAUP to the applicant of its acceptance for consideration, the candidate press shall be regarded as having entered a period of probation, which will last for a period of time no longer than one year, at the end of which, if not sooner, its candidacy will be acted upon as prescribed under the By-Laws, and during which it shall enjoy the following privileges of membership: (a) the right to send delegates to the Annual Meeting at the member rate, and (b) the right to send representatives to all training sessions, workshops, symposiums, and conferences dealing with professional activities of scholarly publishers and enjoying the support of the Association.

A press shall be elected to full, associate, or international membership by an affirmative vote of a majority of the Association's full members at the Annual Meeting or a Special Meeting, a quorum being present, on the recommendation of the Board of Directors. Such action shall be taken by the Board only on the prior recommendation of the Committee on Admissions and Standards, which shall be responsible for determining that the applying press satisfies the minimum requirements for membership. Admission of a new full, associate, or international member to the Association shall take effect immediately following an affirmative vote of a majority of the Association's full membership at the Annual Meeting or a Special Meeting.

Admission to introductory membership shall be made at the discretion of the Executive Director of the Association in consultation with the Board upon receipt by the Membership Manager of a letter of request that includes information about present staffing, reporting relationships, review processes, and any changes or developments proposed in these areas.

To maintain its active membership status, each member press shall be required to submit each year to the Central Office of the Association, for publication in the annual Directory of members, both a roster of its current staff and an indication of the number of books, journals, and original digital publications that it has published in each of the two calendar years preceding and that have been certified as to scholarship by its editorial board or committee.

3. Cancellation

A university press, by its very nature, must be devoted to scholarly and educational ends; the failure of a press to pursue such ends as its fundamental business shall constitute grounds for canceling its membership in the Association. Any accusation of such a failure will be brought to the Committee on Admissions and Standards for a recommendation to the Board. Cancellation of membership shall be effected, on recommendation of the Board of Directors, by a two-thirds' majority vote of the members present and voting at the Annual Meeting or a Special Meeting, a quorum being present.

It shall be the responsibility of the Membership Manager to review each listing of an active press in each annual edition of the membership Directory, and to undertake action as follows when any member seems to have fallen below the qualifying criteria for membership: (a) to notify the Executive Director and the Committee on Admissions and Standards of a member's apparent delinquency under the Guidelines so that the Executive Director may make an inquiry and, if current standards are not being met, offer the assistance and cooperation of the Association in bringing about satisfactory solutions to the member's problems; (b) to advise the President, the Committee on Admissions and Standards, and the Board when notification of an apparent delinquency has been sent and an offer of assistance made; (c) to inform the President, the Committee on Admissions and Standards, and the Board of any response received from the member press following the offer of assistance.

Should the delinquent press fail to resolve its difficulties within one year of the Executive Director's notice, the Committee on Admissions and Standards shall submit to the Board of Directors a full report of the situation, and recommend, for endorsement by the Board and transmission to the membership for ratification, that the membership of the delinquent press be terminated. Two years from the date of its expulsion, a press shall be entitled to apply for readmission through initiation of the application procedures herein prescribed.

E. The Committee on Admissions and Standards

The official agency for the administration of these guidelines shall be the Committee on Admissions and Standards, which shall operate under authority delegated by the Board of Directors, and which shall consist of between four and six members, two of whom, at least, shall be the director of a member press. The incoming President will appoint the chair of the committee from among members of the current committee with at least one year of service. The chairs shall each serve a term of one year as part of their three-year term on the committee and may not succeed themselves in office. The chair shall appoint the remaining committee members. Terms of the committee members will normally be three years each except that in the year that these revised Guidelines take effect shorter terms may be established for some of the members. Committee members will not be eligible to serve more than two successive terms.

PERSONNEL INDEX

Esterly, Laura	93	Forward, Deborah	110
Ettinger, Jacqueline	171	Foster, Cynthia	100
Evans, Barbara	71	Foster, Wendi	107
Evans, Claire	21, 22	Fowler, Marjorie	115
Evans, Justine	51	Frain, Christina	112
Evans, Mary Seldon	150	Francendese, Janet M.	153
Ezzell, Emmy	122	Francis, Lowell	119
Faerber, Justin	56	Francis, Mary	38
Fagan, Teresa	46	Frankel, Ellen	78
Faherty, Robert L.	35	Franklin, Tom	115
Fahmy, Miriam	27	Frankovich, Nick	61
Falaster, Lisa	146	Frazier, Rebecca	156
Falocco, Filomena	88	Frech, Linda	102, 190
Fandel, Jennifer	146	Freels, Amy	21
Fanfani, Tommaso	131	Frey, Gina	33
Faran, Ellen	92	Friedl, Catherine	40
Farkas, Richard E.	84	Friedlander, Anna Eberhard	34
Farlow, Martha	170	Friedman, Rachel	141
Fastiggi, Raymond T.	140	Froehlich, Peter	74
Fauci, Julia	117, 190	Fromm, Devin	132
Faust, Allison	155	Fruehwirth, John	151
Faust, Jana	108	Fuentes, Regina	156
Fay, Stephanie	38	Fuget, Beth	172
Feal, Rosemary G.	103	Fulton, Cindy	39
Fearer, Jaime	35	Furbush, Jake	93
Federico, Don	44	Furney, Laura	50
Felgar, Catherine	41	Gable, Larry	96
Felland, Kirstie	119	Gabriel, BJ	127
Feneron, John	147	Gallaway, Matt	126
Ferber, Susan	125	Galle, Suzanne	82
Ferejohn, Laurel	57	Gammon, Julie	21
Ferguson, Clare	177	Gan, Qi	49
Fernando, Kalyani	82	Ganeles, Diane	149
Ferris, Kristen	111	Garcia, Kristina	110
Ferwerda, Eelco	28	Gardner, Elizabeth	127
Fidlar, Patricia	181	Gardner, Jennifer	158
Fielding, Sandra	160	Garrett, Susan	122
Fifer, Louis	126	Garrison, Patrick	55
Finan, Bill	129	Gasoi, Marta	39
Finkelstein, Edward	138	Gately, Maureen	77
Fischer, Amber	126	Gawronski, William	52
Fischer, Amy-Lynn	39	Gay, Meaghan	25
Fisher, Lynn	162	Gemignani, Nathan	55
Fisher, Michael G.	67	Gendler, Anne	118
Fisher, Miriam	29	George, Derek	156
Fitzgerald, Brenda	170	Gerhard, Corey	39
Fitzgerald, Leslie	171	Gershenowitz, Deborah	113
Fitzgerald, Patrick	51	Gettman, Joyce	107
Fiyak-Burkley, Michele	60	Gibb, Rebecca	181
Fleegal, Stacia	107	Gibson, Ellen	47
Floyd, Doris	39	Gill, Craig	100
Flynn, Dan	150	Giller, Megan	155
Flynn, Robert	66	Gimbel, Despina P.	113
Fobben, Tish	107	Ginsburg, Erica	129
Fogle, Linda	144	Givler, Peter J.	189
Fontana, Viginia	167	Glazer, Adam	126
Forlifer, Linda E.	79	Gleason, Laura	87
Forrey, Scott	166	Gloria, Angela	140
Forsythe, Lisa	152	Gloster, Margaret	119
Fortgang, Adam	134	Goldblatt, Debbie	41

Martin, Roger	88	McKnight, Emily	120
Martin, Shari	34	McKown, Ashleigh	79
Martinez, Donald	156	McLachlan, Shannon	125
Martinez, Mariana	129	McLaughlin, Brenna	189
Martinez, Sylvia	52	McLaughlin, Larin	149
Martinez, Tracy	102	McLeod, John	65
Maruhn, Elaine	107	McLeod, Rebecca	93
Marz, Megan	47	McMenemy, Siobhan	162
Mastromarino, Mark	56	McMillen, Ronald E.	26
Matheson, Laurie	71	McMillen, Wendy	119
Mathewson, Janet	158	McRory, Susan	82
Mathias, Ashley	144	Meade, Deborah	132
Mathis, Steffen	134	Medlin, Karen	160
Matsumoto, Elyse	69	Meehan, Eileen	149
Matthen, Kate	75	Mehring, Adam	178
Mautner, Stephen M.	104	Melvin, Terrence	35
May, Theresa	155	Mendoza, Celeste	155
Mayer, Dariel	169	Merchant, Ann	104
Mayer, Loomis	61	Mesker, Louis W.	72
Mayer, Mary	181	Metro, Judy	105
Maynes, Kerrie	172	Metz, Isabel	101
Mazzocchi, Jay	115	Metzger, Abby Phillips	123
McAdam, Susanne	88	Meyer, Kathy McLaughlin	58
McArdle, Jeff	72	Meyer, Steve	59
McBeth, Barbara	111	Midgley, Peter	24
McBride, David	126	Miles, Elizabeth	148
McBride, Debra	47	Miles, Terry	115
McCall, Linda	189	Mill, George	156
McCallum, Heather	182	Millar, Catherine	79
McCamic, Nathan	115	Miller, Cynthia	132
McCarthy, Ellen	96	Miller, Dan	168
McCarthy, Juliana M.	79	Miller, Kim	189
McCaull, June	93	Miller, Lori	110
McClanahan, Valerie	74	Miller, Luke	115
McClure-Parshall, Sally	54	Miller, Robert	126
McConkey, Jill	162	Miller, Robyn L.	56
McCormick, Mack	85	Miller, Ron	138
McCormick, Monica	113	Miller, Rose Ann	67
McCowan, Claudia	138	Miller, William M.	106
McCoy, Anne	51	Millholland, Valerie	56
McCoy, James	190	Mills, Maureen	63
McCoy, Jim	76	Mills, Nancy	170
McCullough, Michael	56	Mills, Rod	87
McDermott, Kathleen	67	Mills, Ulrike	105
McDonald, Jane	92	Milroy, Peter	34
McDonald, Jessica	87	Milton, Christina	95
McDonald, Leigh	29	Mitchell, Carine	41
McDuffie, John	26	Mitchell, David	55
McEntire, Ila	84	Mitchell, Douglas	46
McGann, Michael	152	Mitchell, Nicole	64, 191
McGilvray, Joan V.	88	Mitchell, Patricia	130
McGonagle, David J.	45	Mitchell, Sue	23
McGuinness, Nina	171	Mitchner, Leslie	141
McGuire, Kristi	47	Miyasato, Terri	69
McIlraith, Don	39	Modica, Luciano	131
McIntire, Karyn	96	Moen, Jeffery	99
McIntosh, Susan	88	Moermond, Sheila	178
McKaskle, James	156	Moir, Robin	100
McKee, Sarah	64	Mones, Mark	170
McKie, Ellen	156	Monroe, Nancy	156

Montoya, Orion	126	Neff, Brett J.	83
Mooney, Joe	96	Nelson, Eric	124
Moore, Alexander	144	Nelson, Ivar	59
Moore, Lloyd	57	Nelson, Kathryn	127
Moore, Mary Peterson	151	Nelson, Stephanie	156
Moorehead, Harold	147	Neugebauer, Lisa	60
Moore-Swafford, Angela	146	New, Carol	41
Morales, Ruth	136	New, Erin Kirk	65
Moreton, Leonard J.	103	Newalu, Clifford	69
Morgan, Clay	92	Newcomb, Paula	96
Morgan, Kathi Dailey	64	Newman, Carey	31
Morris, Ian	119	Newman, Sarah Crane	148
Morris, John	121	Ngueha, Hubert	45
Morris, Meghan	149	Nicholls, David G.	103, 190
Morris, Michael	54	Nichols, Joel	160
Morris, Ryan	149	Nichols, Sally	91
Morrison, Don	118	Nichols, Suzanne	140
Morrison, Pamela	56	Nicola, Christine	59
Morrison, Richard	99	Nicolaes, Chantal	28
Morrone, Cathy	93	Nicolosi, Charles	65
Morrow, David	46	Nielsen, Luci	104
Mortensen, Dee	74	Nieves, Juan	136
Morton, Greg	29	Nikpour, Golnar	152
Mosely, Erin	180	Nishimoto, Kiera	69
Motherwell, Elizabeth	22	Noe, Jason	126
Motomura, Akiko	58	Noonan, Jane	59
Moynihan, Kellie	36	Noonan, Margaret M.	61
Muccie, Mary Rose	79	Noonan, Maureen	181
Muench, Timothy	189	Norell, Randy	25
Muenning, John	47	Norman, Robin	78
Muirhead, Donna	176	Norton, Jennifer	130
Mullen, Tess	47	Norville, Valerie	165
Mullervy, Deirdre	62	Nowak, Emily	174
Munson, Heather	72	Nussbaum, Stephen	127
Munson, Stephanie	55	Nyberg, Karl	152
Muranaka, Royden	69	O'Boyle, Amanda	163
Murillo, Michael	156	O'Brien, Kate	61
Murphy, Diane	172	O'Brien, Katy	115
Murphy, James	41	O'Cain, Stephanie	113
Murphy, Liza	40	O'Connell, Chris	158
Murphy, Paul	138, 190	O'Conner, Chris	143
Murphy, Sarah	174	O'Connor, Devlan	166
Murphy, Tim	104	O'Connor, Noreen	129
Murray, Barb	36	O'Donnell, Joan	68
Murray, Kirt	178	O'Donnell, Robert	140
Myers, Charles	133	O'Donovan, Maria	53
Myers, Patricia	147	O'Halloran, Sylvie	89
Nachbaur, Fredric	113	O'Hare, Joanne	109, 189, 190
Nachtigall, Lisa	126	O'Mahen, Sarah	29
Nadkarni, Alicia	141	O'Malley, Michael	181
Nagasaka, Masayuki	161	O'Neill, Kathy	72
Naimola, Lauren	95	Oates, Paula	117
Nair, Valerie	34	Oblack, Linda	74
Nakassis, Magda	105	Ochsner, Daniel	99
Nakata, Kyle	69	Oeste, Robert	80
Nangle, Leslie	134	Ohlin, Peter	126
Napolitano, Claudia	131	Okamoto, Kazuo	161
Naqib, Nadia	27	Okrent, Marilyn	125, 127
Nathe, Anthony	35	Olson, Andrea	96
Neel, David	158	Omen, Adrienne	179

Quinn, Michele	22	Roberts, Susan	120
Rabinowitch, Janet	74	Roberts, Tony	122
Racette, A.C.	118	Robertson, Beth	137
Rached, Nadine	113	Robertson, Monica	109
Ragsdale, Neil	74	Robinson, Brett	97
Ramirez, Linda	156	Robinson, Kim	126
Ramonda, David	156	Robinson, Lou	54
Ramos, Vicky	158	Rocha, Rogelio Jr.	156
Ranalli, Kathy	129	Rodrigue, Sylvia Frank	145
Rancourt, Suzanne	162	Rodríguez, Miguel	136
Rand, Bonnie	121	Roecklein, Anne	74
Randolph, Ladette	107	Roessner, Maura	126
Rankin, Charles (Chuck)	121	Rogers, Christopher	181
Ratchford, George Ann	146	Rohnmann, Eric	134
Rawitsch, Elizabeth	110	Rohrer, Mary	146
Raykov, Mariana	147	Rold, Alison	107
Read, Cynthia	126	Rollins, John D.	181, 182, 190
Read, Mary	173	Rollins, Leslie	66
Read, Zachary	114	Romeo-Hall, Ange	54
Reaume, Julie	97	Rood, Karen	144
Redding, Jennifer	67	Rosen, Amy	127
Reed, Astrud	121	Rosenberger, Wilma	80
Reed, Sandra	168	Rosenthal, Sam	39
Reed-Morrison, Laura	130	Ross, Allan	40
Reedy, Nora	79	Ross, Daniel J.J.	21, 22
Regan, Ann	98	Rossner, Mike	139
Regier, Willis G.	71	Roupe, George	87
Rehl, Beatrice	40	Routon, Anne	51
Reichlin, Jennifer L.	64, 190	Roux, Michael	72
Reider, Karen	79	Rowe, Niccole	94
Reilly, Elizabeth	134	Rowell, Edd	94
Reimann, Alice	47	Rowley, Linda	96
Reinhardt, Shelley	126	Roy, Krishna	77
Reisman, Don	139	Roy, Michael	26
Reissig, Stopha	155	Rubich, George	41
Remington, Sara	95	Rude, Pam	74
Rennells, Kevin	96	Ruggieri, Elizabeth	60
Renner, Karen	102	Ruiz, Johnny	158
Retel, Pauline	28	Ruiz, Marcia	152
Rhodes, Maya	174, 190	Rush, Deborah	74
Rial, Shelley	172	Russell, Richard A	106.
Ribesky, Mary	172	Russo, Franco	131
Rice, Anita L.	70	Rutledge, Kim	107
Richards, Kent	142	Ryan, Jane	138
Richards, Michael B.	113	Ryan, Suzanne	126
Richards, Todd	174	Sacks, Lisa	33
Rickman, Denise	21	Saenz, Guillermo	105
Riddle, Karen	144	Saffel, Than	176
Ridge, Sam	31	Sagara, Mike	147
Ridgeway, Vicky	102	Sagstetter, Karen	105
Rifkind, Barbara	125, 127	Sajeski, Bob	150
Rimmer, Kim	126	Saleeba, Ashley	172
Rine, Margie	107	Salem, Kate	107
Rinella, Michael	149	Salisbury, Leila	84
Rivers, Shana	22	Salitros, Linda Lou	158
Riviere, Leah	33	Salling, Stacey	156
Roane, Kari	47	Saltz, Carole Pogrebin	152
Robbins, Linda	126	Salveson, Sally	182
Roberts, Conrad	82, 190	Samen, Anita	46
Roberts, Dennis	71	Sanabia, Anibal	136

Sanders, David	120	Sen, Sharmila	67
Sanders-Buell, Sara	105	Sery, Doug	92
Sandoval, Manuel G.	136	Severance, Mary	39
Sanfilippo, Tony	130, 190	Sewall, Martha	79
Sangar, Puja	147	Sewell, David	170
Sanmartín, Cristina	93	Sewell, Vicki	144
Sarraf, Suzanne	105	Sexsmith, Ann	68
Satrom, Ellen	170	Sexton, Mary	96
Saunders, Mark H	170.	Seymons, Ambra	131
Savage, Lisa	72	Shafer, Deb	95
Savarese, Anne	134	Shaffer, Bryan	137
Savir, Tami	41	Shaffer, Harrison	29
Savitt, Charles C.	77	Shahan, Andrea	107
Scallan, Amanda	87	Shanahan, Mary	47
Scanlon, Sonia	181	Shanholtzer, Joshua	132
Scarpelli, Elizabeth	141	Shannon, Tom	125, 127
Schaffner, Melanie B.	79	Sharer, Stacey	65
Schaut, Diane	120	Shaw, Cameron	127
Scheld, Melissanne	40	Shay, Damien	112
Schellinger, Paul	46	Shay, Mariah	105
Schenck, Linny	133	Shayegan, Leyli	152
Schier, Jeffrey	181	Shea, Timothy	182
Schipper, Marike	85	Shear, Donna	118
Schleicher, Wendy	105	Shelly, Mary Lou	75
Schlesinger, Laurie	78	Sherif, Tawhida	27
Schmidt, Karen	66, 190	Sherman, Bo	99
Schmidt, Randy	34	Shestack, Alan	105
Schneider, Naomi	38	Shields, Charlie	30
Schneider, Robert A.	25	Shiflett, Shannon	170
Schnittman, Evan	125, 127	Shilling, Julie	122
Schoeffel, Ron	162	Shimabukuro, Jill	47
Scholz-Jaffe, Kathy	130	Siegelman, Howard	41
Schott, Susan	82	Sieger, Peter	152
Schrader, Rebecca	92, 189	Silay, June	74
Schraeder, Chris	39	Siler, Jennifer M.	154
Schreiber, Rebecca McNulty	71	Silva, Diana	54
Schreur, Robert	80	Simmons, Carolyn	66
Schroder, Alan M.	29	Simmons, Valencia	62
Schroeder, Julie	102	Simon, Rebecca	38, 39, 189
Schuetz, Richard	112	Simpson, Amy	23
Schuh, Lynda	72	Simpson-Vos, Mark	115, 190
Schwalbe, Russell	179	Sims, Michael	92
Schwartz, Eric	40	Sims, Peter	181
Schwartz, J. Alex	117	Singerman, Jerome E.	128
Schwartz, Marilyn	38	Sioles, Lee	87
Schwarz, Angel Collado	136	Sippell, Kelly	95
Schwarzchild, Olive	104	Siress, Janyce P.	181
Scollans, Colleen	125, 127	Sisler, William P	67.
Scorziello, Vinnie	93	Skidmore, Scot	85
Searl, Laurie	149	Skinner, Heather	99
Secondari, Linda	51, 190	Slater, Sarah N.	110
See, Sandy	122	Slatter, Carol	21
Seger, Rebecca	127	Slavin, Michelle	165
Seils, Andrea	126	Sloan, Robert	74
Sekiya, Yoko	24	Slocum, Melissa	107
Selby, Larry	126	Smathers, Parker	175
Sells, Dianna	158	Smith, BJ	115
Seltzer, Joyce	67	Smith, David	104
Semerad, Marilyn	149	Smith, Diane E.	31, 32
Semple, Timothy	110	Smith, Dianne	144

Smith, Greg	150	Sudhir, Pillarisetti	25
Smith, Heather	130	Sullivan, Tim	134
Smith, Ileene	181	Summerfield, Mary	47
Smith, J. Reynolds	56	Suneja, Shilpi	113
Smith, Lyn	102	Suorez, Joa	147
Smith, Marena	65	Sutton, Amanda	112, 190
Smith, Mariellen	128	Sutton, Laura	84
Snoeyenbos, Ann	79	Swain, Beth	29
Snyder, Cindy	55	Swanson, Rosie	100
Soden, Pat	171	Swanson, Tom	107
Soldavin, Susan	35	Sweeney, Kathleen A.	61
Sondervan, Jeroen	28	Swope, Pamela K.	90
Sondker, Juree	51	Szawiola, Kathleen	109
Sorenson, Nicole	60	Szuter, Christine R.	29
Sotomayer, Melissa	29	Tadlock, Susanna	39
Soule, Susan	41	Takahashi, Tomohiko	161
Sparkes, Kathy	112	Takayanagi, Mitsuo	161
Sparrow, Amanda	105	Tallon, Andrew	90
Spaulding, Pamela	57	Tamminen, Suzanna	175
Spence, Edris	80	Tamulevich, Alessandra Jacobi	122
Spencer, Katie	33	Tan, Elisa	79
Speth, Linda	176	Tandysh, Melissa	112
Spicer, Ed	130	Tanner, Annette	97, 190
Spooner, Michael	168	Tartar, Helen	61
Spotswood, Jessica	45	Tate, Ben	134
Springsteen, Sara	107	Tate, Lori	152
Srinivasan, Seetha	100	Taus, Ellen	125, 127
Staggs, Susan	129	Tavarez, Carmen	161
Stahl, Levi	47	Taylor, Jean	173
Stakes, Robert L.	161	Taylor, Joanna	58
Stannard, Eric	126	Taylor, Rob	107
Stanton, Alice	122	Taylor, Robyn	60
Starr, Leslie	175	Teefey, Carrie Downes	174
Starr, Lindsay	160	Teillard-Clemmer, Anne	74
Stascavage, Anne	101	Telikicherla, Puja	63
Stauter, Jason	118	Tempio, Rob	134
Stein, Kathy	26	Tenorio, JoAnn	69
Steinberg, Ruth	170	Thatcher, Sanford G.	130, 189, 190
Steinle, Kim	57	Thomas, Alan	46, 190
Steinmetz, Kay	151	Thomas, Allison	76
Stephens, Wendy	36	Thomas, Teresa	115
Steve, Betsy	113	Thompson, Jessica	75
Stevens, Chelsea	35	Thompson, Karen	151
Stevens, Erika	64	Thompson, Myles	51
Stevenson, Hector D.	136	Thompson, Ren	39
Stevenson, John	172	Thompson, Stephanie	155
Stewart, Lane	64	Thornton, Shirley	107
Stewart-Kruger, Sandra	143	Tierney, PJ	32
Sticco, Maria	132	Tietz, Angelika	121
Stinchcomb, Rick	122	Tifft, Douglas	110
Stone, Colleen	174	Timberg, Robert	106
Stone, Tom	92	Tingle, Leslie	155
Stoner, Julie Finnegan	63	Tjandra, Lia	39
Stowe, Jennifer	72	Toff, Nancy	126
Strauss, David	152	Tolen, Rebecca	74
Strauss, Marc	40	Toller, Amanda	32
Strickland, Sherri	110	Tom, Henry Y.K.	79
Stritch, Jim	182	Tomé, Jesús	136
Suarez, Gary	41	Tomolonis, Michael	141
Suciu, Ioan	63	Toole, Regenia (Jenny)	94

Weintraub, Joe	47	Wolfe, Elisabeth	31
Weiss-Feldman, Rachel	189	Wolfe, Mary	71
Wellner, Fred	151	Wong, Angelina	49
Wellnitz, Clare	51	Wong, Deborah	57
Wells, Phyllis	65	Wong, John	33
Wells, Thomas	154	Wonski, Leah	152
Wells, Vicky	115, 190	Wood, Lori	126
Welsch, Sarah L.	110	Woodard, Nancy	112
Wendland, Ann	50	Woodward, Fred	82
Wenzel, Stephanie	115	Woollen, Susan	35
Werden, Barbara	160	Wright, Charlotte	76
Werntz, Myles	31	Wright, Glenn	151
Werts, Lynn	60	Wright, Michelle	57
Wessels, Cindy	132	Wrinn, Stephen M.	84
West, Linda	80	Wrzesinski, Julie	97
Westcott, Winnie	142	Wu, Suzanne	47
Westlund, Laura	99, 190	Wyllis, Kaila	156
Westmoreland, Cherie	57	Wyrwa, Richard	165
Wetjen, Rhonda	76	Yagan, Sally	127
Whaley, Kathy	75	Yahner, Kathryn	130
Wheel, Brian	126	Yamaguchi, Masami	161
Whipple, George	54	Yamashita, Mina	112
White, Sara Henderson	82	Yates, John	162
Whitehorn, Clark	112	Yates, Steve	101
Whitmore, Anne M.	79	Yen, Cindy	69
Whittaker, Linda	89	Yenerich, Pat	117
Whitton, Elizabeth	34	Yost, Michelle	160
Wicklum, Ellen	110	Young, Emily	56
Widhalm, Bob	108	Young, Mary D.	83
Wiebe, Jeff	66	Young, Mary	117
Wilburn, Judith	68	Youngman, Donna	110
Wilcox, Bruce	91	Yudell, Deenie	66
Wildfong, Kathryn	174	Yup, Carline	113
Wilkie, Craig R.	85	Zachry-Reynolds, Lauren	156
Willamson, Matt	74	Zadrozny, Mark	41, 190
Willcox, Clair	102	Zalewski, Ellen M.	46
Williams, Carmen	39	Zavada, Kara	179
Williams, Isabel	160	Zeitlin, Randy	41
Williams, Kelli	149	Zellmann, Stacy	99
Williams, Stephanie	60	Zenner, Boyd	170
Willis, Kathleen Z.	31	Zielinski, Tammy	69
Willmes, Karen	80	Ziemacki, Richard L.	40
Willoughby-Harris, H. Lee	56	Zimmer, Ben	126
Wilson, Andrea-Jo	163	Zimmerman, Carol	79
Wilson, David	153	Zinner, Eric	113
Wilson, Jean	34	Zoss, Bernadette	74
Wilson, Judy	121	Zotz, John	148, 189
Wilson, Luther	111	Zucca, Damon	126
Wilson, Pam	179, 191	Zucchi, John	88
Wimberly, Pam	39	Zucco, Joeth	107
Winarsky, Hanne	134		
Windham, Darrell	156		
Wingard, Daniel	127		
Wirkus, Melinda	84		
Wise, Amelia	55		
Wisniewski, Cassandra	48		
Wissoker, Ken	56		
Wissoker, Peter	54		
Withey, Lynne	38		
Wolfe, Alex	132		

OTHER PUBLICATIONS AND RESOURCES

AAUP Annual Report
The report provides a summary of association activities.

AAUP Book, Jacket, and Journal Show Catalog
The purpose of the Show is to recognize achievement in the design, production, and manufacture of books, book jackets, and journals. The catalog displays and critiques all titles selected in this annual competition. Gratis to members, $10.00 to non-members.

AAUP Bulletin
The *Bulletin* is a monthly electronic news brief on the programs and activities of the AAUP Central Office and membership. The *Bulletin* is distributed electronically to AAUP members only.

AAUPNET.ORG
The association's Web site features an online directory of members with links to each press's home page; information about AAUP programs, activities, and upcoming events; a job list; general information on scholarly publishing; and much more.

AAUPWiki
The AAUPWiki is a collaborative site designed to help AAUP members learn and share best practices, conference materials, and professional development tools. Hosted by Princeton University Press, and editable by registered AAUP members, the AAUPWiki is open to interested members of the scholarly communications field at: http://aaupwiki.princeton.edu/

Books for Understanding
Books for Understanding is an online resource for anyone looking for in-depth background and expertise on today's news. This service features subject-specific bibliographies on critically important news stories. New bibliographies are compiled when a major news story breaks or heated public debate takes place. This resource is available at: www.booksforunderstanding.org

The Exchange
The association's quarterly newsletter. Now published in electronic-only format, *The Exchange* is available for free to the public. *The Exchange Online* is available at: http://aaupnet.org/exchange/

University Press Books Selected for Public and Secondary School Libraries
An annual bibliography that lists more than 400 university press titles in a wide range of disciplines. A committee of public and secondary school librarians selects the titles. The bibliography is published with support from the American Library Association (ALA) and is now also available electronically at: www.aaupnet.org/librarybooks.